THE BUSHMEN

San Hunters and Herders of Southern Africa

Edited by Phillip V. Tobias

Foreword by Raymond A. Dart

Megan Biesele ▪ Irenäus Eibl-Eibesfeldt
Hans J. Heinz ▪ Ray R. Inskeep
M. D. W. Jeffreys ▪ Richard Borshay Lee
Jalmar and Ione Rudner
George B. Silberbauer ▪ Ronald Singer
Anthony Traill ▪ Alex R. Willcox

Human & Rousseau
Cape Town and Pretoria

The Bushmen was first published in 1978 by
Human & Rousseau Publishers (Pty.) Ltd.,
3-9, Rose Street, Cape Town and
239, Pretorius Street, Pretoria

The Bushmen was designed by
G & G Design, Cape Town
The text was set in 10 on 12 pt Plantin Monophoto
Printed and bound by
National Book Printers,
Goodwood, Cape

ISBN 0 7981 0668 9

Foreword

Emeritus Professor of Anatomy, University of the Witwatersrand,
Johannesburg, South Africa

There are few survivors left of the six scientists who participated in the fieldwork of the first University of the Witwatersrand Kalahari expedition of 1936. We investigated "the linguistically most pure Bushmen known to Dr Dorothea Bleek", the brilliant daughter of the renowned linguist W. H. I. Bleek. The expedition depended upon such equipment and skills as the Department of Anatomy and its staff had managed to attain despite the foregoing years of economic depression but scientific excitement. As one of those survivors I feel particularly privileged to congratulate my successor, Professor Phillip V. Tobias, the editor of this outstanding work on the Bushmen, not only upon it, but also upon the staggering series of twenty-one subsequent expeditions into the Kalahari. The first of these was initiated by him with Nuffield Foundation financial support in 1958, the year of my retirement from the Anatomy Chair after thirty-six adventurous years.

If memory serves me correctly, our initial expedition's modest financial subvention had been limited to £250. We were granted the use of an all-purpose but far from new Albion truck owned by the University and expertly handled by E. W. Williams and H. Hall, my assistants. This and three privately owned cars accommodated the six investigators and undertook the rugged trip over inferior roads, veld tracks and dry river beds. Much time was lost unavoidably digging out not only the cumbersome truck but our own ill-equipped vehicles, so often bogged down in the sand encountered, before we reached the 70 Bushmen assembled by Donald Bain after his consultation with Dorothea Bleek.

So today, in 1976, this multi-authored book concerning the Bushmen and their culture – doubtless regarded as a natural phenomenon by the average citizen – takes me back to a vanished era just forty years ago.

What these field researches represent in ardent work and study can be assessed only when one considers – even if momentarily – their impact upon a single individual such as its leading author. The twenty-one expeditions were completed in the first decade (1958-1967), but by 1975 over seventy scientific publications had resulted from the work stimulated by him or carried out under his aegis.

But this book (lavishly produced by a firm of South African publishers) ranges far beyond those inter-departmental expeditions and their precious scientific data, to present to its fortunate readers a glamorous, synthetic over-view of the Bushmen: who they still are, and where; and what their significance has been from their most remotely known past until today; their colourful mural art and their differing languages; their scientific knowledge, as well as their beliefs, myths and folklore; the variant environments they have mastered and the racial contacts they have survived; their position in the world of today and their potential future.

So readers have at their disposal here a collective work. Most of the other twelve contributors to the book have devoted varying but correspondingly considerable parts of their lives to gaining their knowledge of the Bushmen in southern Africa, but are presently spread apart geographically: from England and Germany in Europe to Australia and South Africa in the Old World, and from Canada to Texas in the New World. Yet the audience for anthropological knowledge is worldwide, and increasing phenomenally. Forty years ago there were few if any more than forty professional anthropologists in the United States; today there are thousands, producing Ph.D. degrees at the rate of over four hundred annually.

Comprehensive books such as this about people as physically and culturally distinctive as the South African Bushmen are needed wherever there are high schools and libraries in our air-linked modern world.   *7th July, 1976*

About the illustrations

The captions of the more than two hundred illustrations in *The Bushmen* have been numbered according to chapter (e.g. 2.3 would indicate the caption to the third illustration in chapter 2). The illustrations themselves bear numbers only where there is a possibility of confusion among various illustrations on the same page.

Editor's Foreword

This book is dedicated to the Bushmen in transition. It is an archive of the old prehistoric and historic life-ways; a record of the people today poised between a long creative past and an uncertain future; and a glimpse of the road ahead – of the Bushmen as part of Tomorrow's Men.

The Bushmen is a book about aboriginal southern Africans who, until the present century, lived the life of hunters and food-gatherers. It was a means of subsistence that had been followed by Man's fossil ancestors, ever since the first appearance in Africa of *Homo habilis* shortly before the onset of the Pleistocene epoch. A way of life dimly foreshadowing this may have been pursued even by some of the later Pliocene populations of *Australopithecus africanus*, the probable ancestors of all later forms of humanity. Yet, although this way of life had stood Man in good stead for at least two million years, the last quarter of the 20th century may well see its final disappearance from the face of the earth.

The fact that for 99,5 per cent of his time on earth Man has been a hunter and a food-gatherer is not to suggest that time stood still for those few million years: far from it, for they were aeons of great advance in Man's progressive mastery of his environment. His tool-kit became ever more versatile and adapted to many different environments. He tamed fire, he learned to shelter within clothing and caverns, he acquired speech, he developed techniques of social cohesion, codes of belief and conduct that bonded groups of people – and so helped them to survive. In time, he spread over all of the Old World, crossing even the deep Wallace Line into Australia, and the Bering Straits into America. All the while he was becoming transformed genetically and culturally in a hundred different ecological niches. Yet, beneath the flowering diversity was a unifying subsistence-base, the hunter-gatherer mode of life.

That is how it was until about ten thousand years ago. Then, in several different areas, two revolutionary ideas changed the pattern of life. They were agriculture and the domestication of animals. The new modes of subsistence spread over most of the globe – and this process continues yet. In the 20th century, only a few small groups of mankind still follow the hunter-gatherer mode of life – and even they are changing rapidly. The Bushmen or San are among these groups.

Fewer than half of the 50 000 Bushmen estimated to be alive today survive by hunting and gathering alone. More and more of them are adopting pastoral habits – and that is why this book is sub-titled "San Hunters and Herders of Southern Africa". We must give up the idea that "the Bushman way of life" – in the last quarter of the 20th century – means a hunting life. By the year 2000, it is most unlikely that *any* Bushmen will be leading the pure, pristine hunter-gatherer life. *That* way of subsistence will linger on only as romantic and nostalgic memories of the "good old days".

The Bushmen embraces the observations, inferences, views and predictions of thirteen scholars. Between them, they have spent scores of years and thousands of hours living with the San and with the fruits of their artistic and technical genius. No attempt has been made here to harmonise conflicting views – for such there inevitably are. Indeed, all viewpoints expressed in this book are those of the individual authors of chapters and neither I nor the Publisher is responsible or answerable for them. We present this book to all who would learn a little about the past, present and future of the Bushmen: for those who would delve more deeply, we append a Bibliography of nearly 300 titles of books and articles, classified according to special areas of interest. For readers unfamiliar with Khoisan words, as well as with colloquial terms in common use in these parts and with more technical language, we include a short Glossary.

Acknowledgements

Directly and indirectly many people have helped to make this book. To name some as especially worthy of gratitude is, however, not to exhaust the list, and I can but apologise to those whose names are inadvertently omitted, but whose support is no less appreciated.

My thanks are due, first, to my friends and colleagues in many parts of the world, members of an unofficial "Kalahari Old Boys' Club", including those who have contributed the chapters of this book and so much else in fellowship and inspiration,

to my incomparable *confrère* "Doc" M. D. W. Jeffreys, who so admired the little yellow people but did not live to see this book completed,

to the writer of the *Foreword*, my much loved and admired predecessor, mentor and friend, Emeritus Professor Raymond A. Dart, who gave me my first opportunity to visit the Kalahari and its people and so changed the direction of my life's work,

to my good companion and leader, the late François Balsan, who in 1951 introduced me, as a member of his Panhard-Capricorn expedition, to the Kalahari San,

to the University of the Witwatersrand, the Kalahari Research Committee and the Nuffield Foundation, who made it possible for me to carry out what little I could in research on the San,

to Jürgen Schadeberg of Johannesburg, Noel Ramettre of Paris, Jens Bjerre of Copenhagen, Kitty Brown of Chantilly, Virginia, Naomi Jacobson of Windhoek and Johannesburg, Mel Konner of Harvard, Nancy DeVore of Anthro-Photo, Captain G. Collender of Johannesburg, Irving DeVore of Harvard, and the Peabody Museum of Harvard University and to the writers of the chapters themselves, for many of the pictures that illustrate the book,

to John Pitts of the Johannesburg *Star,* who made it possible for me to include a photograph of a "new" Bushman of the last quarter of the 20th century,

to Elizabeth Dey, Librarian (Reference and Research) of the William Cullen Library, University of the Witwatersrand, for valuable help with the Bibliography,

to Peter Faugust, Noreen Gruskin, Carole Orkin, Christel Eckert, and, above all, Kay Copley, who helped in a thousand different ways to bring the manuscript and the book to fruition,

to Messrs Human & Rousseau, for their kindly and patient help, and especially to Leon Rousseau for initiating the idea of this book, for giving me exemplary encouragement during the dark days when a myriad other pressures made it seem it would never be completed, and for his ever-ready helpfulness at all stages in production of the book; to Louise Steyn, Hans Büttner and Hermann Koch, who were responsible for seeing it through the press; and Mrs A. M. Kettley, who compiled the Index,

. . . lastly, to the Bushmen themselves, whose ineffable spirit, resilience, charm and good humour cannot fail to captivate all who have the privilege of living and working with them.

Phillip V. Tobias
Johannesburg, 24th July, 1977

Contents

I
Introduction to the Bushmen or San

Phillip V. Tobias

The people of this book have been given many names, such as Bushmen, San or Sanqua, Sonqua, Souqua or Soaqua, Sarwa or Masarwa. They are broken up into numbers of clans or tribes, and these, too, have a bewildering array of names, such as !Kung and /xam and //gana. The symbols ! and / and // are used to convey some of the clicks in the Bushman languages.

In the title of this chapter we have used two of these names. It is appropriate to begin this book by telling how we arrived at these terms, how we use them and how we define the peoples they represent.

So, without further ado, let me introduce them to you.

Who are the Bushmen or San?

The definition of the terms "Bushmen" and "San" is by no means straightforward, because in the past they have meant different things to different people. For some, they referred to people speaking one of a particular group of languages; for others, they conjured up a vision of a way of life, hunting and the gathering of veld foods; for yet others, these names connoted a people of singular appearance, short of size, with yellow skin, tufted hair, flat noses, strong cheek-bones and accumulations of fat over the buttocks *(steatopygia)* and the thighs *(steatomeria)*. These three groups of features are spoken of as linguistic, cultural and physical (or biological), and they are often thought of as the hallmarks of the Bushmen.

If all groups of these people were marked by the special way of life, by speaking one of the distinctive languages, and by the characteristic bodily structure, it would not be difficult to give a single definition of the San or Bushman. However, there is by no means an exact correspondence among all three sets of criteria. For instance, some of the hunters do not speak one of the "Bushman languages". Again, some of those with the "typical San" appearance are not hunters but herdsmen. In other words, as Professor I. Schapera pointed out in "A Survey of the Bushman Question" (1939), the correlation between physical, cultural and linguistic features is not at all exact. As a result, no single criterion – whether language, economy or physical form – would on its own be able to identify all of the people commonly called Bushmen or San. For example, if the hunter-gatherer way of life is our test, we should be obliged to leave out all of those thousands of Bushmen under the name of Sarwa who are today cattle-herds, and also all of those who are living on farms owned by members of other groups. Or, if we used the language as the identifying mark, we should find ourselves having to omit some well-known populations like the Hei-//um (Heikum) and the Nharo (Naron), who on other than linguistic grounds are generally considered to be Bushmen or San, whilst their languages are different.

Similarly, if we used a definition based on all three diagnostic features – language *and* culture *and* physical form – we should clearly end up by omitting a number of groups commonly accepted as Bushmen or San.

Perhaps you may feel that definitions and classifications are not important. Yet, if we wanted to determine, for instance, how many Bushmen or San are still alive today, how should we know whom to include in the census if we did not have a scientifically valid definition? Similarly, if we wished to find out how close the San are, in genetic make-up, to the Khoikhoi (or Hottentots) and the Negroes, we could not do this unless we had a clear idea whom to include in the San population to be compared. What we need is to find that criterion which, if carefully applied, would include the great majority of living San, and would miss out fewer than any other criterion would.

1.1 An elderly San man in the Ghanzi district, north-western Botswana. From the published accounts of early travellers, the San until recently have changed but little since the settlers arrived in 1652.

1.2 A young Bushman girl showing striking San features around the nose and eyes. The physical traits are one means of recognising many members of the San population.

One of our great authorities on these people is Professor I. Schapera, whose book *The Khoisan Peoples of South Africa* (1930) is the standard reference work on them. After pondering all aspects of the problem of definitions very thoroughly, Schapera came to the conclusion that language was perhaps the most reliable single criterion.

In 1951 I was seconded as physical anthropologist to the French Panhard-Capricorn expedition under the leadership of François Balsan of Neuilly-sur-Seine. I began to collect data from all those territories in which Bushmen were known to occur. Immediately I came face to face with the problem of definition. After carefully studying Schapera's discussion of this question, and those of others, I concluded that, for purposes of estimating the numbers of surviving Bushmen, I would adopt Schapera's language criterion, to which was added *the common recognition of individuals and tribes as Bushmen or Sarwa*, both by themselves and by their Tswana neighbours. The word "Sarwa" is the root of "MaSarwa" (singular "MoSarwa"), the term commonly applied by the Tswana-speaking peoples of Botswana to the San or Bushmen. It is the modern practice, in scientific writings, to omit the prefix from African tribal names: hence we use here "Sarwa" rather than "MaSarwa".

Although even this twofold rule of thumb is not without difficulties, it has been used before, and with success. J. W. Joyce employed these two criteria when, for the League of Nations, he carried out an investigation of the state of the Sarwa living and working in the Ngwato Reserve of the then Protectorate of Bechuanaland (1938). He found it a useful working rule – and so did we in 1951-1955 – to determine who are Bushmen or San in the vast majority of instances.

Although suitable, perhaps, for the taking of a census, more exact definitions were necessary for meticulous scientific studies. In 1956, after the French expedition, it was already clear that the term "Bushman", used by students of the culture and languages of the living peoples, was not synonymous with the term "Bush race" or "Bush physical type", which for long had been in use among physical anthropologists, such as professors Raymond A. Dart, Matthew R. Drennan, Alexander Galloway and Lawrence H. Wells. When Monica Wilson and Leonard Thompson produced the first volume of their *magnum opus, The Oxford History of South Africa* (1969), they faced this problem of definitions and terms squarely. They stated: "Because correlations are so far from exact, different terms are used in this book for physical type, language, and economy." They offered three clearly different sets of terms, for the first time.

Two years later, T. Jenkins, on behalf of the South African Institute for Medical Research, and the author, for the Royal Society of South Africa, convened a symposium on the peoples of southern Africa in Johannesburg (June 1971). This was a multi-disciplinary meeting, the forty participants being drawn from the fields of archaeology, social anthropology, history, linguistics and human biology (including human genetics and physical anthropology). One major objective of the meeting was to try to get agreement on the terms to be used by specialists in various branches of the study of man. After much debate, the participants agreed with Wilson and Thompson that there should be different terms for the biological populations, the languages and the economies. The terms agreed upon were not the same as those used in the *Oxford History*, except for those applied to the different kinds of economy. Although the Johannesburg meeting concerned itself with all the populations and ethnic groups in southern Africa, we need take note here only of the recommendations affecting the San or Bushmen, the Khoikhoi or Hottentots and the Negroes or Bantu-speakers. It was agreed to use the following terms:

Biological entity (race or physical type)	San	Khoikhoi	Negro (or southern African Negro)
Language	Bushman	Hottentot	Bantu
Economy	Hunters (or Hunter-gatherers)	Herders	Herders, Cultivators

2

In recommending the use of "San" and "Khoikhoi" as the biological, racial or physical names for Bushmen and Hottentots respectively, the conference followed a usage proposed by Professor Leonhard Schultze Jena of the University of Marburg, West Germany. In his physical anthropological treatise on these two branches of humanity (1928), he drew attention to the word "Khoikhoi" or "Khoikhoin" for the Hottentots – it is their name for themselves and means "men of men" or "genuine people"! He also quoted the term "Sān" as the Khoikhoi's term for the Bushmen, since the latter have no collective name for themselves. From these two designations Schultze Jena proposed the term "Khoisan" ("Koïsan") as a suitable name for the combined group to which he believed the two populations belonged. In regarding them as a single racial group in this way, he followed the earlier views of Theophilus Hahn (1867, 1870). Two years later, Schapera adopted Schultze Jena's term "Khoisan" in the title of his great book.

Thus, in this book, when we speak of the little yellow people as a biological or racial entity, we use the term "San"; when we speak of the cultural group (including language), we refer to them as "Bushmen"; while "hunters" or "Bushman hunters" refers to them as exponents of a particular economy. When it is convenient to refer to the two closely related groups Khoikhoi and San as a single biological entity, we shall use the term "Khoisan".

The three biological labels – San, Khoikhoi and Negro (or southern African Negro) – have now gained wide acceptance and are used in a number of books and periodicals, both in southern Africa and internationally. We hope that the set of names agreed upon at the 1971 Johannesburg symposium will become standard usage.

Now that we have tried to clarify the names San/Bushmen/hunters used in this book, let us take a glance back at their first contacts with Whites, as these may give us valuable information on the former numbers and distribution of the San.

Early contacts with the Bushmen or San

When Jan van Riebeeck and his little band of Dutch settlers stepped ashore at the Cape of Good Hope in 1652, they found the land in the immediate vicinity inhabited by shortish, yellow-skinned people who were cattle-owning herdsmen and whose speech was characterized by curious clicking sounds. These pastoralists came to be known as Hottentots, and more recently as Khoikhoi. It was further afield, to the north of the Cape settlement, that the Dutch settlers in April 1655 first encountered a second group of people, the Bushmen or San. At first known as Sonqua, Souqua or Sanqua, they came to be called *Bosjesmans* (Bushmen) some time later. According to Professor L. F. Maingard, the earliest recorded reference to the name "Bosjesman" is an entry in the account of the first journey of Olof Bergh, under the date 4th November, 1682: ". . . some Hottentots, being Sonquas alias bosjemans". From their described physical appearance and mode of life, there is no doubt that these were members of the San race living by hunting and gathering.

Thus the hunters came to be known as Bushmen, the cattle-owners as Hottentots. From the beginning the distinction made between the two by the Dutch pioneers was a *cultural* one: the two groups differed from each other in language and way of life (see Chapter 3).

As if to confuse the picture, groups of beach-combers had taken to living along the shores to the north and east of the Cape Peninsula. Theirs was basically a hunter-gatherer life; only, instead of catching land-based species of game, they did their hunting in rock pools and along the foaming wave edges and in the water. They became known as the *Strandlopers*. Their remains, bones, tools and shell mounds, are found in kitchen middens and cave deposits around much of the South African coastline. For a long time they were regarded as a third group of indigenous people, distinguished from their landward cousins, the Bushmen and Hottentots, by their beach-ranging way of life. Today, the Strandlopers are no longer considered to have been a separate population group. The term refers rather to a coastal way of life that was adopted by some San and also probably some Khoikhoi.

1.3 Ornaments, dress and weapons of the Bushmen of the first half of the 18th century – from an old engraving.

3

Such, in broad outline, was the cultural and ethnic skeinwork that bedecked large areas of southern Africa before the arrival, a few thousand years ago, of the darker Negroes from the north and, just over three centuries ago, of the light Caucasoid or White settlers from across the sea. Each group brought its own strange new culture, language and life-ways, and its own biological make-up.

The click-speaking peoples of Africa were encountered by travellers from Europe and Arabia long before 1652. From the end of the 15th century, Portuguese navigators had made contact with Strandlopers and other Khoisan folk. Even before this, as far back as the 10th to the 12th centuries, Arab geographers accompanying traders down the eastern coast of Africa described click-speakers whom they called Wak-Wak. At that time, they reported the presence of Wak-Wak at what is now Maputo (formerly Lourenço Marques) and as far north as Sofala. The scanty records from this earlier period include that of the Moslem chronicler Masudi of Baghdad: in his *Meadows of Gold and Mines of Precious Stones* (A.D. 915) he spoke of the little Wak-Wak people in the parts around Sofala; while Idrisi, in his map of south-eastern Africa (A.D. 1154), showed the Wak-Wak inhabiting the Sofala coast – a point some 950 km (600 miles) up Africa from the nearest surviving eastern San, namely those of Lake Chrissie in the Transvaal. So historical records covering a thousand years testify to the former more widespread dispersal of click-speakers over a large part of sub-Saharan Africa. By the time that Van Riebeeck arrived in 1652, it seems, the Khoisan occupied a much smaller part of the subcontinent (see the maps on page 19).

1.4 Side view of the fossilized skull of Springbok Flats – found in 1929 near Settlers on the Springbok Flats in the Central Transvaal. This man, who lived tens of thousands of years ago, may give us a glimpse of what early African man was like, shortly before he diversified into Khoisan and Negroid populations.

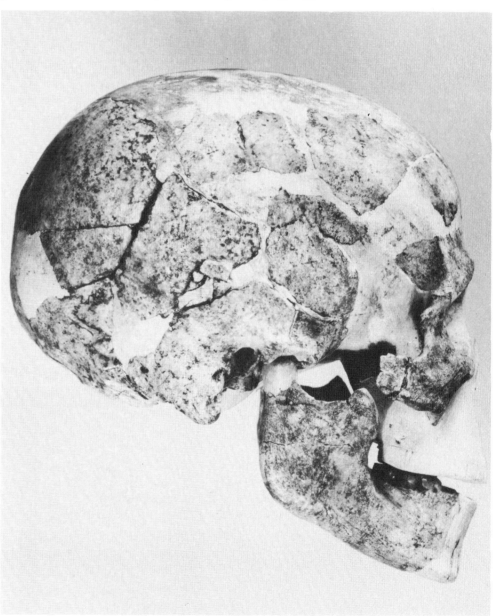

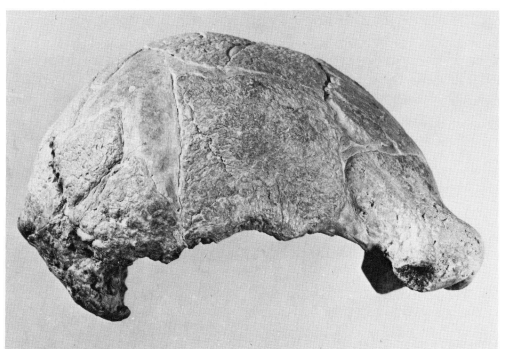

1.5 Two views of the beautifully preserved brain-case of Saldanha Man which was found near the village of Hopefield, inland from Saldanha Bay in the Cape Province, in 1953. It represents an earlier kind of man than that of Springbok Flats: a kind of man that may be transitional between *Homo erectus* and *Homo sapiens*.

The tangle of connections – cultural, linguistic and genetic – among the Khoisan peoples of the southern Cape area was complicated, even before the arrival of the Negroes and the Whites. What were the ties between the San and the Khoikhoi? If each was a distinct ethnic or racial entity, what was their bond of union to each other – and to Africa's major population group, the Negroes? Did the little San have any affinity with the other short peoples of Africa, the Pygmies? How were all these living groups related to the fossil men whose remains have since been found in both South and East Africa – for instance, at Hopefield, inland from Saldanha Bay; at Florisbad, near Bloemfontein; on the Springbok Flats in the Transvaal; at Ingwavuma, on the border between Kwazulu and Swaziland; and at Kabwe (Broken Hill) in Zambia?

These perplexing questions might have been easier to solve if an anthropologist equipped with modern knowledge and techniques had landed from *De Goede Hoope* with Van Riebeeck more than three hundred years ago! Alas, there were no trained observers of mankind on board ship – apart from Commander Van Riebeeck himself, who was a surgeon. There were in fact no anthropologists in

1.6 The great Swedish naturalist Carl von Linne (or Carolus Linnaeus, as his name was latinized), who first classified the human species as *Homo sapiens* and placed it in the Primates.

existence anywhere at that time. Indeed, it was still not customary to regard man as a member of the animal kingdom at all. Only in 1735 did the great Swedish naturalist Carolus Linnaeus classify the human species, *Homo sapiens*, as a member of an order of mammals to which he gave the name Primates – that is, the first among the Mammals. Man, he declared, should be regarded as a primate along with the apes, monkeys and baboons, lemurs and bush-babies.

The first serious studies on the natural varieties of mankind did not appear until 1775. In the latter year, by one of those strange coincidences that enliven the history of science, two men in two different countries each devoted his thesis for the degree of doctor of medicine to a study of the varieties of man. One was Johann Friedrich Blumenbach, and his famous dissertation was published at Göttingen in September 1775. It was through his treatise that the study of anthropology became popular at Göttingen, and he is often called "The Father of Anthropology". The other M.D. thesis was that of John Hunter, published at Edinburgh in June 1775: he was an army physician and *not* the celebrated contemporary surgeon-anatomist of the same name. His work was slight compared with Blumenbach's, and anthropology enjoyed no rise of popularity in Scotland, while it grew to flourish in Germany.

However, these developments were far in the future at the time of which we speak. This has made the task of reconstructing the history and affinities of the various southern African peoples all the harder. We have to rely on the records of the Cape administration, as well as the accounts of observant travellers like Kolb, Sparrman, Le Vaillant, Barrow, Campbell, Livingstone, Chapman, Baines, Andersson, Alexander and Sutherland. Their writings have helped to build up a fair

1.7 The old way of life is fast disappearing among the Bushmen. Where it survives yet, a semicircle of saplings provides the framework of a new hut.

picture. At the time of the first White settlement, Bushmen were living in many districts, especially mountainous areas, of the Cape Province, the Orange Free State, Natal and Lesotho, and certainly in the Transvaal, Botswana and South West Africa. From some of these areas the Bushmen did not entirely disappear until about the beginning of the present century. In the last three territories mentioned, as well as in Angola and, to a slight extent, in Zambia and Rhodesia, Bushmen have survived till today.

By the time a serious study of the peoples began in the 20th century, the picture had been confused by a history of migrations, hybridizations, acculturations and exterminations scarcely, if at all, equalled in any other part of the world. White men arrived in slowly increasing numbers; Negroes pressed southward in their millennial advance down Africa; West Africans were imported as slaves – and so were Malayans, adding an exotic Mongoloid ingredient to the mixture. Thousands of Bushmen were cut down for the crime of hunting the strangely peaceful domestic beasts of the White settlers. Hottentots fought Bushmen; White men pursued Hottentots; Bushmen and Hottentots retreated before Negroes; Negroes were in conflict with Whites. And all the while, as by-products of conquest and enslavement, novel blends of humanity were arising from genes contributed by the Caucasoid, Negroid, Mongoloid and Khoisan contestants. A whole nascent people, the Coloured South Africans, was produced by this era. New tribes – such as the Griqua – were thrown up by the coalescence of varied populations with unprecedented mixtures of human genes. Older tribes, like the Gonaqua, were completely annihilated or, like the Korana, brought to the verge of extinction by intertribal warfare. In 1950, for example, there were only 300 Korana – all that

1.8 Over the scaffolding of saplings, the huts are completed with thatch or with mats made from dry reeds. This technique has certainly been in use for hundreds of years, as this 18th-century engraving shows.

remained of 20 000 estimated to have been alive only a century earlier.

In this racial and tribal maelstrom, we catch glimpses of the San as a palaeolithic survivor in a hostile world of metal, farmlands, domestic animals, property rights – and firearms. We see him being wiped out in the genial, well-endowed parts of the land before the combined pressures of White settlers expanding northwards and eastwards from the Cape of Good Hope, Negroes advancing down the east coast and Hottentots harrying him in the hinterland. Often the men were slain and the women taken captive. Thus the San genes have entered into the genetic composition of many of the living population groups of South Africa. Still other San were left unmolested – these were the desert dwellers, surviving in the most arid and inhospitable parts of the subcontinent, those regions of the Kalahari Desert that none of the invading peoples really wanted. There were still San in Natal in the 'seventies and 'eighties of the last century, and in the Orange Free State and Lesotho in the early days of the 20th century, while a handful of isolated survivors are still to be found in the northern Cape Province and near Lake Chrissie in the eastern Transvaal. So it is only since recent historical times that the San has become almost exclusively a desert dweller.

1.9 The finished product – a temporary hut with fireplace opposite its mouth. The shelter or *skerm* and the use of fire are two cultural techniques that help the San to cope with the cold nights of the Kalahari winter.

The San and other African peoples

In the early days of White settlement at the Cape of Good Hope all of the indigenous peoples encountered were generally lumped under the name Hottentots, as by O. Dapper in 1668 and Willem ten Rhyne in 1686. There was even a tendency to include the more remotely situated darker peoples of Kaffraria as Hottentots. The term Hottentot thus included the Sonqua, Souqua or Sunqua (that is, San). These Bushmen were regarded as Hottentots without cattle – the distinction we drew earlier in this chapter. It is interesting to note that Willem ten Rhyne, a physician to the Dutch East India Company, expressed the view that the Dutch settlers were to blame for the San having no cattle! ("Next are the *Sonquas,* who for just occasion were bereft of their cattle by our countrymen, with the result that they live in the woods and are forced to seek a means of livelihood in the desert, chiefly by hunting wild animals.") This is certainly not correct, and may be one of the "rather fantastic statements suggesting a lack of critical ability or at least a naive credulity" on the part of Ten Rhyne referred to by his 20th-century translator, Professor Benjamin Farrington (1933).

Subsequently, as acquaintance with the Bantu-speaking Negro peoples further to the east and north-east grew, the tendency was to regard the Bushmen (and Hottentots) as extremely different from the Negro Africans. For example, back in 1731, in *The Present State of the Cape of Good Hope,* Peter Kolb – translated from the German by Guido Medley – wrote:

"Some confound the *Hottentots* with the *Caffres* or *Keffres,* and call them by that Name. But the Caffres, who inhabit the *Monomotapa,* tho' encompass'd in a Manner by the *Hottentot* Nations, are a very different kind of People . . . this confounding of the two Nations could only be owing to a great ignorance of both" (p. 28).

Kolb included the Sonquas or San among the Hottentots.

Anders Sparrman, too, sharply distinguished the Hottentots and "Caffres" in his work *A Voyage to the Cape of Good Hope* (1785), and regarded the "Boshies-men" as a species of "wild Hottentot".

Robert Knox, the Edinburgh anatomist who had been involved in the Burke

8

and Hare scandals, wrote in his book *The Races of Men* (1850): "The primitive races of this land are or were two, the Hottentot, namely, or yellow race of men, and the Caffre. No two races differ more from each other . . ." For Knox, the category "Hottentot" included the San, while he considered the "Caffre" superior to the "Negro".

In 1877 there appeared an English translation, under the title *Anthropology*, of an important work by the great French anthropologist Paul Topinard, whilst the same year saw the publication of the American edition of J. G. Wood's *The Uncivilized Races of Men*.

Topinard spoke of the "Negro type", which he divided into Asian and African types. The former comprised the "Papuan" and the "Negrito", the latter the "Guinean, Kaffir and Hottentot" types. The Guinean was considered the most characteristic of the Negroes, whilst, along with other 19th-century systematists, Topinard placed the peoples of Kaffraria in a separate category. The third rubric – the Hottentot – included the Kora, Nama and Bushmen. Subsequently, Topinard suggested that this was too heterogeneous for a single class: he abandoned the Hottentot as a specific type, but promoted the Bushman to that status.

Wood did not seem able to make up his mind how to classify the Bushmen: in the same sentence, he spoke of them as "a singular race" and "evidently allied to the Hottentots" (1877, p. 242).

To read the accounts of these and other early writers is sometimes informative, often diverting. Truly it was a case of "Quot homines, tot sententiae" – so varied were their views on the place of the Bushmen and on the affinities of the indigenous peoples of sub-Saharan Africa.

In the first half of the 20th century, the view that the San was unutterably different from the Black peoples of Africa held sway. Dr Robert Broom suggested that they had affinities with China and were the "stunted and degenerate descendants" of the Korana. Others thought they had descended from another big-headed earlier people, called by some the Boskop race or the Bushmanoid people. The view of their absolute distinctness reached its zenith about 1955, when Dr J. C. Trevor of Cambridge University elevated the Khoisan group to the status of a fifth major racial constellation of the world, which he called the Khoisaniform, alongside the Caucasiform, Mongoliform, Negriform and Australiform branches of *Homo sapiens*.

As a result of the spate of new studies since the 'fifties, we now have a much clearer idea about how the San are biologically related to the other peoples of Africa. The new information is the result of the work of participants in the expeditions of the Kalahari Research Committee, and of such men as Professor Ronald Singer (see Chapter 8), Professor Joseph Weiner, Dr A. Zoutendyk, Professor Trefor Jenkins and Dr George Nurse.

We now know that the San have the same basic genetic make-up as other sub-Saharan African peoples. Careful studies in the field and in the laboratory have shown that the San agree with Negro populations in the frequencies of blood groups and other inherited biochemical traits. All of these characteristics are known as genetic markers. It is especially interesting that the San are not only *typically* African in their genetic patterns, but that in a number of respects they are *exaggeratedly* African. For in many of the genetic respects in which African Negro peoples differ most from non-Africans, the San show such features to the highest frequency in this continent! This suggests that the San may possibly be more closely related in their gene composition to the ancestral African peoples than are other living Negriform peoples.

Soon after it was first realised that San genes display a basically African pattern, professors Singer and Weiner proposed that the definition of the Negro should be extended to include these light-skinned people, namely the Khoisan groups. At that stage, 1963, we had evidence for only a few genetic markers. But the idea of these two men seemed to be supported by the fact that we were able to show that some anatomical traits previously thought to be confined to the Khoisan were, in fact, present as well in the Negro peoples. For example, both steatopygia and a female genital peculiarity known as the tablier were found to be present in southern African Negroes, though not to so marked a degree nor so consistently as in the Khoisan.

Then more and more gene variations (called polymorphisms) were discovered, and we began to realise that the picture was more complicated. All the new data on gene frequencies, such as those collected by Jenkins, Steinberg and Nurse, while confirming the broadly African Negroid picture of the Khoisan gene-set, nevertheless showed that, in numerous genetic traits, the San differed appreciably from the southern African Negro. These differences were apparent not only in genetic markers of the blood and other body fluids, but also in a number of fine anatomical features that had not previously been analysed in detail (for example, colour-blindness, the obliquity of the eye, specific features on teeth, the external genital organs of both sexes, skin colour, hair form and so on).

This mounting tally of differences led us to suggest in 1966 that, although the Khoisan manifestly belong to the same major genic constellation as other sub-Saharan Africans, the evidence points to a lengthy period in which the Khoisan must have developed in isolation from the Negro. This means that the latest common ancestors of the Khoisan and the Negro lived a much longer time ago than we earlier believed. The genetical and evolutionary divergence of the Khoisan and the Negro from each other was not an event of the other day, nor yet of some centuries. It must have occurred many millennia ago, possibly as long ago as 15 000 years or more. This story of the origin and evolution of the San will be picked up in the next chapter.

The San – hardly a "dying race"

It was long customary to regard the San as a vanishing people. For example, in his well-known work *Ancient Hunters and Their Modern Representatives* (1924) W. J. Sollas wrote:

"We have spoken of the Bushmen in the past tense, for they are practically extinct; a miserable remnant of inferior character still lingers on in the Kalahari desert, but even this is slowly dwindling away under the terrible hardships of an unfavourable environment" (pp. 489-490).

The Rev. S. S. Dornan, in his *Pygmies and Bushmen of the Kalahari* (1925), estimated that as many as 10 000 San might be alive. Nevertheless he added:

"They are a dwindling race and in a comparatively short space of time, they will have ceased to exist as a separate people" (p. 199).

In 1930, in his *Human History,* Sir Grafton Elliot Smith was "mourning the disappearance of this remarkable race", which was "almost extinct" and reduced to "a few scattered groups still lingering in the Kalahari Desert". "In a few years the world will know them no more" (pp. 207-208).

Professor I. Schapera's authoritative work *The Khoisan Peoples of South Africa* (1930) placed the total number of San still in existence "at a conservative minimum" of about 7 000 to 7 500. And he added:

"There seems little doubt that the Bushmen are steadily dying out as a race. What relentless persecution at the hands of other peoples has not achieved is being slowly accomplished by disease and racial intermixture. Racially pure Bushmen are already in a minority, and their ultimate absorption by their neighbours is probably inevitable" (p. 40).

However, in 1939 Schapera replaced his earlier figure by a greatly increased estimate of 30 000 San. His 1939 publication appeared just before the outbreak of the Second World War and it does not seem to have become widely known.

Nine years later, the British anatomist and physical anthropologist Sir Arthur Keith could still state: "It is estimated that only about 6 000 of the Bushmen now survive" (1948). Even that great student of the Bushmen, Dr Dorothea F. Bleek, concluded her introduction to A. M. Duggan-Cronin's *The Bushman Tribes of Southern Africa* (1942) with the words ". . . this race, which as a separate entity is doomed to extinction in the near future" (p. 14).

In the face of these pessimistic forecasts, it came as a surprise to many people when in 1956 I published an estimate of 55 531 surviving San as at that date. Most of them were living in Botswana and South West Africa; there were a sizeable number in Angola, and very small numbers in Zambia, Rhodesia and South Africa. The latest position may be summarized as follows:

1.10 A San woman and child in the Dobe district close to the border between Botswana and South West Africa. Despite earlier under-estimates, there are 50 000 Bushmen alive today.

1.11 Another little San baby to add to the 30 000 Bushmen already in the Republic of Botswana.

Botswana: The total arrived at in 1956, based on regional and district counts or estimates, was 31 000, of whom some 10 000 were in the Ngwato Reserve. In 1964 Dr George Silberbauer (the Bushman Survey Officer appointed by the Bechuanaland Government) and the Population Census Officer found the Bushman population to number somewhat fewer, namely 24 652. In his well-known *Bushman Survey* (1965) Silberbauer stated: "This figure does not include persons who might, on grounds of their appearance and ancestry, be considered to be Bushmen, but who have now been accepted as part of the Bantu population. On the basis of follow-up checks, we believe that the total is twenty per cent inaccurate." In the context of the report, it would seem that the figure should be increased, rather than decreased, by twenty per cent. If this were correct, the total for Botswana would be as much as about 29 600, slightly less than the estimate of a decade earlier. It is difficult to know whether this represents a true drop in the San population, or whether it is the result of difficulty in defining who is a San or of marriage or acculturation of San into other population groups.

South West Africa/Namibia: Between 1876, when W. C. Palgrave estimated that there were 3 000 San in South West Africa, and 1939, estimates of the number of

San in this territory have fluctuated wildly, but generally seem to have erred in being on the low side. Schapera's 1939 estimate was 8 000 in all. Nevertheless, the South West Africa Native Affairs Annual Report for 1953 gave a total of 20 582 San in the territory; I used a slightly reduced version of this figure (20 311) in my 1955 estimate. The results of the 1970 preliminary census yielded a figure of 21 909, while the 1974 population estimate gave a figure of 26 000 San, the most recent total available. If these figures are correct, the population of South West African San has increased by 5 689 in the 21 years from 1953 to 1974, or an approximate growth rate of 1,3 per cent per annum.

Angola : Father Martin Gusinde's estimates, back in 1952, indicated the presence of some 3 000 "yellow Bushmen" and 1 000 to 3 000 "black Bushmen" in Angola. On the strength of these assessments, I used a lower total of 4 000 in my 1955 compilations, although the range of figures was 4 000 to 6 000. Professor Antonio de Almeida estimated that there were about 3 500 "yellow" San and 400 or 500 "black" San (1965), that is, approximately 4 000 Angolan San.

Zambia : The small group of some 200 San in the Barotse forests, between the Zambezi and Mashi rivers, were visited by J. D. Clark in 1951. We have no newer information and adhere to that earlier figure.

Republic of South Africa : Schapera (1930) drew attention to a few San living on the shores of Lake Chrissie, near Ermelo in the eastern Transvaal, and "evidently remnants of a tribe that once roamed over the High Veld of the Transvaal". He mentioned that the name "BaTwa" is applied to them by the local Swazi. Later expeditions located some 20 "unhybridized" San there: this figure excludes about the same number of individuals born to unions between one Swazi and one San. There are also a tiny handful of isolated San individuals on farms in the north-western parts of the Cape Province. Dr and Mrs Gerhard Fock of Kimberley have recently brought to my attention a few such individuals whom they found on farms. In 1905 the Transvaal Native Affairs Department, assisted by a Mr Knothe, issued a *Short History of the Native Tribes of the Transvaal*, the first data to become available for that province. Although it did not refer to the BaTwa of Lake Chrissie, it included reference to a few scattered groups of "Vaalpense",

1.12 One of the last surviving Transvaal Bushmen: a farm-dwelling Bushman lady at Lake Chrissie near Ermelo in the eastern Transvaal. She is one of a tiny remnant – numbering today not more than 20 souls – of San peoples who once roamed the easterly parts of southern Africa in great numbers. In this area live another 20 individuals each of whom is the progeny of a union between one San and one Swazi parent. Within another generation this group of San survivors will have ceased to exist as a distinct entity.

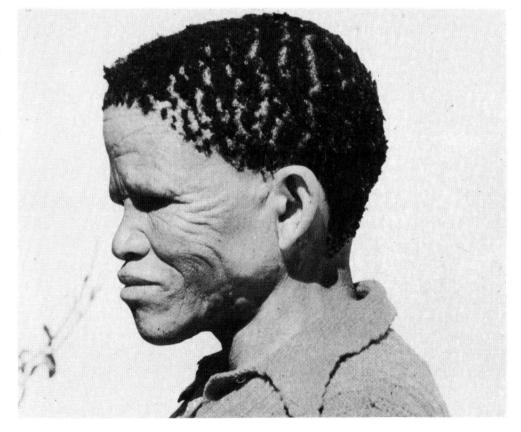

described as "a Hottentot-Bushman people, who are found in the Zoutpansberg and other districts, occupying the sterile plains, especially along the Magala-kween River". The name "Vaalpens" means "dun-coloured belly", and the *Short History* states that this name was "given to them by the Boers owing to their colour, caused, it is said, by their habit of crawling along the ground when stalking game". No reference to this group could be found in Schapera's 1930 book, nor in any other more recent publications. Thus the total estimate of San in the Republic of South Africa today is set at 25, based on the Lake Chrissie and north-western Cape remnants.

Rhodesia: It is possible that there may still be a small number of San in the districts of Dett, the Gwaai Reserve and Masuie. No figures or recent facts are available for this territory.

Total: On these latest estimates, imperfect as they are, it seems that there are about 55 000 to 60 000 San alive today, of whom about half are present in Botswana and about half in South West Africa. The following figures summarize the latest estimates:

Botswana	24 652 – 29 600
South West Africa	26 000
Angola	4 000
Zambia	200
South Africa	25
Grand Total	54 877 – 59 825

These figures are far higher than those believed to exist in the middle of the century. The evidence seems sufficient to deny that the San as a people are dying out. That the old way of life is disappearing is undoubted, but the people as biological or genetic entities are living on in new cultural and economic guises.

The San in transition

Just what proportions of the San are still pursuing the hunting-gathering life, in its pristine unadulterated form, is hard to gauge. Some rough indication may be obtained from Silberbauer's figures for Botswana in 1964. Of the more or less 24 000 San he enumerated in that territory, he reported some 4 000 on the White-owned cattle-farms in the Ghanzi area, either in the employ of the farmers or as dependants of such employees. Approximately 14 000 San, he states, lived permanently, or for most of the year, at Tswana and other Negro villages or cattle-posts, or in close proximity to them, as labourers or clients of the Negro peoples. Approximately 6 000 of the Botswana San were "wild Bushmen", able to subsist on the proceeds of their hunting and food-gathering, and either living in remote areas without moving out on visits, or making only brief visits to farms or cattle-posts for the purposes of trading or finding water and food.

On this analysis, only about 25 per cent of the Botswana San were in 1964 still living the hunter-gatherer life. In South West Africa over 40 per cent of the San are living in the farming area. This means that over 50 per cent are living away from the farms, in the north of the territory. From this figure should be deducted a number who have been affected by a settlement scheme and others who may be dependent on the Kavango and Ambo peoples. We have no information on what the latter figures are, but the impression remains that a slightly bigger percentage of the South West African San than of the Botswana San may possibly still be living as hunters and gatherers.

Of the estimated total of 55 000 to 60 000 San, it is unlikely that as many as one-third (or 18 000 to 20 000) are still hunters and gatherers. A precise figure is almost impossible to obtain partly because of difficulties of definition of San or Bushmen and partly because many regions are for one reason or another virtually in-accessible today.

Moreover, numbers of San are neither "pure" hunter-gatherers nor "pure" settled herders. In varying degrees many pursue a way of life intermediate be-

1.13 San children poised between two worlds – the old palaeolithic ways of hunting and gathering and the new pattern of subsistence by the herding of domestic animals and the cultivation of crops.

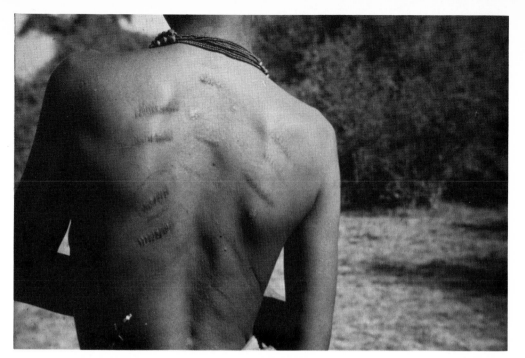

1.14 The complex cultural life of the Bushmen includes powerful elements of ritual and religion. A girl's back is ritually scarified at puberty.

1.15 A male Bushman from Lake Chrissie, one of the few very last surviving Bushmen in the Republic of South Africa.

tween the two extremes. In 1959, the expeditions of the Kalahari Research Committee had to classify the San of western Botswana into five main categories, according to the amount of contact experienced – and these excluded the San living on Tswana cattle-posts. The five categories were:

1. Those born in the veld, who had remained "wild", having little or no contact with settled and pastoral ways. The numbers in this category, we found, were seriously declining: even an apparently very isolated group encountered north of Sonop Koppies possessed a few goats!

2. Some born on the veld came in periodically to the farms or boreholes for food and water in dry seasons, but returned always to the veld.

3. Of the San born in the veld, some had taken up residence on farms, but journeyed forth into the veld to hunt and collect wild foods every now and again.

4. Some of the veld-born San were living on farms and never wandered away to the wilds.

5. Finally, there was a new generation of San, born on the farms, who had experienced no other than farm life and did not hunt or collect wild foods.

The existence of all these transitional groups adds to one's difficulties if one tries to give absolute figures for those San who have abandoned the hunter-gatherer life and those who have not.

There are periods when the tempo of change seems to increase. Just before our 1958-1959 expeditions, there had been five successive years of drought. As a result, the movement of "wild" Bushmen to the water-holes, the farms and the cattle-posts had been greatly accelerated. Hence, between the 1951 Panhard-Capricorn expedition and the 1958-1959 Kalahari Research Committee expeditions, we found that "wild" San, who had had little or no contact with farmers and their ways, had become fewer and further between. The process of moving in to the farms seems to be sensitive to seasonal fluctuations that may modify the pattern and the rate of acculturation.

Why study the San or Bushmen?

What we have just said gives one of the reasons why the Bushmen or San are among the most exceptional of today's humankind. Even now, in the last quarter of the 20th century, many of them, living in the desert wastes of the Kalahari, are still leading the old nomadic life, hunting with poisoned arrows and collecting *veldkos*, or wild foods, with digging sticks. They provide us with a remarkable view of a present-day society – one of the last – living in a Stone Age cultural context.

There is a further reason why the San excite our curiosity. They stand poised between two worlds: the old palaeolithic ways of hunting and gathering and the new pattern of subsistence by the herding of domestic animals and the cultivation of crops. Many San, even within the present century, have adopted a food-producing economy and have settled on the land for shorter or longer periods. As a people, they are hovering on the brink of the great change-over from the palaeolithic existence to pastoral and agricultural life, such as occurred in the river valleys of the eastern Mediterranean some 10 000 years ago (see Chapter 2).

At this very moment, some of them are re-enacting that transition of ten millennia ago. The transfiguration from food-collecting to food-producing is being revealed before our eyes – as though a gigantic time-top had whirled us back to a remote age and far-off places. There are differences, of course. History never repeats itself precisely, but the essentials are broadly alike. By the end of the 20th century, the process will be complete – and it is very doubtful if any San living at that time will still subsist purely by hunting or gathering.

This transitional state is of great importance and a most serious challenge to administrators as well as sociologists, economists and political scientists. For them this is a chance to study the dynamics of the change-over from food-collecting to food-producing. How does the break with the past occur? How does it affect the people undergoing the transformation, and those who are already pastoralists among whom the San live? Is there anything governments can do to ease the metamorphosis? Should administrations encourage settlement schemes? Or should they leave it to the San to decide for themselves, to continue living their old life, happily hunting as the whim or need or opportunity presents itself, gathering veldkos when hungry, migrating when necessary or desirable, adopting such items as they wish from the sedentary economy of other peoples farming in their vicinity?

It is inevitable that, within another generation or two, the hunter-gatherer lifestyle will have become completely extinct among the San. Indeed, this is likely to happen for all such groups in other parts of the world by – or at the latest, during – the 21st century. Should the process of what anthropologists call *acculturation* be deliberately encouraged and accelerated by the governments and agencies concerned, or should things be left to take their own course?

If it is accepted that the administrations have a responsibility to effect the material advancement of the San, should there be complete and immediate settlement, with the teaching of cultivation and pastoral techniques? Or should there be a policy of gradualism, with – initially at least – only minimal steps by government, such as the putting down of boreholes to ensure a supply of water, the proclaiming and fencing of traditional hunting areas and the debarring of farmers and poachers from the San's terrain?

How difficult it is to answer these questions is shown by the fact that quite different policies have in the recent past been adopted by the administrations of the three main territories concerned, namely Botswana, South West Africa and Angola. Some of these problems are discussed at greater length by Dr H. J. Heinz and Dr G. B. Silberbauer in chapters 13 and 14 of this book. It is important to stress here that sound and constructive policies must depend upon a clear picture of the present state of the San, both those who are still hunters and gatherers, those in various stages of transition and those who have already accomplished the change-over. When we reflect that well over half of all surviving San have already abandoned the pure hunting and gathering mode of subsistence, we realise that we should already have at our disposal much invaluable information on the mechanics and dynamics of the adjustment.

Many of the facts recorded in this book will, it is hoped, make a contribution towards the planning of the future of the San, their survival and their welfare.

2
The San: An Evolutionary Perspective

Phillip V. Tobias

Hunters and gatherers of yester-year

Until about 10 000 years ago, mankind everywhere lived off the land by hunting animals and gathering natural food products. It was a way of life that had gone on since the dawn of man. In some areas and at some times game was plentiful, and so were edible fruits, nuts and bulbs. Often bad seasons and even long-term climatic changes led the animals to migrate: and man followed the animals. So many, but by no means all, of the hunter-gatherers were nomadic and their settlements were temporary. The main part of the equipment needed included weapons for the chase, domestic utensils for preparing food, digging tools and water containers. Because his wordly possessions were few, man could travel light, and this was a decided advantage for those hunting peoples who were frequently on the move.

Such a subsistence economy was the basis of human life for over a million years. There were variations on the theme. For example, those who lived near great lakes or marine beaches may have taken to hunting in the water and rock pools – for that is all fishing is! Hunting techniques varied: some people trapped game, others threw spears or used a bolas, two balls connected by a cord which entangles the legs of the quarry; the bow and arrow were invented and the use of poison was discovered. The mastery of fire added a new element to the economy: it brought winter warmth, protection by night, the cooking of food and the lengthening of the hours of wakefulness.

2.1 An old engraving of a hunting scene. Khoisan hunters used short spears as well as bows and arrows. Ostrich eggs not only provide nutrition; their empty shells carried in the net (left) were used as water containers.

Under this pattern of existence, the numbers of human beings grew but slowly. Very gradually, the whole of the Old World was peopled – Africa, Asia, Europe, Australia – and, late in the day, the American continent as well. The Palaeolithic, or Early Stone Age, cultures that accompanied hunter-gatherer subsistence became modified in a hundred different ecological settings. Man adjusted himself to life in the tropics (from which he probably started out), the subtropical and the temperate zones; to extremes of climate: from the frozen circum-polar wastes of northern Eurasia and America to the Sahara, Gobi and Great Australian deserts;

to different environments: from beaches, river valleys and lake-shore habitats to mountain-top elevations, from continental land masses to a myriad great and small islands. As a way of life the hunter-gatherer existence was extraordinarily successful. Its flexibility and adaptability enabled it to meet the challenges posed by nearly every corner of the world, and in all such niches man arrived, established himself, modified his cultural equipment, adjusted his basic hunter-gatherer pattern – and set up "home".

Undoubtedly the nature of this mode of living was a major factor in enabling man to become a dominant global species. However, we must not forget the man himself, who was the bearer of the culture and the economy. Man, as a biological entity, had discovered, invented, explored, innovated and experimented to produce that pattern of existence – and, what is more, to modify, augment and adapt it wherever he carried it. As a species, he possessed the hereditary endowment to do these things. Virtually alone among the animals, his genetic evolution had given him the intellect, the visual and manipulative skills, the foresight and the versatility to develop a set of cultural resources, notions and practices which played an all-important role in his survival. It was almost as though he had evolved extensions of his body to help him solve the problems posed by his surroundings.

Yet, while man became utterly dependent on his cultural survival kit, he remained the most resilient and unspecialized among the mammals. His biological inheritance – his genes and chromosomes – laid down the blueprint for a bodily design and a style of functioning that could persist and flourish in the most varied environments, with only a bare minimum of evolutionary modification. True, he did diversify genetically into geographical varieties, such as those great groups of humanity known as the Australoid, Caucasoid, Mongoloid and Negroid peoples. However, this division of man into broad varieties did not in any way tie each population down to a narrow ecological compartment or to a specialized manner of existence. Despite biological diversification, the different human branches remained largely unspecialized, as animals go. Furthermore, whatever adaptive gains followed in the wake of such differentiation are far outweighed by the advantages and the plasticity of the hunter-gatherer lifestyle and the palaeolithic cultures of which it was a part. These two factors – the absence of bodily specialization coupled with the possession of a universal, and highly pliant, hunter-gatherer culture – largely account for the world-wide evolutionary success of our species, *Homo sapiens*.

The Neolithic or Agrarian Revolution

From about 10 000 to 20 000 years ago, a revolutionary new mode of human life gradually made its appearance. Up till then, man had been content to take what Nature offered – from nuts and berries to warthogs and birds' eggs. Since the end of the Ice Age in the Northern Hemisphere, man has progressively learnt to control his own food supply – and so to control Nature. His lifestyle became altered from a subsistence economy based on hunting and gathering to a food-producing regimen. These far-reaching changes are sometimes called the Neolithic or Agrarian Revolution.

Man began to plant, cultivate and improve by selection edible grasses, roots and trees. For example, he domesticated certain kinds of wild grasses to produce wheats and barleys. By deliberately selecting and cultivating the seed of the best plants, and by accidentally or consciously crossing varieties, man produced grains that are far larger and more nourishing than any of the wild grass-seeds. In different areas, a variety of plants were cultivated and came to provide a staple diet – plants such as millet, rice, maize, sweet potatoes, yams and bananas. Agriculture was born and man's life was unalterably changed from its million-year-old former fabric. The way was opened for the development of all the more complex societies and civilisations that followed.

Man's farming activities were not, however, confined to plants. He succeeded in taming some species of animals that became firmly attached to his person and his place of living. These domesticated animals became dependent on man for the fodder and for the protection that he was able to provide. Man, for his part, came to depend on his domestic animals, such as cattle, sheep, goats and pigs, for meat

and for milk – and later for other uses, such as to provide wool and hides for clothing, to serve as pack animals, or to furnish dung for use as fertiliser. In certain societies, the adoption of this pastoral or agricultural mode of life by no means brought an end to the nomadic ways followed by most hunters and gatherers; but for some, nomadism soon gave way to a more sedentary life.

The most significant evolutionary change that followed in the wake of the Neolithic or Agrarian Revolution was the first human population explosion. The appearance of the earliest farmers was followed by new patterns of human settlement and social organization. Village-building and city-dwelling entered on the scene. The processes of civilisation were set on foot – and man came increasingly to cocoon himself within his man-made social fabric and cultural milieu.

The new patterns of food production arose independently in several different parts of the world, such as the Middle East and the Nile Valley, India, China and the New World. They spread gradually westwards and northwards across Europe, northwards across Asia and southwards down the African continent. Over the ensuing millennia, more and more human populations came to adopt the new ways of life. The ripples of agriculture and pastoralism spread in ever-expanding circles from the original centres. By the 20th century, almost all mankind in the entire world had adopted food production as the basis of life.

Hunters and gatherers of today

Only here and there, in scattered and remote corners of the globe, are there still little groups of men and women living as hunters and gatherers. R. B. Lee and I. DeVore estimated that they comprised 0,001 per cent of the human population in 1966, 15,0 per cent in 1492 A.D. and 100,0 per cent some 10 000 years ago. So the hunters and gatherers are a dwindling minority of the world's human population. In general, it would not be accurate to speak of them as "living fossils", since most of them do not represent the survival of an otherwise extinct kind of man. It is rather their *way of existence* that is a living fossil, for it represents the persistence of a lifestyle that has all but vanished from earth. You may find this nearly extinct pattern lingering on in the Central African forests, in East Africa, in parts of India, in the Andaman Islands and Malaya, in the "outback" of the Australian Desert, among the Eskimoes of Greenland and the far north of Canada, among some tribal populations of North and South America, and among the San or Bushmen of southern Africa.

These living exponents of hunting and gathering ways of life provide us with rare and precious glimpses of man's past. When we dig up burials, stone imple-

18

ments and other cultural objects in archaeological sites, there are always big problems of interpretation. For what purpose were these tools used? What part was played in the economy by artefacts made of perishable materials that have not survived? How did these people hunt? How was their society organized? What beliefs, traditions, ritual observances, ethical concepts, social structures, family and inter-group relationships informed their culture? Our inferences cannot but be tentative. But when we have a Stone Age society living today, it is possible by careful study to provide answers to all of these questions, and many more besides. Hence, to the student of man the survival of hunter-gatherer communities is invaluable in providing possible clues to the past. Of course, we cannot assume that Stone Age man of 25 000 and of 50 000 years ago lived exactly as the surviving hunters do today; but at least these survivors provide us with living models. And, by cautious comparison of the lifestyle of different groups of living hunters, we may be able to detect common threads running through them. This is what Richard B. Lee and Irven DeVore have done in their book *Man the Hunter* (1968). Our inferences about prehistoric man are likely to be more valid if they are based not only on what can be learned by digging up the past, but also on what is known about living hunter-gatherers.

Present and past distribution of the San

Today the remnants of the San live mainly in Botswana, South West Africa and Angola, with very small numbers in the Republic of South Africa and in Zambia. There is little doubt that the San were formerly far more numerous than at present, and that they occupied a large part of Africa. When the first White settlers landed in Table Bay in 1652, the San must have inhabited almost the entire territory now included within the Republic of South Africa, South West Africa, Botswana, Lesotho and Swaziland, as well as parts of Mozambique, Rhodesia, Zambia and Angola.

Still earlier, as we have seen, Arab historians reported the little click-speaking Wak-Wak, who were probably San, on the Sofala coast of Mozambique: this would place them in the eastern part of Africa as far north as 20° South latitude. In contrast, in the hinterland of Rhodesia, Zambia and northern Botswana and the Caprivi Strip, the San are still to be found as far north as 17°S, whilst in the western part of the subcontinent, in southern Angola, 15° S represents the most northerly latitude occupied by the San.

If, however, we wish to go back before recorded history in Africa, we have to rely on archaeological remains. Excavations have revealed a number of skeletons very similar in their anatomical features to the bones of known recent San. Most of these have come to light within the area of southern Africa known to have been

2.3 In prehistoric times a people with skeletons similar to those of the San inhabited a very large part of Africa – estimated as the area shaded. The sites of individual discoveries are shown by dark dots.

By 1652, when the first Dutch settlers under Jan van Riebeeck reached the Cape Peninsula, the estimated distribution of Bushmen had already greatly diminished.

Today, despite the harshness of the terrain, the Bushmen are to be found almost exclusively in parts of the Kalahari desert in Botswana, South West Africa and Angola. Their territory has shrunk to a minute fraction of what it was formerly.

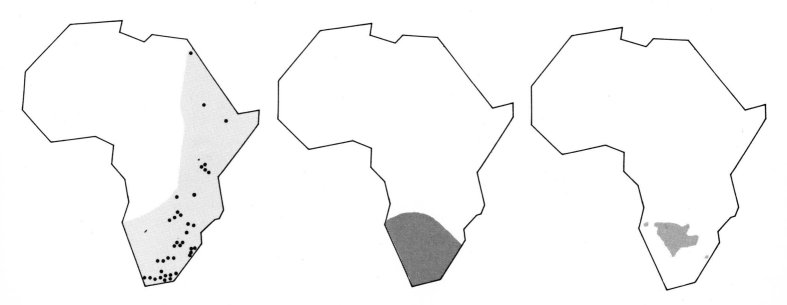

19

inhabited by San in historical times (see map). A sprinkling of skeletons with San features and dating from the Later Stone Age onwards has been found well outside the known historical limits of the San. These remains, as shown on the map, suggest that people with skeletons like those of modern San might have lived in Central and East Africa, and possibly even throughout the north-south extent of Africa, at least in its eastern half, about 10 000 to 15 000 years ago.

Thus, over ten millennia, the San have been dramatically rolled back as their numbers have been decimated, until today they are left living for the most part under the arid, semi-desert conditions of the Kalahari.

The San and the Kalahari

The Kalahari basin has been described by the geomorphologist L. C. King in 1951 as "perhaps the greatest expanse of sand-veld in the world". This semi-desert zone has in most areas a low average annual rainfall varying from 125 to 380 mm (5 to 15 inches), but years of drought are frequent. The sand – of red, yellow and white hues – is covered by a mantle of grass and scrub, quite bare stretches of sand

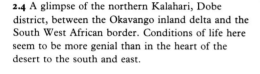

2.4 A glimpse of the northern Kalahari, Dobe district, between the Okavango inland delta and the South West African border. Conditions of life here seem to be more genial than in the heart of the desert to the south and east.

being rare. On the other hand, some areas inhabited by the San are somewhat moister and the vegetation cover is more luxuriant: such, for instance, is the Dobe area, where Dr R. B. Lee studied a group of San who are manifestly better off than most of the Kalahari dwellers. In the northern Kalahari, the rainfall rises to nearly 760 mm (30 inches); the vegetation is dense, gradually increasing until it merges with the woodland-savanna to the north.

2.5 A San girl at puberty: she shows the bulging forehead, flat nasal bridge, folded eyelids and other anatomical features reminiscent of childhood structure.

Thus, most San live under dry to semi-arid conditions, where lean years are common and the vegetation is drought-conditioned, though surprisingly extensive and varied for regions of low rainfall. Much game is encountered, including springbok, gemsbok (oryx), blue wildebeest (brindled gnu), eland, giraffe, kudu, duiker, steenbok, and other antelopes; a variety of carnivores, including members of the cat and the dog family; warthogs, spring-hares, ant-bears and porcupines; water-loving species in the swamp area to the north; birds, reptiles and insects.

2.6 The broad low-bridged nose of San people is correlated with climatic conditions, for people who live in hotter climates generally have broader noses than those who live in more temperate climates. This is one feature of the San that is of particular adaptive value for life under warm conditions.

Natural water is scarce, as there are not many water sources. River-beds are nearly always dry, often resembling silver ribbons snaking their way across the reddish sand. Even at times of flood, as Professor King has pointed out, virtually no surface outflow escapes from the Kalahari.

2.7 The neotenous or child-like features in the facial and cranial structure of the Bushman mother are readily apparent in this picture of a Central Kalahari San mother and child. Note also the small ear with over-rolled helix or rim and the tufted or "peppercorn" distribution of hair over the scalp, especially in the baby.

Such is the physiographic background of the modern Bushman: how he copes with life in these circumstances will be considered below and in later chapters of this book.

The singular San

A most striking feature of the living San is their unusual bodily structure. Basically they are a short people, the average height for virtually all San groups falling below the mean height for most groups of southern African Negroes.

In addition to the pygmoid size of the San, the structure shown by many parts of the body resembles that of juvenile human beings in general, irrespective of racial or ethnic affinities. Some of these juvenile traits are to be found in the soft tissues of the body and some in the bones. The main soft-tissue features recalling the anatomy of the infant are a relative lack of hair on the face and body; light skin pigmentation; lips of only moderate thickness, or even thinnish and inverted; a fold of the upper eyelids, especially over the inner corners; transversely placed nostrils; the short, often nearly horizontal penis, with high, compact scrotum; and some cerebral characteristics. The infantile features in the skeleton are largely to be found in the skull: they include the low, flattened cranium, often with strongly developed bulges in the front, at the sides and at the back, giving the skull a pentagonal shape when looked at from above; the small mastoid process behind the ear-hole; a generally smooth brow above the eye sockets; a vertical or even bulging forehead; a small, flat face; the wide distance between the eye sockets; a flat nose bridge; poor development of the sinuses that open into the nose; a brain case that is fairly large in relation to the size of the face; jaws that protrude slightly, if at all; a low, squat branch of the mandible or lower jaw.

Of course, as in all human beings, each of these features varies greatly among San individuals. None the less, the length of the list – which is by no means complete – shows how many of the peculiar features of the adult San may result from the carrying into adulthood of anatomical traits normally associated with the bodily structure of human infants. It should be noted that this does not apply to sexual, functional, emotional or mental maturity – only to the observable architecture and proportions of the body. All of these features occur in the young of *Homo sapiens,* at a stage in the unfolding of the adults – whether of Australoid, Caucasoid, Mongoloid or Negroid peoples. The fossil evidence confirms that such features marked the young of the ancestral San, too; though as the pre-San children grew up, the infantile appearances were outgrown and replaced by typically adult-like form and proportions. At an early period in the evolution of the San, changes seem to have occurred in consequence of which some of these infantile traits came to persist into adult life.

Such retention of juvenile anatomical features into adulthood is well known in other members of the animal kingdom. The phenomenon is known as *neoteny.* It has been suggested that neoteny was an important factor in the transition of an ape-like ancestor into a member of the family of man. Also, it may have played a part in the formation of some varieties of the human family, such as the San. The late Professor M. R. Drennan first stressed this neoteny (or paedomorphism) in the anatomy of the San, and both he and Professor R. A. Dart frequently wrote on this subject. For Drennan, the Bushmen were verily morphological Peter Pans!

Although some of the infantile likenesses could perhaps be laid at the door of poor nutrition, the rise of genetics suggests another explanation of neoteny. The genes are the basis of our biological inheritance. They produce their effects by altering the processes of development. Some alterations are qualitative, such as the formation of a new type of pigment; some are quantitative and amend the timing, direction, threshold or speed of a process. A large class of mutant genes either accelerates or retards the processes of development, and so indirectly modifies the ultimate finished product. If a mutant gene operates early in embryonic development, it may affect a variety of processes; its impact may thus ramify through many parts of the embryo's body. If one of the rate-retarding mutant genes operated early, it could lead to the retardation of divers processes of development, thus producing the persistence of infantile features. It may be that such early-operating, rate-controlling mutant genes provide the key to neoteny.

The San as a desert dweller

We have looked at two extraordinary facts about the San. First, they possess a peculiar and, in some respects, extreme bodily structure. Secondly, they inhabit a

restricted and, in some respects, extreme environment. Is there a connection between these two facts? It seems but a short step from the fact that the stunted and neotenous San live in the desert to the claim that their anatomical peculiarities are the "specialized" or "degenerate" products of desert conditions. Is such a claim justified?

The idea that the San's curious bodily features are the result of, or adjustments to, life in the desert has bedevilled the literature for decades. Indeed, for a long time this view was so strongly held that it largely distracted attention from other aspects of the San's ecology. As long ago as 1918 the great American physical anthropologist E. A. Hooton suggested that steatopygia (the large fat deposits over the buttocks of many San and Khoikhoi) was an evolved means of overcoming drought – like the camel's hump. In 1936 J. R. H. Marett, in a large book entitled *Race, Sex and Environment*, proclaimed the San as "the one form of man specialized for desert conditions". Among many other reasons, he held that steatopygia represented a peculiar capacity to economize water. He also tried to relate the San's small stature to the level of activity of the hypophysis, or pituitary gland, which he believed to be low in order to check loss of water from the body. The yellow skin and the eye-fold he regarded "as a primary character evolved in the desert cradle-land of this race" and the tufted or "peppercorn" hair as an adaptation to withstand heat. Similarly, C. S. Coon cited the San as a human illustration of the "desert-fat rule", namely that in those that dwell in hot deserts fat is not spread evenly over the body, but "is deposited in lumps, where it will not interfere with body-heat loss or locomotion" (1955).

2.8 An accumulation of fat on the buttocks (steatopygia) and on the thighs (steatomeria) provides one of the most eye-catching characteristics of Khoisan ladies. A San female photographed in the south-western Kalahari more than forty years ago.

It is implicit in all such views that the San is not only a present-day desert dweller, but that he is an ancient son of the desert, and that he has developed his bodily peculiarities while living in the desert, *as adaptations to desert conditions*.

We no longer believe this. A moment's glance at the earlier distribution of the San is enough to disprove the idea. We now know that the San lived all over southern Africa, including the well-watered and lush uplands of Natal, the rolling, hilly country of the eastern Cape Province and the luxuriance of the southern Cape mountain and forest belt. From the evidence of early travellers' descriptions and pictures and of exhumed skeletons, we know that the San in these richly endowed areas showed the same bodily characteristics as do their present-day relations in the Kalahari. Anatomically speaking, the San looked like the "desert Bushmen" long before their descendants became exclusive desert dwellers!

The fact that the San developed infantile features before they became desert survivors rules out the possibility that neoteny in any way adapted the San to desert life. We cannot even say that neoteny is a necessary adaptation to the hunting and food-gathering way of life, for there are hunters and gatherers like the aboriginal Australians who do not show infantile features. Why the development-retarding mutant genes should have been selected in the ancestors of the San remains a mystery. It is difficult to conceive of any especial advantage that neoteny might have conferred upon a people in a Pleistocene African setting. The Negroes of Africa do not show these infantile specializations, although they live in many areas in similar surroundings, yet they have flourished over large parts of the continent. Whether there is some subtle tie-up among African climes, low food intake, trace elements and other food minerals, retarding and accelerating mutant genes, the secretions of the endocrine glands and the architectonics of the body – all this remains a fascinating and pregnant speculation.

Infantile structure and small pygmoid stature do not necessarily go hand in hand. Some of the ancestors of the San seem to have combined neoteny with moderately large stature. At different times, it seems, these early African people underwent two kinds of change – development-retarding and growth-retarding. The archaeological record shows that the last step in this transformation was the tendency towards dwarfing of larger ancestors. Dwarfing, too, has been regarded by some as a result of life under desert conditions. Again this theory is contradicted by the former widespread distribution of *small-sized* San over some of the most fertile parts of southern Africa.

Late Pleistocene dwarfing in Africa was not confined to man. Dr M. D. W. Jeffreys assembled data on a variety of wild and domesticated mammals of which dwarf forms exist today. Examples include the pygmy buffalo, antelopes, hippopotamus, elephant, dormouse, leopard and chimpanzee, in addition to dwarf cattle, goats and sheep. Pleistocene remains from a yet earlier period contain fewer dwarf forms and, at some stages, more giant species. It is possible that late Pleistocene conditions in parts of Africa may have favoured and strongly selected dwarf forms. We should remember that man, too, is a mammal and that human dwarfing in Africa ought perhaps to be viewed against this background.

Genes, glands and calories

It has been suggested that the internal secretions made by the endocrine glands of the body may have something to do with the small size and juvenile features of adult San. One of these glands is the hypophysis, or pituitary gland, at the base of the brain. The hormones manufactured in this gland affect many parts of the body and a number of different processes, including growth. If the pituitary produces too little growth hormone, for instance, a miniature human being results – and many of the pituitary midgets have infantile anatomical features! In other words, normal, healthy San adults have two important groups of characteristics that are shown by human beings with an underactive pituitary gland. Is it possible that the setting of the pituitary gland in the San was different and perhaps lower than that in other kinds of modern man?

When we first put this suggestion forward many years ago, no research work had been done on the internal secretions of the San. We had at that time no knowledge about whether the setting of the endocrine glands in the San differed from that of other races. We were aware, of course, of differences between the small, neotenous San and the small, neotenous pituitary midgets. For example, a pituitary midget is a sporadic and rare occurrence among human populations, whereas small stature and juvenile features in the adult are very common – one might almost say the rule – among the San. Secondly, in true pituitary midgets, infantilism commonly affects the reproductive system, so that sexual underdevelopment and even sterility may result. In the San sexual functioning is not affected, even though there are some possibly infantile features in the anatomy of the male and female genital organs. Thirdly, although the features of infantilism and dwarfing are combined in many pituitary midgets and in modern San, the ancestors of the San seem to have become infantilized *before* the onset of dwarfing changes. So, although the San's structure bears a superficial resemblance to that of a pituitary midget, the processes at work in the two kinds of human being show some clear differences.

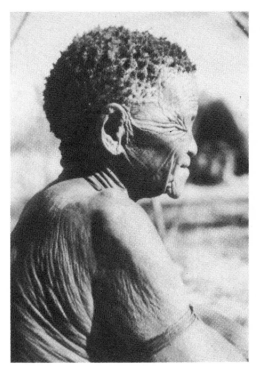

2.9 This elderly San lady beautifully illustrates the tiny face and large brain-case that is one of the juvenile traits retained into the adulthood of the San.

2.10 A San midget with an underactive pituitary gland: this miniature Bushman named Oubaas lived on a farm in the Ghanzi district of Botswana. (The author, appearing with him in the left photograph, is himself on the short side.)

Even steatopygia has been blamed by some on an out-of-step pituitary gland! The curious thing, though, is that steatopygia may develop in a woman with an *over*active pituitary, as in the condition known as acromegaly. Stranger still are the changes that acromegaly produces in the bones: the skull becomes heavy-browed and overgrown, to produce a picture not far from that of Neandertal man, whose anatomy was poles apart from that of the San. Hence we should be guilty of oversimplifying the picture if we were to attribute San steatopygia to an *over*active pituitary gland.

Despite the contradictions, however, the build of the San leaves a strong feeling that, somehow, his balance of internal secretions is different from that of most other kinds of modern man. From other parts of Africa there is already some evidence that the functioning of the endocrine system in Negroes or Blacks displays a pattern that differs somewhat from that in Caucasoids or Whites. For instance, it has been claimed that another of the endocrine glands, the suprarenal (or adrenal) cortex, is smaller in Negroes and produces less steroid hormone than in Whites.

So we set out to learn something about the endocrine system of the San. Much remains to be done, and we do not yet know whether the hypophysis of the San produces a diminished amount of growth hormone. However, we did find one important sign of a different endocrine centre of gravity. Adult San *males* produce a very high level of *female* sex hormones (oestrogens). This is known to be high in many African peoples, but our work showed it to reach extreme values in San, perhaps the highest yet found in the world. We may well wonder if some of the anatomical distinctness of the San should be laid at the door of this factor. Lifelong exposure to too much oestrogen could perhaps produce such effects as the San's hairlessness and retention of juvenile traits.

The diet plays a major part in determining the level of oestrogen: on a poor diet, the level is high; as the diet improves, the level drops. Is it possible that the diet of the San, which in most areas seems to be very poor, results in the high level of oestrogen – and that this, in turn, may have an effect on the form of the San body? If this proves true, we should be forced to conclude that some of the features we consider distinctive in the San may change over the coming years as the diet improves. That is to say, not all of the distinguishing features of the San would, on this view, be genetic.

Already we have evidence that the San are growing taller than they were formerly. We have been able to compare measurements taken in the 1970s with those taken in the 'fifties and 'sixties, between the two world wars, before the First

24

World War and even in the latter part of the 19th century. Over a period of something like three-quarters of a century, the San have undergone an increase in average height of some 6,6 cm (roughly 2⅝ inches) in adult males and 3,4 cm (roughly 1⅜ inches) in adult females. This kind of change in the San is due to environmental factors like diet, and probably not to genetic changes. We call this tendency for populations to grow taller with the passing years and generations a *secular trend*. While it has long been known to have occurred in many parts of the world, in Caucasoid and Mongoloid peoples, our demonstration of this trend in the San was the first from Africa. Apart from the San, very few other African populations have shown the tendency towards increased average stature of adults; indeed, a number of African populations have shown a tendency to *become shorter* over the past 25 to 50 years.

Although the San have grown somewhat taller than they were earlier, they remain a fairly short people. To what extent their increase in height will continue over the coming generations we can but speculate. At some point, we must assume, the San will reach an upper limit set by their genes, just as some North American and European populations have begun to reach their genetically determined upper limits of stature.

If environmental changes can alter one of the bodily features we have long considered to be the hallmark of the San, perhaps other features may become altered too. As the diet improves and the sex-hormone levels change, it is possible that some of the other anatomical traits of the San will change too. Possibly the complex of features we have called infantile or neotenous may gradually become less evident, so that the San will come to look more like the other peoples of sub-Saharan Africa. All this could happen without the necessity for any genes to mutate.

We shall therefore have a look later at just how close the genetic make-up of the San is to that of other Africans.

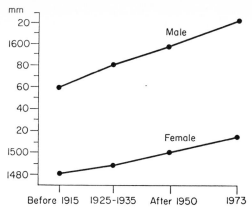

2.11 These graphs show how the average stature or height of San men and women has increased over the last three-quarters of a century. In the Central Kalahari, adult male San have shown a steady increase in height, the total increment being some 6,6 centimetres (or 2,6 inches). During the same period, adult female San have increased by 3,4 centimetres (or 1,4 inches). The increase in the mean height of the males has thus been greater than that of the females. This is possibly because males, being more sensitive to adversity than females, were more severely affected by the very poor conditions at the beginning of this century than were the women. When conditions improved over the ensuing 75 years, men had more leeway to make up than the women had; thus, the superiority in height of adult men over adult women has become *greater* under improved circumstances of life.

Bodily adaptations in the San

We have seen that none of the special bodily characters of the San – whether pygmoid stature or infantile anatomical features or steatopygia – seems to be an adaptation to life in the desert. This is not to say, however, that the San show no anatomical adaptations whatsoever.

Professor J. S. Weiner has shown that the body build of the San, as reflected in the ratio between height and weight (stature and mass), differs but little from that of other African peoples living in hot, though not desert, conditions. People who live in hot climates tend to have a lower body weight than those in temperate and cooler climates. This may be coupled with a relative increase in the surface area of the body. The San are thus better able to cope with life in hot conditions by possessing a much greater cooling surface relative to their body weight. This feature the San share with other Africans. The fact that present-day, desert-dwelling San do not show it in more marked degree than other Africans who do not live under desert conditions confirms again the general absence in the San of biological features specifically related to life in the desert.

The San likewise share a low-bridged, broad nose with other Africans. This feature seems to be correlated with external climatic conditions. In general, peoples who live in hotter climates have broader noses than those who live in more temperate climates. Here we find a probable difference between the San and other African groups. Many studies on living San and on San skulls have shown that this group possesses lower and broader noses than most other groups in Africa. Is this a distinct desert adaptation, or is it simply a reflection of the more infantile lineaments of the San cranium? Here, too, there seems to be little or no difference, on the average, between the noses of desert-dwelling San and those of San (or their skulls) from other, better endowed areas. So we may say that the broad, flat noses of the San are of particular adaptive value under warm conditions, though not specifically under a desert regimen.

We must examine one more possibility before leaving the adaptations of the San. Dr Alice Brues has suggested that the bodily build of human groups, past and present, may be correlated with their way of life, their habitual activity, their

2.12 These dancing Bushmen illustrate the slender though muscular build of many African dwellers in hot climates. The light yellow skin colour contrasts sharply with the darker hues of other inhabitants of the African sub-continent.

culture. In other words, we should seek evidence for bodily adaptation not only to the physical but to the cultural environment. As examples, she suggests that the heavy, muscle-bound physique of Neandertal man was well adapted to the use of bludgeon-like weapons, while the slender or linear build of some other precursors of *Homo sapiens* was physically well adapted to the use of spears as projectile weapons. The broad build and strong shoulders of the central Mongoloid peoples may have been correlated to the use of the bow, and a generally heavy build to the sustained labour required by an emergent agriculture. Most of the peoples of Africa, on this analysis, have retained to a greater or lesser extent the linear build of the idealised spearman.

Where does the San stand on this analysis? As far as weaponry goes, he is primarily an archer. Yet his build is slight and linear with stringy muscles. At first sight, these features would seem to contradict Dr Brues's suggestion that strong shoulders and a broad, sturdy build go with archery. However, the explanation may lie along these lines: the Bushman bow is small and light. His rather fragile arrows do not usually wound severely any animal which they strike; he relies rather on the efficacy of the poison smeared over the arrow points. Instead of requiring heavy shoulders to wield large, strong arrows from long-bows, the San depends rather on his fleet-footedness and extraordinary tracking skills. These qualities enable him to come very close to a herd before letting fly his arrows. A scratch is generally sufficient for the poison to penetrate the animal, but its effect is fairly slow and the animal is able to run away with the herd. It may be many hours or even a day or two before the hunter, following on foot, is able to close in on the dead or dying animal. So his very hunting methods have placed a premium upon other qualities than broad shoulders, namely smallness and lightness of build, staying power (which is commonly associated with the slender or ectomorphic body-build) and an acute reliance on veld-craft in the tracking of wounded animals.

Perhaps, then, it is to aspects of his own culture that the body build of the San has become adapted, rather than to the challenge of desert environs. We cannot yet say how valid this interpretation of the San's physique is, at least until Dr Brues's hypothesis has been worked out over many more human populations.

26

In brief, the San shows some general African adaptations to life in hot climates. Nevertheless, the very structural features which distinguish him from other Africans cannot be attributed to desert adaptation. In this respect he differs from the mountain dwellers of the Andes, who show clear-cut bodily adjustments to the special problems of living, breathing and working at high altitudes.

Acclimatization among the San

Genetic adaptation is a slow, long-term process: it affects populations rather than individuals and is one of the mechanisms of evolution. Acclimatization is a shorter-term process, whereby the functions of an individual's body become adapted.

Over many years of research in the Kalahari, Professor C. H. Wyndham and his colleagues have given us some answers to the question: Is it possible that the San are well acclimatized to conditions of the desert, even though their body structure may not be genetically adapted? We now know that the San are well acclimatized to high temperatures and fairly intense radiation – to both of which their habitat and their way of life expose them. Thus, in tracking down and pursuing wild game, they exercise actively in high temperatures and are exposed to rather intense radiation.

Man adapts to heat by an increased volume of sweat, by greater dilution of the sweat so as to conserve precious salts in the body, by a decreased acceleration of the heart rate during activity, and by dilution of the blood. Such internal adjustments affecting the individual's body during his lifetime help the San to cope with conditions in the Kalahari. But he does not show a marked degree of acclimatization – more than, say, members of other populations coming into similar conditions for short periods. Professor Wyndham and his colleagues were in 1956 and again in 1964 led to conclude that the small stature and light weight of the San do not confer any advantage on him in his heat responses, as compared with much heavier Whites or Caucasoids exposed to the same conditions.

Similarly the San do not show any marked difference from Whites in cold adaptation. The Kalahari nights in winter can be bitterly cold; yet the way in which the San's bodily mechanisms cope with the problem is scarcely different from that of other peoples. Indeed, the only real difference in his physical or physiological equipment against cold seems to be that the San has far less fat under the skin. With a poor insulating layer, it is not surprising to find that during cold nights the skin temperatures of the San fall more than those of Whites.

In sum, the work of Wyndham and his colleagues has shown that the San's bodily responses to heat and cold differ only to a very slight degree from those of other Africans and of Whites.

An interesting feature that emerged from our expeditions was that the San do not show a rise of blood pressure with age. In most peoples studied, especially developed communities, the average blood pressure rises with the advancement of age. In our studies it was found that the average blood pressure of San males and females remains at approximately the same level as they advance into old age. In another study, made by medical men on the !Kung San who were being studied by Dr R. B. Lee (see Chapter 7), it was found that the average blood pressure actually fell with age in adult San males. One suggestion that has been made to explain this finding is that the San do not eat salt. Perhaps other aspects of the San way of life have something to do with it. At any rate, the San are one of several populations in which this has been found. It makes us realise that, if our conditions of life were otherwise, it is not impossible that the entire human species would attain old age without an increase in the average blood pressure.

Another thought-provoking finding is that the cholesterol level in the blood serum of the San is among the lowest in the world – despite their eating meat. However, Professor A. S. Truswell has pointed out that the meat of wild buck has virtually no fat around it, while Dr M. A. Crawford has shown in Kenya that the small amount of fat in the muscles of wild antelopes is entirely poly-unsaturated. What is more, the San's diet is characteristically a *mixed* one, as Truswell has stressed, as more than half their calories stem from vegetable foods (see Chapter 7 by Dr R. B. Lee). So the low cholesterol level is probably related to the nature of the diet, although the high levels of oestrogens or female sex hormones may play a part as well.

From their studies on the Dobe San, Professors A. S. Truswell and J. D. L. Hansen concluded that the San do not develop obesity, except for a few who live with Negro pastoralists in the neighbourhood. Among the Dobe San, they found no signs of frank malnutrition, except where some illness or injury had occurred; neither were there signs of vitamin deficiency.

Cultural adjustments of the San

We have seen that very little in the bodily structure or physiological responses of the San can be regarded as specific adaptations to their harsh desert milieu. There is yet a third means of adjustment available to man: he is able to undergo "cultural acclimatization" and to adapt his way of life to the conditions of his environment. This process is far swifter and simpler for resourceful man than either the long-term genetic adaptation or shorter-term physiological adjustment. As Marston Bates has pointed out, ecology in man includes the study of not only climate, soil, vegetation and all the other things that it connotes in animals and plants, but also the impact of cultural features that may themselves modify physical and biological factors. Culture modifies the man, but modifies also the environment. Hence, according to Bates culture may be viewed "at one moment as a part of the man and, at another moment, as a part of the environment".

Man's plastic and versatile culture enables him to don fur-lined clothes and to heat his dwellings in cold climates; he does not need to grow a hairy skin to survive an ice age, as did the mammoth and the rhinoceros! Indeed, man's biological evolution has, to a large measure, given way to cultural evolution. No longer is he the passive victim of his physical milieu: more and more he is able to control his environment and, especially, those parts of it that formerly dictated the direction of evolutionary change.

There is little doubt that the Bushman has undergone this type of adaptation: he has adjusted his pattern of culture to his historically recent way of life as a refugee in the desert. Here are a few examples:

In some areas, to protect himself, he coats his skin with plant juices and, when obtainable, animal fat or blood. For instance, among some of the southerly San an ointment made from the *tsamma,* a wild melon, is smeared over the body and vigorously rubbed into the skin. To this greasy surface a fine layer of Kalahari sand may adhere. This protective mail shields him from absorbing unduly large amounts of solar radiation. So thick and dark may this layer become that the unwary observer doubts, at first, that the San is as light in skin colour as he is reported to be. This "pomade and mud-pack" treatment of his skin is a cultural adaptation that helps the San cope with heat.

Cultural, too, are his techniques of water conservation. The rainfall is sudden and sporadic. The earth blossoms briefly. The San stores all the water he can in the empty shells of ostrich eggs and calabashes, carefully burying them in the cool earth or concealing them in a tree against a later day of thirst. Such supplies are rapidly exhausted in the dry season, and he then resorts to eating quantities of water-rich plants, such as the fruits of the tsamma and the gemsbok cucumber and other species with juicy storage organs.

We have seen that it is not any greater proclivity for metabolic adjustment that protects the San against the cold. Instead, his culture helps him to build a micro-climate around him on cold winter nights. He makes skilful use of his shelter, or *skerm,* as a windbreak; of his kaross or skin cloak within which he curls himself up; and of his fire. A fourth element may be added: he may scoop out a shallow bed in the sand, within which he is somewhat protected from cold air movements. Professor Wyndham and Mr F. Morrison showed that the temperature under the skin cloak over the trunk is 25° C to 26° C. Thus the San creates a bearable micro-climate about himself. Such cultural adaptation carries the Bushman through the cold, wintry nights of the Kalahari Desert.

Interesting is the fact that of the three main devices used by the Bushmen – the windbreak, skin cloak and fire – only the first and last are used by the hunting and gathering aboriginal Australians. However, these people frequently sleep with their dogs for extra warmth, sometimes speaking of a "two-dog night" or a "four-dog night", according to the temperature!

2.13 The skin-cloak or kaross is one of the cultural devices used by the San to cope with the cold Kalahari winter nights. Others are the wind-break and the fire. Sometimes, too, they hollow out a sleeping-place just below ground level.

Other cultural adaptations relate to hunting and food-gathering. Closely related to these questions are the social practices that regulate the size of Bushman bands; the nature of nomadism and territoriality; the implements of hunting and digging. All these and many other examples of cultural adaptation are described in various chapters of this book.

Our final picture, then, is of a people whose curious anatomy plays little part in adapting them to desert life, whose physiological responses acclimatize them to hot, dry conditions, and whose cultural pattern essentially makes it possible for them to bear the extremes of heat and cold that characterize their desert environment.

The evolution of the San

In tracing the development of the San, we should take note of several pointers. First, although the San were formerly more widespread in Africa, there is no convincing evidence that they originated elsewhere than in Africa, more particularly in southern, Central or East Africa. We shall therefore avoid explanations based on fanciful and speculative theories about migrations from outside Africa. Secondly, the earliest San-like skeletal remains date from the Later Stone Age or, perhaps, even from the latter part of the Middle Stone Age; they are from archaeological deposits that have been excavated in South Africa and in Zambia. These items of evidence, though sparse, suggest that men showing some of the anatomical features of the San people have been in this subcontinent for at least tens of thousands of years. All earlier skeletal remains – which may be said to be pre-Negro and pre-San – are of people who were larger and had bigger heads than the San.

The evidence of these bony remains tells us that the San was a peculiarly African line of human evolution. It can be traced back well into the Later Stone Age, and perhaps even to the Middle Stone Age, possibly over 20 000 or 25 000 years. The proto-San peoples were themselves descended from still earlier fossil populations, such as the groups represented by the human skulls from Hopefield, inland from Saldanha Bay in the Cape Province; Florisbad, near Bloemfontein in the Orange Free State; the Cave of Hearths, Makapansgat, in the northern Transvaal; Kabwe (Broken Hill) in Zambia; and Lake Eyassi in northern Tanzania. This earlier group of fossils is by no means homogeneous, but all of the crania have big brain cases and strongly developed brow ridges; where there are lower jaws, they have no bony chin and are heavily constructed; where limb bones are present, they are large and robust. The bones represent an extinct race that has been called *Homo sapiens rhodesiensis*.

For such a population to change into a people like the San of the prehistoric past and of today, two main breaks with the past would have had to occur. First, the sturdy, adult-like, bony features would have had to give way to a more lightly constructed skeleton with a number of infantile architectural features. From the fossil evidence, this may have taken place first – before the end of the Middle Stone Age.

Secondly, the medium-sized pre-San people would have had to diminish their stature. These dwarfing changes, leading the San to become a smaller people, might well have occurred about the beginning of the Later Stone Age. By the time this second set of changes had taken place, the subcontinent would have been peopled by small San probably indistinguishable from those of today.

That part of the story has been pieced together from a study of modern San anatomy and of the fossil record. All fossil records are imperfect, as Charles Darwin stressed in *The Origin of Species* (1859), and only a minute fraction of all the creatures that have ever lived have become fossilized. Hence new discoveries, when they are forthcoming, may lead us to alter the above reconstruction of events.

There is a second way of digging up the past, apart from excavation with an archaeologist's shovel and brush. This other way is to use the genetic markers we have been speaking about as tools to probe the events of antiquity. By carefully weighing the resemblances and the differences between two or more groups, we may be able to infer how closely they are related, how long it is since they diverged from one another, which of them is closer in genetic make-up to the last common ancestor. When we apply this technique to the San and the Negro, we may arrive at the following sequence of events.

It is rather likely that the last common ancestor of the Khoisans and Negroes had a set of genes not very different – at least in broad outline – from the gene-pattern in modern Khoisans. This kind of early African man would have provided the proto-Negriform ancestors of all later sub-Saharan African peoples. They may well have been the possessors of those earlier skeletons that were not yet infantile or neotenous, nor small in stature. This proto-Negriform population, it is postulated, split into two major branches, which were to become Khoisans and Negroes. The separation must have begun a long time ago; certainly, on the archaeological evidence, it must have been upwards of 6 000 years before the present. Indeed it is more likely that the divergence had begun by the onset of the Later Stone Age, between 15 000 and 25 000 years ago.

In the long history of human evolution, this still means a fairly recent common origin. The subsequent micro-evolution of the two sub-groups has led them to diverge from each other, but not so far as to obliterate their basically similar genetic constitution. Hence, we may infer that Khoisans and Negroes both belong to the same major racial constellation, the Negriforms.

Once the dichotomy was established, there followed a fairly lengthy period in which the Khoisan line and the Negro line were geographically isolated from each other. The Khoisans seem to have gravitated mainly to eastern and southern Africa, while the further development of the Negroes took place mainly in equatorial and tropical Africa. Geographical isolation means reproductive isolation. As long as most members of one group were not in a geographical situation where they could mate with members of the other group, the two groups would have been genetically isolated from each other. During the period of isolation, certain genetic differences arose; new mutant genes took root in both populations. Some of these new mutants would have gained a foothold because they conferred advantages on their possessors. The genes which were favourable in one geographical and ecological zone, for example those for darker skin nearer the equator, would not have been the same ones as those that proved helpful to the other group, the Khoisans, in the more southerly sub-tropical environment. So gradually the two isolated lineages would have acquired a number of genetic differences from each other.

On the whole, it seems likely that the Khoisans departed rather less from the probable ancestral gene-set. Contrariwise, the Negroes, by a variety of genetical and evolutionary processes, seem to have departed rather more from the presumed ancient genetic picture. Very high gene frequencies became "watered down" to moderate values. The adoption of a new way of life by the Negro line – agriculture – may itself have speeded up biological change among some Negroes. For instance, the clearing of large tracts of tropical rain forest for purposes of cultivation multiplied the number of breeding places for the mosquitoes that carry malaria. This man-made change in the biotope created excellent conditions for the increase of malaria in West Africa. We know that malaria was the major environmental factor leading to the natural selection of some mutants, such as a gene for the sickle-cell trait in the blood. This mutant gene produces an unusual form of haemoglobin in the red blood-cells that helps its bearers to cope better with the onslaught of the malarial parasite. People who were not excessively exposed to malaria, like the Khoisans of the south, do not possess this unusual genetic variant of haemoglobin.

From this single example, we see how the nature of the gene-pool in the two evolving lineages would change with time. Thus man's cultural and economic changes could have acted as catalysts of genetic changes. Since agriculture was adopted by the Negro populations, but not by the Khoisan, this could have provided an additional factor encouraging more gene differences between the agriculture-dependent Negroes and the non-agricultural Khoisans. Always the direction of micro-evolutionary change seems to have been carrying the Negroes genetically further away from the ancestral pattern. On the other hand, little seemed to happen in the life of the San line to carry them far from the ancestral gene-set.

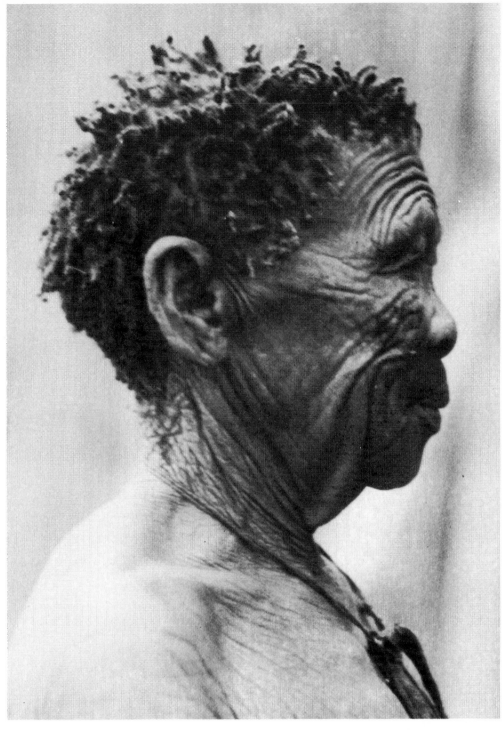

2.14 The wrinkled skin of an aged San woman. It is possible that the genetic make-up of today's San is closer to that of the ancient African peoples from whom Negroes and Bushmen are descended than are the gene-pools of any other living peoples of Africa.

Thus the San lived on in isolation from the rest of what was rapidly becoming "Black Africa", inhabited by recognisable Negroes wielding a new kind of food-producing economy. In the southern parts of the subcontinent, it was the Bushmen, or San, who were the aboriginal inhabitants, as George W. Stow stated in his famous work *The Native Races of South Africa*. All the rest, he pointed out, were without exception mere intruders. Even the Khoikhoi, or Hottentots, were intruders of but a few thousand years ago, for they were Khoisan who had acquired the art of the pastoral life further to the north-east and had moved south with it, before the agricultural Negroes turned southwards.

In the south, we see the San as a compelling reminder of what the earlier pre-Negro and pre-Khoisan inhabitants of Africa south of the Sahara may well have looked like. In this sense, in the sense that their gene-set may well provide us with some telling clues as to the gene make-up of ancient Africa, we may regard the San as being living fossils, not only in their hunter-gatherer way of life, but perhaps even in their biological heritage.

31

Much, much later some of the Negro peoples who had evolved further north and acquired a new way of life – agriculture – and a new set of cultural techniques, including iron-smelting, turned southwards and moved across the subcontinent. They occupied new ecological niches that suited their cultivation procedures – and they encountered their long-lost fellow Africans, the Khoisan. To each, the other was unrecognisable. Even the languages had changed. Twenty thousand years is a long time for two members of a family to remain apart!

Hence the numerical and regional expansion of the Negroes broke down the geographical isolation which had for so long obtained between them and the Khoisan. This in turn brought to an end the long phase of reproductive and genetic isolation. Although there were many fights between the various groups, there were, too, undoubtedly many examples of "hybridization", of blending of genes between the groups. Such hybridization brought some of the new San mutant genes into the genetic composition of the southern African Negroes. The consequences are apparent in the lighter skin colour of many southern African Negroes, in the form of their skulls, in many other bodily features and in some of the San blood genetic markers present in the southern African Negroes. To some extent, too, genes flowed in the reverse direction, from the Negro to the San.

Thus, the gene-set of divers southern African Negro groups came to be altered by the inclusion of "Khoisan genes", varying in proportion to the amount of genetic contact between the newly arrived populations and the Khoisan. In the reverse direction, whatever gene-flow occurred from Negro to Khoisan must have been largely overshadowed by the gradual extermination of the San at the hands of all the intruders coming from the north and the south, the north-east and the north-west. The San whose blood might have told us a story of such admixed Negro genes are no more; the San of the Kalahari are the sole survivors. We can never know how much Negro genetic influence had entered into the make-up of the rest, who have perished.

That is the story of the rise and the decline of the aboriginal Africans, the Bushmen. They nearly went the way of the Tasmanians, extinct now for about a century. Only, in Africa the Kalahari provided a refuge: those Bushmen who walked that desert earth were exposed to the ravages of a most exacting terrain – and ironically enough they survived. Those who lived the good life in the lush and well-watered valleys of Natal and the mountains of the Cape Province paid the ineluctable price of inhabiting the best part of the country; only their stone tools, their fireplaces, their burials and their vivid rock paintings remain as poignant reminders, mute though eloquent messages from the past.

3
The Bushmen in Prehistory

Ray R. Inskeep

In the previous chapters the Bushmen have been defined, and their numbers and geographical distribution commented on. Unless we are to suppose that they were suddenly and magically scattered across the landscape just in time for the earliest European travellers and their scientist successors to discover and remark upon, we must suppose that the Bushmen have a history: or more correctly, because there are no written records older than the earliest European accounts, a prehistory. It is the purpose of this chapter to say something about that prehistory, but the task is not altogether straightforward, and it will be worth while to pause and explain why.

The definition of "Bushmen" in the prehistoric period

In 1652, when the first Dutch settlers under Van Riebeeck landed in Table Bay, where Cape Town now stands, they met with a number of different indigenous peoples, of whom tantalisingly brief descriptions have come down to us. There were the *Strandlopers* or *Watermans* (the "Beach-rangers" or "Watermen"), numbering 40 or 50 souls, who occupied the Cape Peninsula and the area around Table Bay. They are said to have depended almost entirely on molluscs and roots, but some of them may have had a few cattle. There were people called "Fishmen", of whom perhaps 500 lived beyond the mountains east of the Cape, towards Mossel Bay. These people are said specifically to have caught fish from the rocks, with a line; they sometimes owned a few cattle, but no sheep. It is not entirely clear whether these people are the same as, or a branch of, the people later referred to as "Sonqua", "Soaqua" or "Souqua". The third principal group encountered were the "Saldanhars" or "Saldanjamen", who lived north of Table Bay, towards Saldanha and St Helena Bay. They moved into the area of Table Bay with vast herds of cattle and sheep during November, and generally left in January. These people were true nomadic pastoralists, but their movements were far from random; they appear to have had a well-defined territory through which they moved with some regularity. All of these people were referred to from time to time by the earliest Dutch settlers as "Hottentots", a name apparently given them on account of their strange-sounding, "stuttering" speech. One thing that the three groups had in common was that they possessed livestock, although the "Watermen" and the "Fishmen" seem to have done so only in a rather limited and somewhat "unprofessional" way. It is clear from records of the mid-17th century that all three groups had the use of the bow and arrow and the spear. All three supplemented their diet by hunting and collecting various kinds of wild foods, but there is nothing to suggest that it might be possible to distinguish these three groups one from the other archaeologically. It may be more probable that old shell mounds along the sea-shore were the result of "Watermen" or "Fishmen" encampments, but it would be unwise to assume that none of them was the result of encampments of "Saldanhars".

In addition to these three groups, early Dutch records speak of a fourth people, the "Sonqua", "Soaqua" or "Souqua". They were encountered in groups of three to thirty, generally in the mountains to the north of Table Bay. Jan Wintervogel, sent inland by Van Riebeeck on a journey of exploration, reported them as being "like these Hottentots and speaking almost as they do". In December 1660 an expedition to Monomotapa "had come across a poverty-stricken band of tiny people, who had helped them cross the first range (of mountains north of Table Bay) and had been very friendly to them, giving them some honey and dried fish. These small people . . . live in a state of poverty in shabby, low huts made of branches. Our explorers had found some of these standing empty here and there and it seemed to them that these little fellows use them during the night. They are well provided with bows and arrows, and they are adept at using these for shooting all kinds of game for food. Honey also forms part of their diet. They dress like the Hottentots, but they use very poor skins of wild animals. They are not so greasy as the Hottentots, for greasiness is a sign of prestige and wealth in cattle, etc . . . and their complexion and speech are the same."

What impressed the early Dutch settlers was the apparently "wild" way of life of these "Sonquas", and their complete lack of livestock. No distinction was made on the basis of language, for the languages of all groups were, to the Dutch, unintelligible, and on account of their "clicks" all sounded broadly the same. Van Riebeeck's diaries (1652-1662) refer to the hunters throughout as "Sonqua", "Soaqua" or "Souqua", save in one instance, where it is suggested that the "Fishmen" are the same as the Soaqua. The name is apparently derived from the plural of *San,* the term by which these hunters were known to the local cattle-herders. But by 1685 the name "Bushmen" *(Bosjesmans, Bosmanekens, Bosies-mans)* was in general use by the Dutch. It seems likely that this "nickname" was suggested either by the environment in which the people lived, or perhaps by the small huts of branches in which they often sheltered.

The point is that the people we are supposed to be writing about, "the Bush-men", were distinguished from others *only* as people who subsisted by hunting and gathering and who did not possess livestock. It would be an oversimplification to suppose that in the late prehistoric period in South Africa we had to deal with only two societies: cattle-owning "Hottentots" and non-cattle-owning "Bush-men". It is clear from Van Riebeeck's diaries alone that within 160 km (100 miles) of the settlement at Table Bay three, if not four distinct groups, Watermen, Saldanhars and Soaqua/Fishmen, each pursuing its own way of life, were to be found, apart from the great Namaqua nation of pastoralists to the north. Despite the enormous disturbances consequent upon the spread of pastoralism in southern Africa – partly at the hands of Bantu-speaking peoples, and partly by Khoikhoi-speakers – and the more recent and more devastating effects of European col-onisation, it is still possible to point to the existence of no fewer than four distinct

3.1 Map showing the distribution of Wilton and Smithfield industries, and of the "Bushman" (San) and "Hottentot" (Khoikhoi) languages, as known from surviving or historically documented examples *(after J. D. Clark and E. Westphal).*

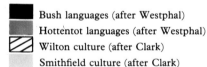

Bush languages (after Westphal)
Hottentot languages (after Westphal)
Wilton culture (after Clark)
Smithfield culture (after Clark)

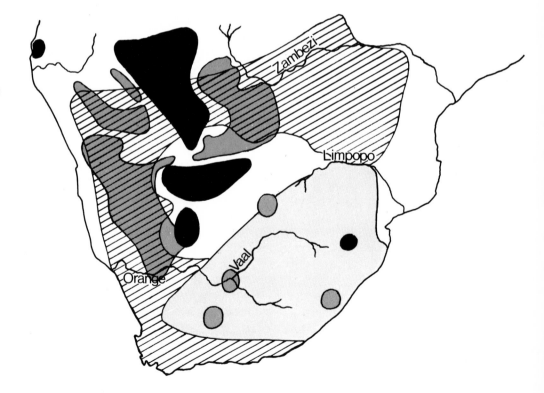

"Bush" language *families* and four Khoikhoi languages (Ill. 3.1). There can be little doubt that a number of others, perhaps many, have been irretrievably lost within the last 500 to 1 000 years.

We have no reliable evidence as to the languages and/or dialects spoken by the peoples encountered by the settlers and explorers of the 17th and 18th centuries. Hence we have no real basis for proposing that all pastoralists belonged to one language group (Khoikhoi), whilst all hunter-gatherers belonged to another (San or "Bushman") language family. Indeed we have already noted that amongst the historically known hunter-gatherers no fewer than four language families may be involved; at least one group of people regarded as "Bushmen" are reported to speak a pure Khoikhoi language. When we survey a collection of archaeological specimens from a prehistoric site, or the site itself, we have no way of knowing what language was spoken by the people involved. Thus an identification of "Bushman" dependent on language is beyond the scope of the archaeologist, and he must limit himself to other things.

In the 17th century and later, writers occasionally essayed to describe the physical appearance of the hunters and the herders, but their observations were generally superficial, and not always entirely objective. The light skin colour was noted, the facial features, and the sparsely distributed, tightly coiled "peppercorn" hair, but these generally applied to both the hunters and the herders. The one possibly distinguishing feature that crops up is stature: the hunters have repeatedly been described as small people. However, this factor must be used with care, for diet may greatly influence stature, and it may be unwise to underestimate the effect of milk in the diet of the herders. At any rate stature is a very variable factor, which it might be difficult to apply as a criterion even were only two population groups involved. However, linguistic and historical studies indicate a vastly more complex situation at the moment when prehistory began to become history, and there is nothing in the skeletal remains from the last 10 000 years or so

3.2 and 3.3 Although archaeologists are able to make many ingenious deductions about the way of life of long-dead peoples, we must always remember that only a part of the life of the past is reflected in the Stone Age remains. Aspects of culture such as dancing (above) and singing and clapping to make the musical accompaniment (on the following page) are among the social pursuits of bygone peoples that leave no mark in prehistoric living sites.

35

to suggest that these people formed a single homogeneous population, or were simply divided into two.

If the archaeologist's prehistoric "Bushmen" can be singled out neither on the basis of language, nor on the appearance of the fossil remains of their skeletons, we are obliged to turn to the way of life and the material culture. How might we know, when we view a site and its contents, whether we are looking at a settlement of pastoralists or of hunter-gatherers? The rather meagre descriptions of material culture that have come down to us from the 17th and 18th centuries provide no basis for a distinction. Both groups used the bow and arrow and the spear, and there is no indication that the forms or armature of these varied significantly. Both groups clothed themselves in skins; and although the cloaks of the pastoralists were often made of sheepskin, as distinct from the skins of wild animals, the survival of such materials is so rare that they are unlikely to be helpful. Both groups used beads made from the shells of ostrich eggs as personal adornments, and again there is no indication of regular differences in the use of these between hunters and herders. (In any case the beads rarely turn up in archaeological contexts with their original arrangement preserved.) Both groups made use of tortoise-shell in various ways, so this too cannot be used as a means of distinguishing one group from the other.

The chief potential for distinction would seem to lie in the possession of sheep and cattle by the pastoralists, and in the architecture and arrangement of the settlements. There is no indication that the hunters ever constructed shelters more substantial than little dome-shaped structures made from a few branches, although in stony areas these might be anchored by slabs or blocks of stone which might remain in place long after the branches have decayed and vanished. In reality such tell-tale stone circles are rare indeed. The encampments or kraals of the "Saldanjamen" and their fellow pastoralists to the north (the Nama) have been well described from the mid-17th century onwards. They were clearly much grander and – to us, at any rate – better organised than the encampments of the hunters. Large huts were made of long poles set in a circle, bent inwards and secured to form a dome, which was then covered with rectangular mats. The huts were laid out in a great circle, and might be surrounded by a fence of reeds or brushwood. When the time came to move, the huts were dismantled, bundled and packed on the backs of oxen. Unless stones had been collected and placed at the bases of the hut walls or the surrounding fence, little might survive to show that people had ever lived there. Stone circle complexes in the Riet River valley apparently belonged to pastoral settlements of the 17th or 18th century. Southwards only one apparently pastoral settlement is known, on the spit of land south of the entrance to Saldanha Bay. This recently discovered site has not yet been tested by excavation. Thus, intriguing though they are, architecture and settlement plans have little to contribute at present to the recognition of pastoralist and hunter in the prehistoric period.

The discovery of remains of sheep, cattle or goats in Stone Age sites would be of interest more as a commentary on the date by which livestock were present in the locality than as an indication of the economy, for we know that the hunters were only too happy to raid the farmers' herds if the opportunity presented itself.

3.4 A San matron holding a tortoise-shell receptacle. The way in which living Bushmen use such objects throws light on the practices of their prehistoric ancestors.

37

In the face of all these difficulties, about the only definition we can accept for "Bushmen" in the prehistoric period is "those people associated with the remains which the archaeologist assigns to the Later Stone Age in southern Africa". It must be clearly understood, however, that such a definition will almost certainly include people who did not look particularly like what we think a "San" should look like, people who may have spoken languages quite different from the "Bushman" languages known to us today, and some who may, in the last 2 000 years, have tended herds or flocks of their own.

The Later Stone Age and the problem of archaeological "cultures"

Occasional objects of wood shaped by man have survived from several hundred thousand years ago, and convincing arguments can be produced for wood, fibre and skin having been used from very, very much earlier times. But conditions suitable for the preservation of organic materials are rarely encountered. For the most part we have to be content with those tools and weapons (or parts thereof) which were made of stone, and the stone debitage resulting from their manufacture. These pieces betray two things: the shapes and sizes of artefacts, and the techniques by which the stone was worked. More rarely they may reveal something of the uses to which the artefacts were put. It is primarily on the basis of similarities and differences in the forms of things made of stone, and the techniques by which they were fashioned, that the archaeologist has divided the 2,5 million years of human activity in Africa into three great parts: the Early Stone Age, the Middle Stone Age and the Later Stone Age.

It is generally true that in a given region those stone-working techniques and artefact forms classed as Middle Stone Age are younger (or more recent) than those of the Early Stone Age and older than those of the Later Stone Age. But this, too, is an oversimplification, for the three stone ages are not three separate creations with clear-cut beginnings and ends; nor is there any evidence at present to suggest that the transition from one to another, locally, was the result of intrusion into southern Africa of new ideas or new peoples. It is probably more correct to think in terms of localised evolutionary changes in the patterns of stone tool-making, occasionally influenced by ideas borrowed from other quarters and accompanied by biological evolution of the stone-tool makers. If this view is adopted, that the Later Stone Age of southern Africa evolved out of the Middle Stone Age of the region (in contrast to European culture, which was thrust into the country by settlers from outside), it becomes difficult to define a point within the evolutionary sequence at which we might agree to say that the Middle Stone Age had ended and the Later Stone Age had begun. By the same token it is equally difficult to decide just when we should start talking about prehistoric Bushmen rather than their prehistoric non-Bushman ancestors. But we may attempt, presently, to indicate the timing involved.

If we were asked to summarise very briefly the differences between Middle Stone Age (Ill. 3.5) and Later Stone Age (Ill. 3.6) tool-kits, we might suggest the following generalisations. In the Middle Stone Age the majority of shaped stone tools were made on flakes, which were commonly irregular in shape, but were quite often deliberately struck in such a way as to produce roughly triangular or rectangular forms; many of the triangular flakes are very uniformly and symmetrically shaped. Secondary working was applied to a small percentage of the flakes so as to produce working edges suitable for scraping skins or for adzing or paring wood (such specimens are often referred to as "scrapers"), whilst others were trimmed on one or both faces into neat triangular or leaf-shaped "points", which may have been used as spearheads or as knives. In some areas squat triangular flakes are given deeply denticulate, or toothed, edges. In the course of being worked, the parent nuclei, or "cores", from which these flakes were detached often assumed a flattish bi-conical shape ("disc-cores"). The striking platforms designed to receive the blow that would detach the flake from the core were carefully prepared by the removal of a number of very tiny flakes, producing a faceted area of which part came away with the flake. These flakes with finely faceted platforms are also a fairly common feature of Middle Stone Age workmanship. Shaped bone tools are very rare, even when bone is preserved in a site; only

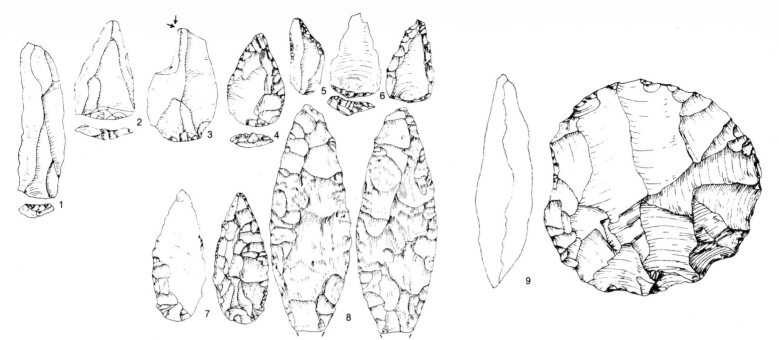

one wooden artefact (a throwing stick) is known from the Middle Stone Age, and no examples of fibre or skin have been found. It is difficult to generalise about size, but most of the flakes and flake tools would fall between 25 and 100 mm (1 and 4 inches) in maximum dimension.

In the conventional Later Stone Age a number of changes are apparent (Ill. 3.6). Faceted platforms on cores and flakes have gone out of fashion, and disc-cores are rare or absent. Very commonly elongate, parallel-sided pieces, termed "blades", were struck from small cores which, as a result, assumed a fluted form.

The triangular and leaf-shaped "points" disappear, and the "oak-leaf" survives only in a somewhat changed form as small, denticulate pieces of varying shape which bear little resemblance to the Middle Stone Age form. Small flakes and blades are often given an abrupt, blunting retouch (Ill. 3.6) along a straight or curved edge to produce so-called "backed blades" and "segments" (often erroneously called "crescents"). The scrapers are commonly much smaller than those of the Middle Stone Age. Perforated stones designed to add weight to digging sticks (Ill. 3.7 and 3.8) are fairly common, as are rod-like and pointed stones used in the perforating process (Ill. 3.7). Grindstones and rubbers, which are rare in the Middle Stone Age, are abundant in the Later Stone Age. In addition there are many artefacts of bone, ivory, shell and wood, and occasionally more fragile objects of fibre and leather have survived.

It has long been held that within the framework of the Later Stone Age there were two great cultural complexes, the Wilton culture and the Smithfield culture. Whilst the validity of this concept is somewhat in question today, the terms are

3.5 Some typical Middle Stone Age artefacts. Numbers 1 and 2, a blade and a triangular flake, both with faceted striking platforms; 3, a burin or grooving tool; 4, a unifacially trimmed point; 5, obliquely truncated blade; 6, a denticulate flake; 7 and 8, probably lance-heads or knives, one partly and one wholly worked on both faces; 9, disc-core. (⅓ of natural size)

3.6 Typical Later Stone Age artefacts. 1-3, cores from which bladelets have been removed: 4-10, segments ("crescents"); 11-13 and 20-23, small "scrapers", which may well have served as blades for adzes comparable to the Australian *tula* adze; 14-19, "crescent adzes", comparable to the Australian *eloura* adze blades; 24, 25 and 27-29, backed blades; 26 and 40, drill points. (Natural size)

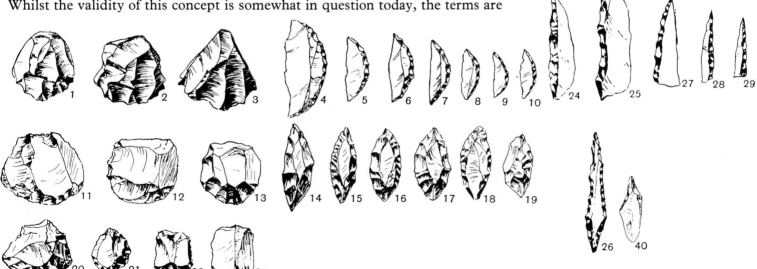

3.7 A bored stone and reamer (⅔ of natural size)

3.8 Digging stick with bored stone weight. Late 19th century. The stick is about 1 metre long. (*Photo: Pitt Rivers Museum*)

firmly entrenched in the literature, and for the time being form a useful point of reference. The distinction between Wilton and Smithfield is partly a question of the types of artefacts found in association, and partly a matter of distribution (Ill. 3.1). It remains to be seen to what extent chronology also is involved.

These, in a general way, are the criteria which lead the archaeologist to distinguish between Middle and Later Stone Age, though there are industries that do not fit well into either category. More will be said of them later. But although much remains to be learned of the chronological details, we can learn something if we look at the latest dates of industries showing affinities with the Middle Stone Age, and the oldest dates belonging to the Later Stone Age.

The following are some industries displaying "late" Middle Stone Age characteristics and their associated dates (see Ill. 3.9 for sites):

Site	Date
Mufo, Angola	11 189 and 14 503 BP*
Abercorn, North Zambia	9 950 BP
Kalambo Falls, North Zambia	9 550 BP
Pomongwe, Rhodesia	15 800 BP
Bushman Rock shelter, Transvaal (less certain)	12 510 BP

These dates suggest that Middle Stone Age traditions were still extant over a large area of southern Africa between 9 000 and 15 000 years ago.

For "Wilton" industries the following are some of the earliest dates:

Site	Date
Nelson Bay cave, Robberg Peninsula	8 650 and 6 020 BP
Matjes River cave, near Plettenberg Bay	7 750 BP
Wilton type site, near Alicedale, eastern Cape Province	8 260 BP
Melkhoutboom, eastern Cape Province	7 660, 7 300 and 6 980 BP
Montagu cave, Little Karroo	7 100 BP
Rose Cottage cave, Orange Free State	6 850 BP
Pomongwe, Rhodesia	7 690 and 7 610 BP

*BP = Before Present; a conventional way of expressing very early dates determined by the radiocarbon method.

So the Wilton "culture" had already emerged 8 000 or 9 000 years ago in a form that was to last for at least 6 000 years. On the other hand, industries of the classic Smithfield culture in the type area of the Orange Free State appear to be not much older than 2 000 years.

However, there are a number of industries known from sites as widely separated as the Lusaka region in Zambia, the Matopos Hills in Rhodesia, the Orange Free State, the eastern Cape, and the southern Cape coast that are devoid of Middle Stone Age characteristics, and yet cannot properly be bracketed with the "Wilton" or the "Smithfield". These industries seem to occupy a chronologically intermediate position, with dates ranging from 9 410 BP to upwards of 20 000 BP. But our knowledge of these industries is so imperfect that it is impossible at the moment to say just how they relate to the Middle Stone Age industries that precede, or the "Wilton" industries that follow them.

If we exclude those industries sometimes referred to as Smithfield "A", and which may belong with the industries described in the preceding paragraph, the remaining expressions of the "Smithfield culture" and the "Wilton", while displaying some differences, have much in common. Together they form the mainstay of the Later Stone Age of southern Africa. As indicated earlier in this chapter, it might well be wrong to suggest that at all times and in all places our

3.9 Map showing the location of the principal sites mentioned in the text.

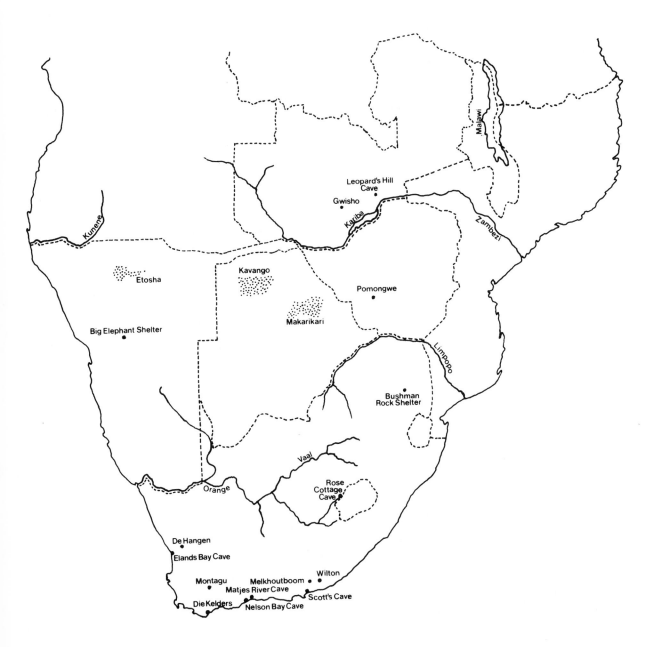

Later Stone Age populations bore a close resemblance physically or linguistically to the anthropologist's historical Bushmen. Yet there can be little doubt that the way of life of the prehistoric Bushmen, or their ancestors, could legitimately be inferred from the evidence culled by the archaeologist from remains of the Later Stone Age. What does this evidence amount to?

Technology in the Later Stone Age

This must necessarily be a brief survey. Much has to be left out, but at least some salient points can be sketched.

Artefacts of stone

Stone was used extensively, for a wide variety of purposes. Hard or soft, coarse or fine-grained stone would be chosen, depending on the use to which it was to be put and on its availability. Stone might be worked in several different ways, but flaking by percussion was undoubtedly the most common. Softer rocks might be ground to shape, using harder, abrasive rocks, or occasionally actually cut or gouged into shape with a hard, sharp piece of stone. Hard stones were "pecked" or "bruised" into shape by hammering with another hard stone.

One of the hallmarks of the Later Stone Age is the "bored stone" (Ill. 3.7). This was used to give weight to the digging stick (Ill. 3.8) for grubbing up roots and bulbs, termite larvae or anything else that had to be dug for, and for the digging of pitfall traps. The stone might be a cobble that, apart from being perforated, was little modified regarding size and shape, but it is clear that on occasion considerable labour and care were devoted to imparting a meticulous symmetry and finish to the stone by pecking and grinding. The sticks with their stones attached are sometimes represented in rock art, but not in use. The evidence for usage is historical. While the great majority of the bored stones are of a size and weight that would make them eminently suitable as digging-stick weights, they do display considerable variation in size. At the extremes are very small stones (down to 27 g, or 1 oz.) and very heavy, or otherwise cumbersome, stones that would be quite unsuitable as weights on digging sticks. The heavy, cumbersome stones could have been parts of game traps, but the small ones remain quite enigmatic.

If historical evidence can be relied upon, the work of making the bored stones belonged to the women – who would also be the users. The general procedure seems to have been to hammer away at opposite sides of the stone, creating two funnel-shaped depressions which would ultimately meet in the middle to form an hour-glass perforation. This work involved the use of a rod-like piece of hard stone, which might be a natural splinter or might be flaked into shape. Once the hole was through, the same stone, or one of similar shape, would be employed as a reamer (Ill. 3.7), being rotated backwards and forwards in the hole to enlarge the central part of the "hour-glass" and impart a smooth finish to the perforation. This reaming operation results in a tell-tale abrasion of the angles of the reamer.

Related to the bored stones, and made by generally similar techniques, are "edged discs". These are flattish, lenticular (or lens-shaped) discs made of soft rock such as shale, and finished by grinding the entire surface, bringing the circumference to a sharp edge. Sizes vary from 13 cm (5 inches) to 6 cm (2¼ inches) in external diameter, while the perforations vary from 7 cm (2¾ inches) to 1 cm (3/8 inch) in diameter. Of the 82 specimens on record only three or four would fit over the wrist of a small adult, and most would be too small even for a child. The purpose of these pieces therefore remains a mystery. Whilst they are comparatively rare, they none the less have a wide distribution.

Shale, which was used widely for the edged discs, and occasionally for bored stones, was used also for the manufacture of flat, often oval "palettes" (Ill. 3.10) of unknown use, and on the southern coast for small grooved pellets (Ill. 3.11) believed to be sinkers for fishing lines. Grinding, as a means of shaping, was applied also to tablets or small blocks of harder rock, commonly sandstone, to make so-called "grooved stones" (Ill. 3.12). The grooves may be V-shaped or U-shaped, and the stone may be carefully shaped or irregular. Stones with U-shaped grooves were apparently used in the final process of shaping beads from ostrich-egg shell. Those with V-shaped grooves were probably used for grinding the

3.10 "Palette" of shale. These are generally oval or elliptical in outline, and their use is unknown. (Natural size)

42

3.11

3.12

points of bone or ivory arrowheads. There is some evidence that the latter were used also in the application of poison to arrowheads, the poison being contained in the groove and the arrowhead being rotated carefully in it.

Last but not least among the objects of ground stone are grindstones and rubbers. On the basis of ethnographic parallel, it is assumed that these were used primarily in the preparation of foodstuffs. It is commonly supposed that they were intended mainly for vegetable foods, but it might be wrong to suppose that meats or seafoods were never pounded or rubbed, while on occasion it seems grindstones were utilised in the grinding of ochres in the manufacture of paint. Certainly they are very common in coastal sites. The nether stone may be any suitably sized slab of rock of the required texture, and at the coast large water-worn cobbles were commonly used. The rubbing stone was often quite small, of a size that could be comfortably held in one hand, and commonly developed one or more flattish facets. Sometimes a small dimple is found, pecked at the centre of a facet; this seems to have been done to give the stone some "bite" during the rubbing process. Whatever may have been the everyday uses of this grinding apparatus, the nether stones commonly ended up being placed in graves. One or more grinding stones were commonly placed above the body in the grave. In a number of cases, on the southern coast, these were embellished with simple paintings (see Chapter 4).

By far the commonest use of stone was for flaked stone tools. For this purpose fine-grained rocks such as chalcedony, agate or silcrete were favoured; these flake easily and yield a tough, sharp edge. But for some classes of tools, or in areas where these were not obtainable, other rocks such as lydianite, quartz and quartzite were used. Basically the process involved detaching flakes of stone from the core by carefully directed blows with a "hammerstone" or with a baton of hard wood or bone. The resultant flakes might then be used just as they were, or they might be modified by trimming, or secondary working, to impart a particular kind of working edge, or a particular shape, or both. Where careful shaping or special working edges are present, we need have no hesitation in recognising the specimen as a tool of some sort. In the case of untrimmed pieces, use may have resulted in wear or damage to the edge, which may tell us that the piece was actually put to a use. But many flakes would not have been used at all, while others might have been used on soft material that imparted no tell-tale damage to the edge. Sometimes the stone-worker would deliberately detach narrow, parallel-sided flakes that are termed blades, or bladelets, for conversion to tools.

One of the tool types traditionally associated with the Later Stone Age, and with the Wilton culture in particular, are the pieces termed "lunates" or "segments" (Ill. 3.6). These small pieces have a sharp, unretouched chord, while the arc is shaped and blunted by the removal of many tiny flakes so as to form a "back" that is almost at right angles to the two surfaces. Allied to these are "backed blades" (Ill. 3.6), which also have a sharp edge apposed to a blunted edge (somewhat like a penknife blade). The precise function of these small artefacts is not known, but it seems certain, from their small size, that they were hafted to make composite tools or weapons. By analogy with what has been found in Egypt, Israel, north-west Europe and Australia, we may surmise that such specimens formed the armature of arrows or spears, or the cutting edges of knives. Although none has yet been found with its hafting preserved, two grooved wood specimens (Ill. 3.13) from the Later Stone Age levels of the Melkhoutboom cave in the eastern Cape may well have been intended for the hafting of such pieces.

3.11 Line sinkers for fishing, made from small pieces of shale. (Natural size)

3.12 Two grooved stones. These have U-shaped grooves, worked on the edges of elliptical pebbles. Commonly the grooves are made across the surface of a flat tablet. (Natural size)

43

3.13 A slender point of wood with several overlapping slots, probably intended to contain settings of stone, perhaps backed blades or segments. From Melkhoutboom *(after H. J. Deacon)*. (Natural size)

3.14 Two views of a hafted stone tool from a cave at Touw River, Cape Province. One face has had the mastic cut away to expose the stone and reveals the remains of the wooden handle and its socket. (Approx. ⅔ of natural size)

3.15 Large, waterworn pebble flaked to provide a cutting or chopping edge. (½ of natural size)

Perhaps the commonest of the flaked stone implements are the "scrapers" (Ill. 3.6). These vary a good deal in size from place to place and at different times, but commonly they are rather small, about the size of the end of your thumb. Indeed they have often been loosely named "thumbnail scrapers". Basically the scraper is made on a flake or blade by removing a series of small flakes from some part of the edge of the flake in such a way as to produce a strong working edge with an angle of about 45° to the main, flat under surface of the flake or blade (rather like the bevel on a chisel or plane blade). The preparation of skins involves the processes of scraping unwanted matter from the inside of the skin after flensing and of removing hair from the outside. Whilst a variety of tools may be used for these tasks, it is possible that flaked stone scrapers figured among them. On the other hand there seems little doubt that some of these specimens, hafted to a wooden handle with a vegetable mastic, were used as adzes in the manufacture of wooden tools, weapons and utensils. Several specimens have been found with mastic still adhering (Ill. 3.14), and in a few cases the wooden handle has been preserved. It is suggested that these tools were used in the same manner as recent Australian stone-bladed adzes. Another small form of adze blade is the "crescent adze", which resembles the Australian *eloura* adze blade (Ill. 3.6). This tool type resembles a rather thick, backed segment on which the chord edge sometimes shows severe utilisation damage, but more often it has been given a scraper-like retouch which imparts a tough cutting edge less likely to suffer damage.

Of much less frequent occurrence are stone awls and drills (Ill. 3.6). Stone awls may have been used in leather working, while the drills would have served for perforating beads made from ostrich-egg shell, tortoise-shell containers or bone or shell pendants. But whilst there are a few tool types whose function we may justifiably speculate about, there must be many "informal" tools whose use will always elude us. There would be little profit in attempting here to describe some of the less frequent and more elusive forms. Whilst all the flaked stone tools mentioned tend to be small and light-weight, the coastal sites commonly produce much heavier tools (Ill. 3.15). Their purpose is not clearly understood, but presumably relates in some way to the business of obtaining and dealing with sea foods, perhaps for detaching shellfish from the rocks, or for butchering marine animals. Large, unretouched stone flakes may have been used in the scaling and filleting of fish.

From about 2 000 years ago pottery (Ill. 3.16) was in use among people living along the southern coast. Unless it can be shown that the pottery industry was learned from coastal traders from outside southern Africa, we must suppose that it was a local invention.

3.14

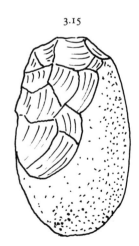

3.15

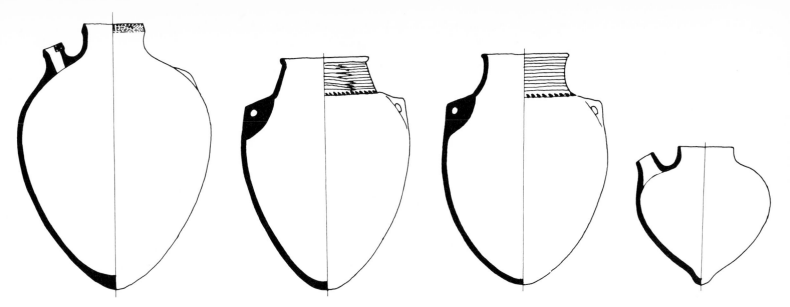

The use of organic materials

Almost everything usable seems to have been used. There are fragments of arrow shafts made from the stems of reeds, and bound with sinew just above the nock (the notch which received the bow string) and at the distal end (which received the arrowhead) to prevent splitting. Specimens of arrowheads and linkshafts show that the composite type of arrowhead (Ill. 3.17) in use among the Bushmen in recent years has been known for at least 5 000 years. At Lochinvar in Zambia wood was used, but generally (perhaps because they survive better) known specimens are of bone and occasionally of ivory. No examples have been found in which stone forms part of the armature of the arrowhead, but early travellers among the Bushmen described how barbs were made by attaching slivers of stone, or the tip of a porcupine quill, to the arrowhead. We may suggest that some of the small flakes and particularly backed specimens may have been used in this way. Support for this suggestion is found in the rather crude specimens made by a captive Bushman at Cape Town in the 19th century (Ill. 3.18). In addition a number of flaked stone specimens appear to represent a more conventional form of stone arrowhead (Ill. 3.19). The simple tanged point from Robberg Peninsula was made about 2 500 BP; the remainder are unfortunately not dated.

The Bushman bow is small, and the one fragment of bowstave from a pre-historic context in the south-eastern Cape (Scott's Cave) follows the same pattern. The small bow with its light reed arrows was not in itself intended to be a lethal weapon; its function was really to deliver poison, applied to the arrowhead, to the bloodstream of the quarry. The delicate, composite arrowhead parts from Lochinvar in Zambia suggest that this method of using poison has been known for at least 4 000 years.

Reed stems were used for making mats. These, one may suppose, were made in a variety of forms to suit different purposes, such as sleeping, or as winnowing trays for separating termite eggs from sand.

The fibrous stem of *Cyperus textilis* was used in the manufacture of twisted cord (Ill. 3.20), as well as in bound bunches of fibre such as would be useful for carrying handles (Ill. 3.21). The cord itself must have been put to many uses. Among these was the making of nets, which might have been used either as containers for carrying, or perhaps in the trapping of small game or birds. The cordage of a specimen almost 6 000 years old from Melkhoutboom (Ill. 3.22) in the eastern Cape is very fine, some 2 mm in thickness; the mesh is 10 mm and the knot is the traditional non-slip knot used universally by fishermen today and for at least 7 000 years in Europe. At Melkhoutboom plant fibre is seen to have been used as a binding on a stone flake (Ill. 3.23), presumably as part of a hafting system. At De Hangen in the south-western Cape, the broad leaves of a lily, bound with fine cord, were used to make a pouch in which several large black mussel shells had been carried from the coast some 60 km (37 miles) away. Various grasses were collected for use as bedding at inland caves, while at the coast the soft, ribbon-like "sea grass" was used wherever it was available.

3.16 Examples of pottery from middens on the southern coast *(after J. Rudner)*. (⅓ of natural size)

3.17 Composite arrowhead (historic Bushman) of bone, showing the slender, sharp-pointed arrowhead, and the thicker linkshaft, joined by a sinew-bound section of reed. (⅔ of natural size)

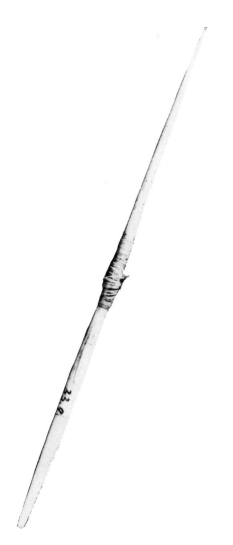

45

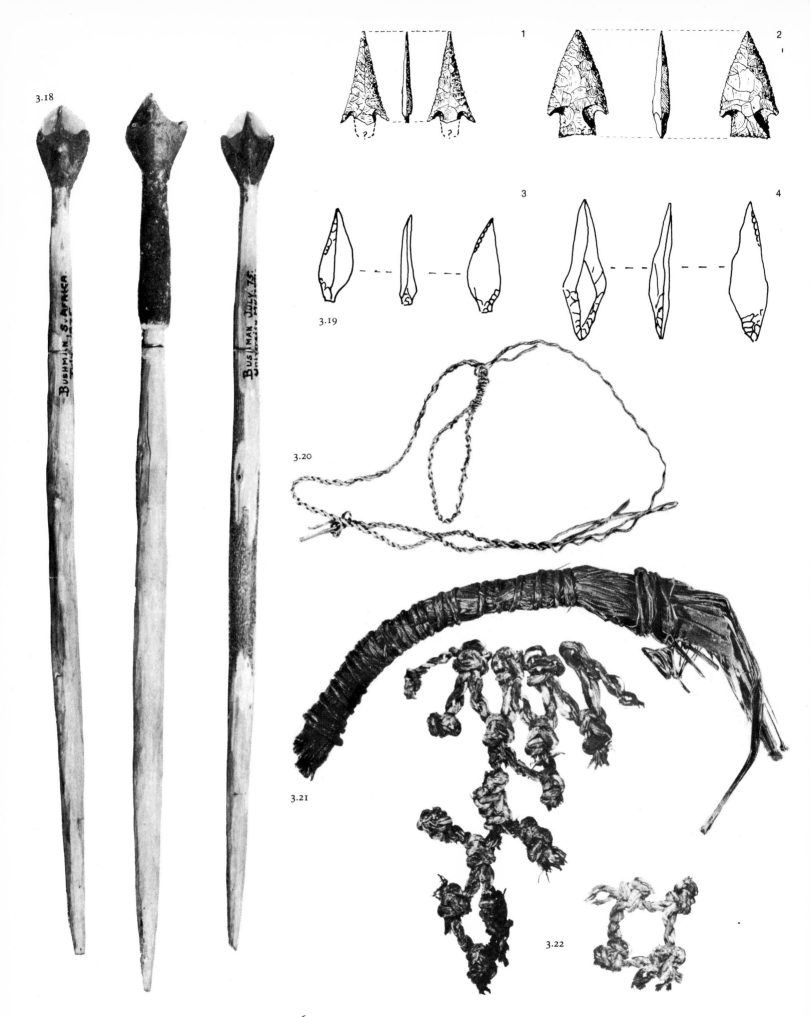

3.18

1

2

3

4

3.19

3.20

3.21

3.22

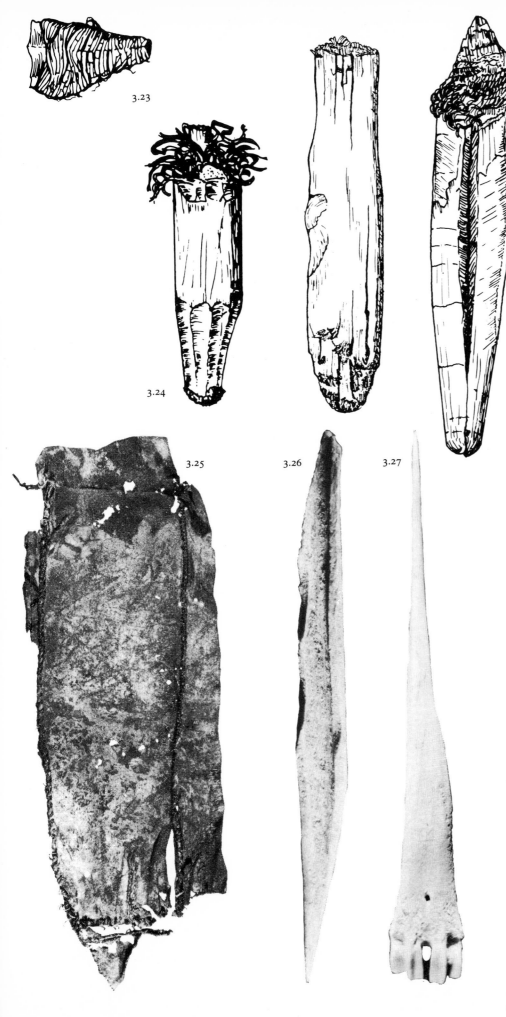

3.18 Three wooden arrowheads tipped with tiny flakes of quartz (or glass) set in a vegetable mastic. These examples were made by Bushman prisoners at Cape Town in the 1870s, and whilst very crude, none the less show a traditional method of arming arrows with stone. *(Photo: Pitt Rivers Museum)* (Natural size)

3.19 Flaked stone arrowheads. 1 and 2, barbed and tanged, bifacially flaked specimens from the Orange Free State. None of the examples of this kind is dated. 3 and 4, from Nelson Bay cave, are about 3 000 years old. Whilst of a simpler kind, they are still thought to be arrowheads. (Natural size)

3.20 Fine twisted cord, probably of *Cyperus textilis*, from De Hangen. *(Photo: J. E. Parkington)* (Natural size)

3.21 Carrying handle (perhaps for a lugged pot) made by binding a bundle of fibres, from De Hangen. *(Photo: J. E. Parkington)* (Natural size)

3.22 Fragments of fine netting from Melkhoutboom. *(Photo: H. J. Deacon)* (Twice natural size)

3.23 Fragment of a tool, possibly the head of a spear or arrow, or a knife blade, made on a flake, and still bearing a fibre binding, presumably intended to make the hafting more secure. Melkhoutboom *(after H. J. Deacon)*. (Natural size)

3.24 Three wooden pegs cut from pieces of stick. Sometimes these are apparently pieces cut away in the manufacture of something else, but others show clear signs of having been used as pegs. Melkhoutboom *(after H. J. Deacon)*. (Natural size)

3.25 A piece of finely sewn leather from De Hangen. *(Photo: J. E. Parkington)* ($\frac{1}{2}$ of natural size)

3.26 Awl made on a splinter of bone. (Twice natural size)

3.27 A fine awl made on the cannon bone of a small antelope. Such awls were presumably used on soft materials such as leather. (Twice natural size)

47

Wood must have been used extensively, but little has survived to enlighten us. We have mentioned the bowstave from Scott's Cave, and the wooden arrowheads from Lochinvar. Digging sticks which have been found at several sites provide another point of similarity with the equipment of the modern Bushmen, and it is likely that such a simple but useful implement is very ancient indeed. Wooden pegs much burred at the end by hammering (Ill. 3.24) seem to be common, and in at least one site (Melkhoutboom) several were found hammered into cracks in the wall of the rock shelter, doubtless to serve as pegs for suspending bows, quivers, carrying bags and any other items of equipment that needed to be kept off the ground. Such pegs may also have been used for the pegging out of skins for cleaning, and perhaps for securing small game traps. Fire is important in every society, and whilst prehistoric Bushmen, like their modern descendants, undoubtedly did their best not to let their fire go out, when on occasion it did, it was rekindled with the aid of the fire twirl. Evidence of this exists in the form of the small cones of wood with rounded, charred bases which served as the working bits of fire twirls, and of the hearth sticks with their charred depressions.

Leather garments are clearly represented in many rock paintings, and a few scraps have come down to us. We have a well-preserved and finely stitched piece of leather from De Hangen (Ill. 3.25), a large fragment with loops and thonging from Melkhoutboom, and a well-preserved sandal from the Big Elephant shelter in the Erongo mountains in South West Africa. The existence of these leather garments and sandals serves as a reminder that the manufacture of such pieces is likely to have involved a variety of tools (skin-dressing equipment, awls) which we might expect to find and identify.

The commonest organic remains are those of bone (and occasionally ivory). Bone is a hard, tough material which can be shaped by flaking, grinding or sawing, and all three methods were employed by prehistoric Bushmen. Bone also takes a good polish, and was occasionally used for the making of personal adornments such as beads and pendants. But the commonest artefacts of bone are probably the group classed as "awls". These may be made on flaked splinters of bone (Ill. 3.26) or on fragments retaining an articular end, commonly the cannon bone of a small antelope (Ill. 3.27). Bone was employed for the heads and linkshafts of composite arrowheads, and some among the former are beautifully symmetrical and finished with a high polish. Small tubes of bone were cut, generally from the humerus or ulna of a bird, by first sawing or cutting a ring around the bone and then snapping it. These "bone tubes" vary considerably in diameter and length, and are often finely finished with (or acquire) a high polish (Ill. 3.28). Not infrequently they are embellished with incised decorative motifs (Ill. 3.29), and occasionally such decoration is applied to the whole, unaltered bone (Ill. 3.30). Spatulate pieces of massive bone, carefully cut and flaked to shape, with a ground, bevelled edge (Ill. 3.31), may have been employed in preparing skins; the working edge commonly displays quite a high polish, and no signs of chipping or battering.

Rock paintings suggest that body painting may sometimes have been practised, but the commonest evidence of personal adornment lies in the tens of thousands of beads of ostrich-egg shell (Ill. 3.32) that have been found in archaeological contexts. Occasionally these are found in graves in such a way as to indicate their uses in waistbands, necklets, wristlets or head ornaments. The variety of uses was probably every bit as great as among living Bushmen. In coastal sites one not infrequently finds *Conus* shells and other species perforated for uses as pendants or components of necklaces (Ill. 3.35). The little *Glycemeris queketi* shells (Ill. 3.36) are found in abundance in some sites. They were undoubtedly collected on the beaches for use as beads, but in these specimens the neat, round holes are made by a carnivorous gasteropod that preys on the little bivalves. Bone, ivory, seashell and ostrich-egg shell were also used in the manufacture of pendants (Ill. 3.37) or sequins. Perhaps the most remarkable of these small objects, which one supposes were ornamental, are the delicate rings made from part of the carapace of a tortoise (Ill. 3.38). These are usually a little over 1 cm in diameter and clearly were not intended as finger rings. Tortoise shells were converted for use as bowls by the removal of the basal plate, or as buchu containers by being blocked at one end and suspended by a cord passed through two holes drilled in the basal plate at the other end.

3.28 Bone tube showing high polish. One end seems to have been slightly roughened as if to give purchase to some attachment. ($1\frac{1}{2}$ × natural size)

3.29 Decorated bone tubes from Nelson Bay cave. One of the three (a) is complete. Figures c, d and e show three different views of the same piece. (2 × natural size)

3.30 Complete bird bone showing notched decoration. ($2\frac{1}{2}$ × natural size)

3.31 One ivory and three bone tools with strong, bevelled working "bits" at one end; probably skin-dressing tools. Nelson Bay cave. ($\frac{2}{3}$ of natural size)

Food-getting and life patterns

Little can be deduced from surviving artefacts about food and food-getting. The bow and arrow may be taken to imply hunting, whilst the digging stick must surely relate to the women's foraging for edible roots and tubers, and perhaps breaking open termite nests and grubbing up mice. The same device may have been used for digging pitfall traps, presumably by the menfolk. Our knowledge of dietary habits is derived chiefly from surviving remains of the food eaten, and animal remains generally survive better than plant remains.

If we may judge by recent ethnographic studies of hunter-gatherers in various parts of the world, and of the Kalahari Bushmen in particular, we should expect a

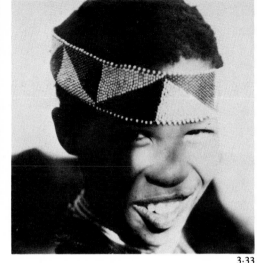

3.32

3.33

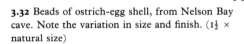

3.34

3.35

3.36

3.32 Beads of ostrich-egg shell, from Nelson Bay cave. Note the variation in size and finish. ($1\frac{1}{2}$ × natural size)

3.33 An elaborate headband is proudly worn by this little girl, //okama. Beads are often found on the prehistoric living floors of Later Stone Age times.

3.34 N≠isa of Dobe, Ngamiland: an attractive teenager complete with necklaces of ostrich-egg shell beads. Such body ornaments are frequently brought to light in archaeological digs.

3.35 Pierced *Conus* shell, presumably part of a necklace. ($1\frac{1}{2}$ × natural size)

3.36 Seven shells of marine creatures with perforations made not by man but by a carnivorous gasteropod which preys on them. The shells were presumably collected to form parts of necklaces. Nelson Bay cave. ($1\frac{1}{2}$ × natural size)

pattern in which collecting of such things as roots, fruits, shellfish and small, slow-moving game (such as tortoises) was in the hands of women and older children, whilst men engaged in the more strenuous and dangerous task of hunting. It also seems likely that whilst the produce of hunting would have been highly esteemed, as it is today, the bulk of the daily subsistence would have been provided by the industry of the women. Hunter-gatherers usually range over a well-defined territory which they know exceedingly well, and which will normally provide for all their requirements in raw materials, food and shelter throughout the year. Usually the territory is defined in relation to the availability of certain staples at different times of year; these would generally be items collected by the women and whose supply was normally reliable. So far as possible such resources, while providing security, would be conserved by advantage being taken of less reliable though perhaps more favoured supplies whenever the opportunity arose: the men's contribution of meat would belong to the latter category. It would be very rare, though not impossible, for a group of hunter-gatherers to have all their requirements met in one locality all the year round. Most things, and in particular plants, have their season, and in the absence of means of storing things from one season to

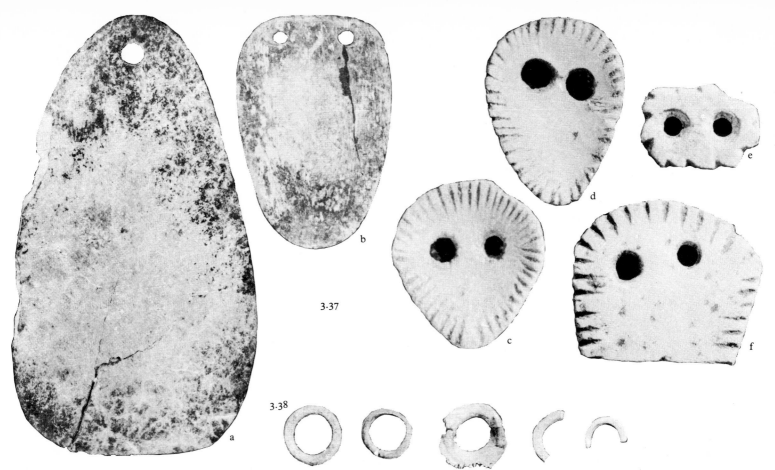

3.37

3.38

3.37 Pendants of various materials: a and b, ivory ($1\frac{1}{3}$ × natural size); c, d, and e, seashell; f, ostrich-egg shell. ($2\frac{1}{2}$ × natural size)

3.38 Rings made from tortoise carapace. Nelson Bay cave. (Natural size)

the next, the group would have to move from one locality to another according to the availability of food. Such movements would not be random, but would be made deliberately, and probably regularly, on the basis of a sound knowledge of where and when resources are available.

One of the more interesting exercises in archaeology is to try to discover just how prehistoric communities exploited their environment, and how their patterns of livelihood were built around such exploitations. This is not an easy thing to do. It requires very careful recovery and analysis of information from a number of sites in an area under investigation; and even then the quality of the results will depend very much on how well organic remains have survived in the sites investigated.

Oral tradition has preserved a record of the movements of a group in the eastern Cape who spent about two months on the Tsitsikamma coast in summer, and went inland to winter in a group of caves in the Baviaanskloofberg; in between they occupied sites along one of the tributaries of the Kouga River. In the western Cape there is archaeological evidence – not yet conclusive – that is suggestive of a somewhat similar pattern of movement between the mountains that lie between the Doorn and Olifants rivers and the coastline to the west. In this case, however, the seasons seem to be reversed. The abundance at the De Hangen site of fruits, berries and root-stocks, which could have been collected only in the summer months, together with numerous juvenile *dassies* (*Hyrax* or "rock-rabbit") and tortoises, all point to a summer occupation, and it is thought that a reliable collected food supply might be non-existent there in the winter months. There are clear evidences at De Hangen of contact with the coast. A site investigated at Elands Bay, 60 km (37 miles) away, on the coast, appears on the evidence of the young seals taken there to have been occupied in the winter months. The suggestion is that the roots, fruits, nuts, tortoises and dassies provided a reliable basic diet in the summer months in the mountains. In the winter the plant foods would not be available and tortoises and dassies might be harder to come by; so the group migrated to the coast, where shellfish could be collected in abundance, and where, for a few months during the winter, yearling seals were obtainable. It is likely that intermediate sites were occupied in the Olifants valley, but at the time of writing this has not been tested archaeologically.

51

On the other hand, in the bush country of the eastern Cape, it seems likely that an acceptable livelihood could have been maintained all year round from a single base. The same might prove to be true of some situations on the southern coast, such as Knysna and Plettenberg Bay, and investigations currently in progress in the latter area may shed some light on the problem.

It is apparent then that no blanket statement will suffice for all groups of prehistoric Bushmen. The pattern of livelihood would have varied from region to region and would depend very much on variations in what the environment had to offer.

The faunal remains from a number of sites show us that small animals such as hares, dassies, tortoises, lizards, snakes, frogs and birds formed an important part of the meat diet, and that almost any of the larger mammals were taken when the opportunity arose. Some sites have yielded remains of food plants, including a variety of bulbs or corms and the beans of the tree fuchsia *(Schotia afra)*, but preservation of vegetation is so limited that these do little more than point up the deficiency. We can only suppose that use was made of whatever edible plants the environment offered.

Those bands that lived close to the sea-shore, or that made seasonal visits, were able to take advantage of a wealth of food resources peculiar to the marine environment. Whales and seals sometimes fall victim to high seas or other disasters, especially during the calving or pupping seasons, and we see this reflected in the bones from archaeological sites. On the southern coast many species of fish, large and small, may be stunned or killed by sudden upwellings of cold water induced by south-easterly winds in the summer months, and such occurrences can produce enormous quantities of fish simply for the collecting. No doubt such gluts were greatly appreciated, but we have no idea whether any of the surplus was preserved in any way (by drying, salting, smoking, etc.). But apart from this fortuitous supply of food from the sea, there is clear evidence in the archaeological record of deliberate, premeditated and systematic exploitation.

Small, grooved pellets of shale (Ill. 3.11) have been found associated with fish remains at two sites on the southern coast (Robberg Peninsula and the Storms River mouth) and have been interpreted as having been sinkers for use with fishing lines. No recognisable fish hooks have been found, but experiment shows that unmodified thorns will suffice, or possibly even sharp fish spines. Certainly the sinkers are capable of taking down a line with a baited thorn attached. Furthermore, the range of species represented in some sites is such that line fishing seems almost certain. The evidence is strengthened by the presence of species not affected by cold-water upwell and not normally to be found in intertidal rock

3.39 Intertidal fish traps at Still Bay, on the southern coast of the Cape Province.

pools. At the site of Elands Bay, north of Cape Town, there have been found numbers of carefully shaped, slender slivers of bone, about 6 cm long, sharpened at both ends; these have been tentatively interpreted as having been fishing gorges, though we should remember that such devices may also be used for catching certain kinds of birds, such as gannets. At the site of Bonteberg, on the Cape Peninsula, crayfish seem to have formed a regular and substantial element in the diet.

Probably the most impressive fishing devices are the stone-built fish traps (Ill. 3.39) found intermittently over 1 600 km (1 000 miles) of coastline, from the Mozambique border to just north of Cape Town. These are likely to be found wherever there is a combination of gently shelving beach and an abundance of boulders. The traps are made by clearing an area of boulders to deepen it into a pool and piling up these boulders to raise a low, broad wall around the pool. All this must be done in such a way that the enclosures formed are completely submerged at high tide, so that fish can swim into them, whilst at low tide the walls provide a barrier preventing the fish from escaping. The walls are really more like low banks, in order better to withstand wave attack.

These fish traps may generally produce only a low yield of fish, although on occasion they will catch a whole school of quite large fish that have come inshore to feed, and fish would then dominate the diet for a while. But they are interesting for their social as well as their economic implications. A single trap consists of a wall enclosing a pool, and the construction of such must involve a considerable amount

3.40 Rock painting from the Drakensberg depicting a fishing scene. It shows spears being used from boats or rafts, one of which is apparently anchored with a stone. ($\frac{1}{2}$ of natural size)

53

of labour. Often they are built in pairs or groups, one such group containing as many as nine or ten enclosures. Such undertakings imply concerted effort on the part of a group of people, with the implications of shared catches and sustained usage. Such large works would scarcely be undertaken for a casual season's use. We must suppose that the locality of the traps was either occupied continuously by the group, or revisited at regular intervals, perhaps as part of a seasonal pattern of movement. We shall not know exactly how the traps fitted into the lives of the people who made them until extensive investigation of adjacent sites has taken place.

But fishing was practised not only at the coast. Fish remains have been recorded from sites in Zambia and Lesotho, and there are paintings of fishing scenes in Rhodesia and at several places in the Drakensberg mountains (Ill. 3.40). These show not only the use of spears and line, but also some kind of water craft – in all probability a bundled reed float or raft.

From at least the 4th century A.D., and possibly earlier, a significant change occurred in the economy of some groups with the acquisition of domestic sheep (present at Die Kelders in the 4th century). We do not know yet when or whence these animals were acquired, but it seems unlikely that they were obtained by contact with Iron Age farmers (Bantu-speaking Negroes) to the north. It is tempting to imagine the arrival of sheep and pottery at points on the south-eastern coast about 2 000 years ago, or a little more, independent of any Bantu movements or contact.

Archaeology sheds little light on the sizes of prehistoric Bushman bands, or on the construction of their dwellings and the way in which these were grouped within the community. Until evidence is found to confirm or refute the suggestion, we must suppose that circumstances were much as they are among Bushmen today. In rocky areas circles of stone sometimes outline the bases of former windbreaks (Ill. 3.41). In a few carefully excavated rock shelters, occasional enigmatic post-holes point to the former existence of screens or the like erected to supplement the natural shelter. There is some evidence that coastal settlers sometimes sought the shelter of hollows in the sand dunes, and may have erected flimsy shelters within them. The best-preserved example comes from a shelter in the dry Erongo mountains of South West Africa, where four well-defined living areas were preserved, each screened off from the others, and each with its sleeping area and hearth (Ill. 3.42). The units probably relate to individual families, and it is thought that twelve or fifteen people may have lived in the shelter. About the only other archaeological evidence relating to group size comes from a study of rock paintings in the south-western Cape, which suggests that in that area bands would have averaged about thirteen or fourteen people. This

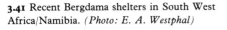

3.41 Recent Bergdama shelters in South West Africa/Namibia. *(Photo: E. A. Westphal)*

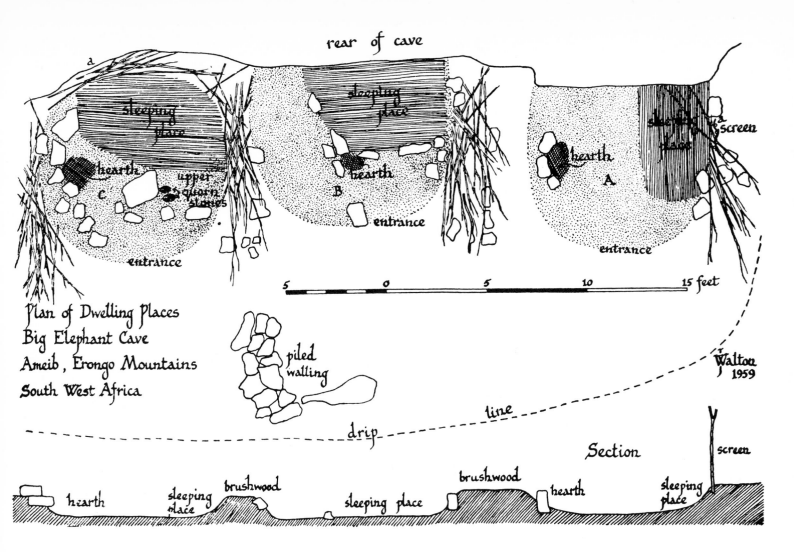

rear of cave

sleeping place

sleeping place

hearth

hearth

upper quorn stones

hearth

sleeping place

screen

entrance

entrance

entrance

5   0   5   10   15 feet

Plan of Dwelling Places
Big Elephant Cave
Ameib, Erongo Mountains
South West Africa

piled walling

Walton
1959

drip   line

Section   screen

hearth   sleeping place   brushwood   sleeping place   brushwood   hearth   sleeping place

calculation agrees very well with 18th-century records for Karroo Bushmen, and though it is a smaller figure than those observed recently for Kalahari Bushmen, the differences may be in part environmental. We should be cautious, however, about attaching too much significance to such figures, for contemporary studies show that band sizes tend to fluctuate considerably in response to a number of factors, the chief of which is probably the quest for food.

3.42 Ground plan and section of a part of the Big Elephant shelter, showing the arrangement of screened living areas, each with a sleeping place and hearth *(after J. Walton)*.

Conclusion

If we wish to think about "prehistoric Bushmen", it is perhaps wiser to avoid thinking in terms of archaeological "cultures". The simple truth is that we cannot really talk meaningfully about *the prehistoric Bushmen;* we can only talk about prehistoric peoples who may have contributed much or little, physically or culturally, to the development of those peoples who have become known in historical times as *the Bushmen.* These prehistoric societies would almost certainly have been mystified by any suggestion that they were related to the numerous scattered groups that the archaeologist necessarily lumps together as his "cultures" or even as "regional variants" of such cultures. We shall come far closer to the truth if we think simply of the essence of these people as seen through the surviving archaeological evidence.

We note the confidence and ingenuity with which they handled a wide variety of raw materials, both organic and inorganic. We can never see things as they saw them, but there is a respect for detail and finish in much of their art and craftsmanship which is surely comprehensible to craftsmen and artists of any age or society. We recognise that some of the environments in which they lived were harsh, while others were much more generous. But without exception we see that they were masters in the art of living off what nature offered. The evidence suggests that in many cases their lives must have been close to what we should call "idyllic" – a life in which ingenuity ensured an adequate (and perhaps often more than adequate) food supply, well-made clothing, shelter and a pleasing degree of personal adornment. Skeletal remains may sometimes reveal injury and pathology, and although we can know almost nothing of their medical practices, historical evidence suggests that they may often have employed sympathetic and effective methods of treatment. It would be foolish to pretend that there was no pain, discomfort or suffering. But by and large it seems likely that, individually and corporately, suffering and anxiety were not at a higher level than in our own society – indeed, they could have been at a lower level.

There is nothing in the archaeological evidence to suggest that the prehistoric ancestors of the Bushmen did not know their territory every bit as intimately as the historical Bushmen did. Indeed, there is more than a little circumstantial evidence to suggest a very good knowledge of the environment and what it had to offer. We still have much to learn about the patterns of exploitation in different areas and at different times. Yet the pattern common to many recent hunter-gatherers of reliance on a staple with a fairly sure supply, supplemented by whatever else could be won, may well be reflected in the high frequency of remains of tortoise and dassie (low bulk yield but reliable supply?) at De Hangen, and in the large quantities of molluscan remains in so many coastal sites. The evidence of De Hangen and Elands Bay in the south-western Cape suggests a seasonal exploitation, perhaps involving a regular movement between inland areas (summer) and the coast (winter). Certainly there is evidence further east of a reverse pattern of movement of groups between the Langkloof mountains (winter) and the coast (summer), with intermediate staging localities between. Elsewhere – and Robberg may have been such a place – conditions may have permitted year-round occupation. In the far north of our area, at the Gwisho sites in the Kafue valley, the extraordinary range of mammals represented, including many large and medium-sized species, argues for a high success rate in hunting, and if vegetable resources permitted, these sites may also have seen year-round occupation.

When viewed in terms of archaeological "cultures", these people vanish into a sterile background of tool types and tool frequencies. But when favourable conditions preserve for us a range of plant and animal remains, they come more sharply into view and we may see them as lively, mobile societies dividing their time between work and relaxation. We may imagine the women and younger children moving off in the morning with digging stick and collecting bag, knowing precisely the right direction to take to collect edible roots or fruits, or moving along the rocks to collect shellfish; or the menfolk, stepping lightly in single file, with bow, quiver and arrows, spear and knife, and perhaps a net bag with water containers of ostrich-egg shells, in search of something more substantial. We can imagine the smoke rising from the long-dead hearths and catch the smell of roasting meat. Among the hubbub of domestic chatter and romping children a man sits shaping a bow or refurbishing an arrow, and if we look carefully we may see deft hands skilfully shredding sinew or sewing leather, shaping minute beads and forming them into simple or ornate decorations for wrist, arm, head, waist or leg. One may make a mat, while another twists cord from fibre to make a line for fishing, or twine for snares. If the call comes to dance or to sleep, the work is quietly set aside for another day.

For many thousands of years prehistoric "Bushmen" have lived this peaceful, industrious, idyllic sort of life. Yet, in a few centuries they have been swept from nine-tenths of their former hunting grounds, while for those who are left the die is cast; they must be absorbed into the "civilised" pattern of life, or perish.

4
Bushman Art

Jalmar and Ione Rudner

Rock art, in the form of paintings and petroglyphs, is to be found all over the world – in Europe, Asia, the Americas, Australia and more than anywhere else, in Africa, from the Sahara in the north to the southern extreme of the continent. In South Africa alone more than 3 000 rock art sites have been recorded, and the actual number must be much larger (Ill. 4.1).

Not only is rock art widely distributed, but it also covers a great range in time. The palaeolithic cave art of France is thought to go back about 30 000 years, while some aboriginal Australians still paint on the rocks. In this sub-continent Bushmen are known to have made the last rock paintings about a hundred years ago.

In South Africa the rock paintings have commonly been referred to as "Bushman" paintings, but there is little doubt that the rock art in southern Africa was produced by different population groups in the past. Before we discuss the art of the Bushmen, it is necessary to explain which rock art we believe can be associated with them and why.

The rock paintings in southern Africa may be divided into several main styles belonging to different areas, periods and people. The most widespread style, which is found from Rhodesia and the northern part of South West Africa right down to the south-western Cape, has been named the *Formal School*. A more lively and colourful art style, found mainly in the Drakensberg and the eastern Cape, has been called the *Dynamic School;* its final phase is associated with the historical Bushmen. On the inland plateau of South Africa is found a cruder and

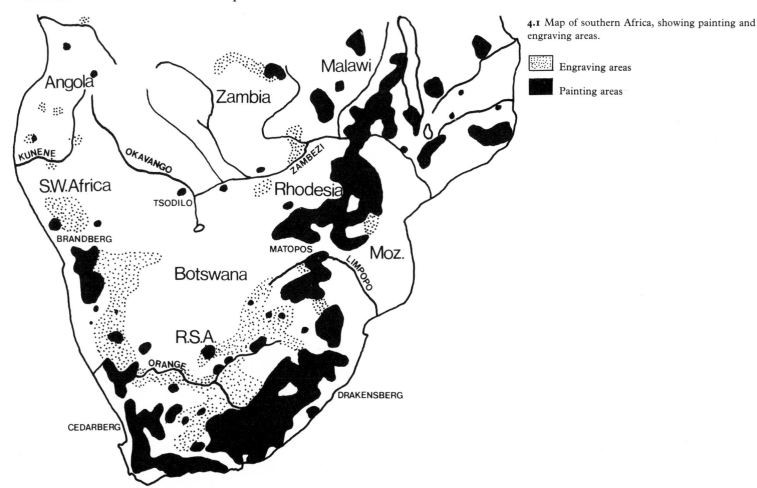

4.1 Map of southern Africa, showing painting and engraving areas.

░ Engraving areas

■ Painting areas

probably late style termed the *Cape Schematic School;* this can probably also be attributed to Bushmen. In the Transvaal and Rhodesia a late, crude style of painting, mainly of animals in white, was probably associated with early, Bantu-speaking Negro people. In northern South West Africa and southern Angola there are two localized styles which may have been associated with the Bergdama and Cuissi people respectively. The *Central African Schematic School* of rock painting in Angola, Zambia and East Africa was most probably the work of Negro artists, but there are also remains of an earlier style. White people have added their contribution in recent centuries in the form of numerous painted or engraved names and scribblings in caves and on rock faces.

The petroglyphs, commonly called rock engravings, have been studied somewhat less than the more spectacular and colourful paintings, but they may possibly extend over a still longer period of time. Variations in style and techniques occur at different periods as well as in different geographical areas. The latest engravings on the South African inland plateau were certainly associated mainly with the Bushmen, but the cultural and human associations of other engravings in Rhodesia, South West Africa and Angola are still enigmatic. In historical times Bantu-speaking Negro peoples, such as the Tswana in the north-western Cape and the Zulu in Natal, made engravings.

The term "Bushman" is used here to refer to hunter-gatherers in southern Africa who speak not only various Bushman languages but also Nama, a Hottentot language. (The Bergdama of South West Africa, who were hunter-gatherers and speak Nama, are however not included.)

Some early travellers, such as Anders Sparrman, wrote of "Bosjesman-Hottentots" – for they regarded the Bushmen, as well as the Strandlopers (or Beach-combers) along the coast, as tribes of Hottentots. In South West Africa some Bushman tribes, such as the Heikum, are Nama-speaking and slightly taller than the small Cape Bushmen. Dr H. Vedder called them "Saan Bushmen", as opposed to "pure Bushmen". He considered them to be hunter-Hottentots who probably preceded the coming of cattle-owning Hottentots. Such differences in language and physique among different Bushman tribes may indicate a diverse history, which would help to explain the presence of different art styles during the Later Stone Age in southern Africa.

Other Later Stone Age people were the Hottentots – or Khoikhoi, as they called themselves. Like the Bushmen, they preceded the coming of the Bantu-speaking Negro people to southern Africa. They are believed to have introduced the breeding of sheep and cattle to southern Africa, although they were in part also hunters and gatherers. They may also have introduced the art of pottery which, at the southern extreme of the continent, goes back at least 2 000 years, as may the breeding of sheep.

The Strandlopers of the South African and South West African coasts were related in language and culture to the Hottentots, but some of their skeletal remains suggest a relationship to both Hottentots and Bushmen.

Rock art and the Bushmen: historical evidence
As early as 1752 an expedition to the eastern Cape found rock paintings near the Kei River and ascribed them to the "Little Chinese", or Khoisan people. Sir John Barrow, who travelled in South Africa in 1797 and 1798, went in search of Bushmen near "Waay Hoek" in the eastern Cape and found one of their retreats in the mountains:

"On the smooth sides of the cavern were drawings of several animals that had been made from time to time by these savages. Some of the drawings were recognised to be of recent execution; but many of them were remembered to exist from the first settlement of this part of the colony."

With one exception, there is no authentic record of any trained observer actually having seen a Bushman artist painting on the rocks.* The closest to direct evidence is perhaps that of the missionary S. S. Dornan: in *Pygmies and Bushmen of the Kalahari* (1925) he recounts how early this century he saw a "half-bred"

*This exception was a young Drakensberg Bushman (see Chapter 5, page 84, by A. R. Willcox) – Ed.

Bushman painting on a granite boulder; he smoothed the surface with a pebble and then painted a zebra, using first a crayon, then warm, liquid paint. He was paid to do it, which somewhat detracts from the authenticity of the evidence. G. W. Stow, a geologist, told of a Bushman who was shot in the Witteberge in 1866 for stock theft; he had ten small horn pots hanging from a belt, each of which contained a different colour. In *Rock Paintings of the Drakensberg* (1956) A. R. Willcox quotes a statement by a Negro who lived among the Bushmen in the Drakensberg from about 1850: the Bushmen painted well, he said, using earth colours and brushes of wildebeest hair. The missionary V. Ellenberger in *La fin tragique des Bushmen* tells of a very old Sotho woman, born about 1856, who when she was young visited a Bushman headman in a large cave. There she saw three men painting, each in his corner. A few others recorded similar, indirect evidence. There is perhaps sufficient historical evidence to indicate that Bushmen must have been responsible for at least the latest paintings in the eastern Cape and Drakensberg areas.

We have very little historical evidence of the identity of the artists of the rocks in other parts of South Africa. The south-western Cape is rich in rock paintings of the Formal School, while a few late paintings in a cruder style show ships, White men with horses and wagons, and women with crinolines. The art in this area must therefore have survived until at least the end of the 17th century, though no written records of those art practices have been found. The south-western Cape was mainly a Hottentot area, but Bushmen (Sonqua) did live in the mountains. The last of the Formal paintings include pictures of fat-tailed sheep, but none of cattle, so it appears that this art period must have come to an end after the arrival of sheep, but before the arrival of cattle. Sheep were already in this area about 1 500 years BP, according to recent radiocarbon dating of excavated sheep remains.

On the inland plateau of the Cape Province the rock art consists mainly of engravings portraying animals and designs, but in some more mountainous areas, such as the Kareeberge near Carnarvon, there are also rock paintings of an abstract nature, representative of the Cape Schematic School. At least in historical times this area was populated mainly by Cape Bushmen, while Hottentots lived along the Orange River and other river courses. The only historical reference to rock art in the northern Cape Province is the missionary Robert Moffat's mention of Tswana herdboys making engravings north of the Orange River, but there is little doubt that the Cape Bushmen made not only some of the last engravings, but probably also the Schematic paintings south of the Orange River.

In South West Africa paintings and engravings are often found in the same area, even sometimes at the same site. In 1879 Theophilus Hahn, a trader at Bethanie, reported that in the south of the territory the Bushmen still made abstract paintings. This, of course, does not necessarily mean that all the paintings there were made by Bushmen.

Cultural associations

Rock art is no longer practised in southern Africa. As even the memory of it has died out, we must turn to archaeology for further information, and try to associate the rock art with other cultural remains found at the art sites. A cultural association between the art on the rock wall and the floor deposit can be proved only when careful excavation reveals fragments of painted rock from wall paintings, or painted stones, in archaeological deposits which can be identified and perhaps radiocarbon dated. Unfortunately the number of excavations at rock art sites in southern Africa is still relatively small, and occurrences of rock art in these deposits are extremely rare.

There is, however, another possible cultural association which, though less reliable, should not be ignored: cultural material is almost always found on the surface at both engraving and painting sites. If only one stone industry is present, and if it is repeated at other similar art sites, it can be assumed with a fair amount of certainty that the stone industry was probably associated with the people responsible for the art. A study of the type of cultural material found at rock art sites all over southern Africa shows a fairly consistent relationship between certain Later Stone Age industries and styles of rock art, a correlation which must be more than coincidental.

In Chapter 3, an outline has been given of the features of the Later Stone Age and of some of its varying industries. Those referred to as *Smithfield N* and *Smithfield B* industries are found in painted shelters throughout the Drakensberg and eastern Cape regions, where paintings are mainly of the Dynamic School, while the so-called *Smithfield B* industry is found on the inland plateau of the Cape Province, at engraving and painting sites of the Cape Schematic School. This distribution agrees more or less with the early historical distribution of the Drakensberg and Cape Bushmen, and we have little hesitation in attributing these industries to the Bushmen. There is also some historical evidence for this association. Archaeological evidence for the association between early Bushmen and Smithfield-like industries in the western Transvaal has recently been provided by Professor R. J. Mason.

In Rhodesia, South West Africa, the south-western Cape and the rest of the Cape coastal belt as far east as East London, the lithic industries found with the paintings (mainly of the Formal School) and with some of the engravings generally belong to the microlithic *Wilton* complex of industries. In this cultural phase we include what was formerly called *Smithfield C,* as well as an underlying, cruder, macrolithic industry. These industries are common also in the Strandloper shell middens along the coasts of South West Africa and the Cape Province. Wilton artefacts are particularly numerous in areas historically associated with the Hottentots, such as the Saldanha Bay area and the region around the Cape Peninsula. Painted burial stones have been discovered in shelters containing such shell middens along the southern coast of the Cape Province. In the light of this evidence, it has been suggested that Khoisan people other than Bushmen may have been mainly responsible for the rock art of the south-western Cape, South West Africa and Rhodesia, most of which is so different from that of the Dynamic School of the Drakensberg regions.

The eastern Cape is of particular interest to the student of rock art, as it was here that two commonly recognised cultural traditions met – the Smithfield of the inland area and the Wilton of the coastal belt, the Dynamic School of rock paintings and the Formal School. In some shelters both art traditions are represented. None of these shelters has as yet been excavated to establish the archaeological sequence.

Anatomical evidence in paintings of the human body such as steatopygia and *penis rectus* suggests a Khoisan origin of the art. By contrast most of the relatively few painted profiles of human figures seem to depict a different people. The rock paintings portray aspects of the life of a hunter-gatherer people. Pictures of White and of Black people belong to the final stage of this art, as do horses, cattle, guns, shields, stabbing spears and knobkerries. The weapons of the men in the paintings are usually bows and arrows, while spears and knobkerries are less common. The women have digging sticks, sometimes weighted with bored stones. All this points to the Bushmen and their way of life, but also to some Hottentot (including Strandloper) hunters, and even perhaps to the Bergdama in South West Africa.

Main styles of painting

We shall describe the paintings of the Dynamic School, which are known to be true Bushman paintings; those of the Cape Schematic School, which were probably also made by Bushmen; and the Formal School paintings, which were probably made by ancestors or relatives of Khoisan peoples.

The Dynamic School

The greatest concentration of rock paintings in southern Africa is along the eastern mountain spine of South Africa – the Drakensberg and its outrunners in the eastern Cape. The paintings occur in sandstone shelters and on rock faces in the south-eastern Transvaal, Swaziland, Lesotho, Natal, the eastern Orange Free State and the eastern Cape Province. These mountains provided shelter, water, game and veld food for the little hunter-gatherers and served as a retreat when they were driven from other areas. The last mountain Bushmen in Lesotho survived until almost the end of the 19th century, or even later.

The Drakensberg areas are the home of the Dynamic School paintings. They

are colourful and lively, often tell a story and sometimes even show a humorous spirit, all features which are absent from the paintings of the Formal School. Often entire scenes are depicted: some may be actual historical events. They show cattle raids, many battles with White or Black enemies, inter-tribal fighting (Ill. 4.2), trekking family groups, hunting scenes and lively dances (Ill. 4.3), as well as smaller scenes of a domestic nature. There are also numerous pictures of animals, particularly of the favourite species, the eland (Ill. 4.4).

Undoubtedly the painters favoured the eland over a long period of time, to judge by the various ways in which it was painted and the many superpositions – in the Ndedema gorge in Natal seven different styles were said to have been found. Thousands of pictures show the eland singly, in small groups or in large herds. They were frequently painted in red, or red and white, but a striking development

4.3 Post Catherine, Wodehouse district, eastern Cape Province: Girls dancing and clapping, painted in red.

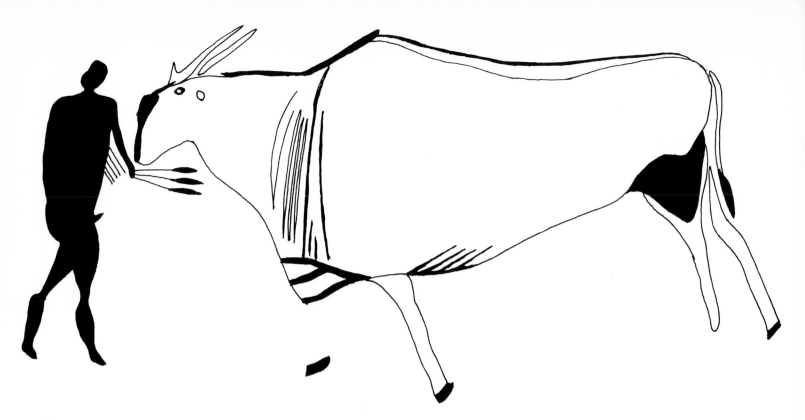

4.4 Camp Siding, Queenstown district, eastern Cape Province: Monochrome man and polychrome eland. The painting of the man is possibly older than that of the eland.

of these pictures was in the shaded polychromes, a distinctive feature in the Dynamic School paintings. The back and main parts of the eland's body were painted darker than the head and belly, where the colours were faded out. Reds, yellows, orange and white were used, and features such as hooves and horns were generally painted black. A three-dimensional effect was enhanced by the further legs of the animals being painted in a lighter colour than the near legs.

The artists depicted the eland in various attitudes – reclining, with heads turned away, or facing the viewer. All four legs, both ears and both horns were usually included. This technique of indicating perspective in animal pictures rarely occurs outside the Drakensberg areas. But despite the care for detail, the sex of the animal was rarely shown, a feature found in all rock art in southern Africa.

Other popular animals depicted in the paintings were rhebuck (Ill. 4.5), hartebeest (Ill. 4.6) and other small buck. Elephants, rhinoceroses, hippopotamuses, zebras, wild pigs, ostriches, baboons, lions and leopards also occur, as well as snakes, fish, birds and even insects. Pictures of cattle and horses are very common in some areas and sometimes even outnumber those of eland. Only the pictures of cattle can compete with the eland pictures in colourfulness. There are some paintings of sheep.

Pictures of people abound, and in some areas they are more numerous than pictures of animals. The figures are often lively and very active, with exaggerated movements, such as those of men running with legs outstretched horizontally to denote speed. They occur singly, in groups or in large scenes – hunting, fighting, dancing, sitting, lying down, standing, walking or running. People were painted mainly in red, sometimes in black, especially when Negro people were portrayed, but there are also polychromes. On the whole the pictures of people are not as carefully detailed as those of the eland, although many show body painting and ornaments, apart from clothing and equipment. Others are merely stick figures. Sizes vary considerably and heads have a variety of stylized shapes. Facial details are generally lacking. Sometimes the face was painted in a light colour, such as yellow or white.

It is generally possible to tell the sex of the human figures, either by physical features or by clothing and equipment. There are more pictures of men than of women and children, and they are often depicted with body paint in the form of stripes and other patterns. Sometimes the figures wear long or short garments or cloaks, sometimes a head covering. The men usually carry weapons and other equipment such as skin bags, while the women often carry digging sticks.

The pictures of people frequently indicate who they are. Many are clearly Bushmen, shown by the semi-erect penis (Ill. 4.4), the small bows, the quivers and typical composite arrows, as well as the large buttocks and digging sticks of the women. Others, sometimes painted black, are southern African Negro people with spears or shields, typical ornaments such as large ear-rings, and big, splayed toes (Ill. 4.7). People in European dress are sometimes shown with guns or astride horses.

An important group of paintings typical of the Drakensberg areas and the Dynamic School consists of pictures of animals of the imagination, probably originating in the myths and legends of the Bushmen. There are strange, winged creatures, others with human features or half animal, half human figures. Among these may be included figures in long garments or karosses (skin-cloaks), with "leggings", hooves and the heads of antelope. They may carry large loads or dead buck. Other human figures have eland masks or heads. Perhaps some of these figures may be hunters disguised to deceive the game, or they may be people dressed for ceremonies. The numerous eland pictures and the creatures with eland heads or masks may reflect an extensive cult.

The narrative style has been described as belonging to a period of unrest, when the Bushmen were being driven out of their old hunting areas to take refuge deeper in the mountains where, on the rocks, they told the story of their struggles. Despite this their art reached its peak during this period. Among the latest paintings are small handprints, finger-dots and finger-smears, lines and crude animal pictures, all obviously made with fingers dipped in paint, and showing a decline in the art. Similar pictures occur elsewhere in southern Africa, especially in the south-western Cape, and seem to belong to a final stage of both the Dynamic

4.5 Buffelsfontein, Wodehouse district, eastern Cape Province: Two rhebuck in white and another bichrome buck.

4.6 Klipspruit, Aliwal North district, eastern Cape Province: Hartebeest in red and white.

63

and Formal schools. The small handprints conform in size to what we know of Bushman and Hottentot hands.

The Formal School

The Formal School is probably the oldest of the rock painting schools. It is associated with the Wilton group of Later Stone Age industries all over southern Africa and may have originated in the granite shelters of Rhodesia. From there it could have spread west to South West Africa and continued south to the south-western Cape and east to the eastern Cape – all areas where these paintings occur.

The paintings may have begun as crude monochrome silhouettes of single animals standing still and showing only two legs and one horn, also a feature of some of the earliest rock engravings. In time the pictures developed into bi-chromes and polychromes, stilted but naturalistic animal pictures.

Man was the favourite subject of the artists. The human figures are stylized to a varying degree and their movements are generally sedate – they stand or walk, but seldom run, and often seem to march. They depict tall, dignified men clad in karosses or shirt-like garments (in the south-western Cape; Ill. 4.8), or they are naked, without even a loin-cloth. The people are depicted with taller proportions than most of those of the Dynamic School, and on the whole the actual painted figures are larger (Ill. 4.9). The men have long bows, unlike the small Bushman bows, and baggy quivers, larger than those of the little Bushmen, and they often carry bags on their backs (Ill. 4.10). The womenfolk are generally nude and often have prominent buttocks (steatopygia; Ill. 4.11). They may carry digging sticks, sometimes weighted with bored stones, such as those found at Later Stone Age camping sites. In the south-western Cape they sometimes wear beadwork around their hips, leg rings and pointed caps (Ill. 4.9). These features agree with historical reports about the Nama Hottentots (or Namaqua).

The heads of the human figures are generally stylized. The hair is shaped like the curve of a sickle or hook, sometimes with vertical lines at the back, indicating long, possibly artificially straightened hair. (The Nama Hottentots were reported by several early observers to have had "long" hair.) In a few paintings faces can still be seen as concave shapes of faded white, pink or yellow (Ill. 4.12; 4.13), sometimes with painted patterns or stripes, as in the Cedarberg. Where the faces have weathered away only the red or black hook-shape of the hair remains, hence the name "hook-head style". There are other head shapes, too, such as a baboon-like profile common in Rhodesia. Actual profiles are sometimes shown, especially in South West Africa, but they are rare. As in the Dynamic School, the men generally have a semi-erect penis, often infibulated (Ill. 4.14),

4.7 Brakfontein, Cradock district, eastern Cape Province: South African Negro warriors, in black, red and white.

4.8 Pienaarsvlakte, Cedarberg, Clanwilliam district, south-western Cape: Hook-headed men and elephants.

64

except in the south-western Cape. There is no information about infibulation in southern Africa, except what is seen in rock art.

The artists used false perspective, showing the shoulders from the front while the head and the rest of the body are seen from the side, a well-known feature in other early art, such as that of Egypt and the Middle East.

Most of the animal pictures in the Formal School are monochromes or bichromes in different shades of red, as well as in black, white and yellow. The choice of animal in the paintings varied with its distribution, but there were also regional preferences. While small buck were the most popular subject everywhere, as well as the most commonly hunted game, the preference for larger buck varied. In Rhodesia it was kudu, sable and wildebeest, in South West Africa oryx or gemsbok, kudu, wildebeest and hartebeest, while in the south-western Cape the eland (Ill. 4.12) and hartebeest were preferred by the artists. The choice of other animals was: in Rhodesia, elephants and giraffes (Ill. 4.15), followed in popularity by hippopotamus, buffalo, zebra, rhinoceros and ostrich, but there are no pictures of cattle, and only one site with pictures of fat-tailed sheep is known. In the Brandberg in South West Africa the giraffe was popular, followed by the ostrich, zebra, elephant, rhinoceros, leopard and other animals, with one picture of a fat-tailed sheep. In the south-western Cape, the elephant (Ill. 4.8) was a favourite animal of the artists, followed by the zebra, baboon, ostrich, rhinoceros, hippopotamus and others. There are several sites in that area with paintings of fat-tailed sheep and even dogs, but there are no cattle among the Formal School paintings. Large mythological animals and snakes with animal heads have been found in all these areas.

Later the Formal School became a little more lively and more colours were used in polychrome pictures. In Rhodesia and South West Africa, new people seem to have appeared in the rock art, with different equipment – perhaps the fat-tailed sheep were theirs, but there were no cattle as yet. These people may have been sheep-owning Hottentots moving down via South West Africa to the south-western Cape, where they were encountered in historical times.

To this period belong some beautiful polychrome animal pictures in the Brandberg, such as the strange, okapi-like animal in the upper Brandberg, wounded by the arrows of tall, black-painted, infibulated men with red hair or caps or head-dresses (Ill. 4.14). Painted profiles in northern South West Africa seem to depict Bergdama and, possibly, Herero. In Mashonaland, Rhodesia, enigmatic scenes seem to depict burials of chief-like figures, such as at Diana's Vow. These pictures represent the peak of the art of the Formal School in South West Africa and Rhodesia. What followed were crude white or red pictures, probably associated with Bergdama in South West Africa and with Negro peoples in Rhodesia.

4.11 Right figure: Brandberg, South West Africa. Left figure: Glen Craig, Albany district, eastern Cape Province.

4.12 Kriedoukrans, Clanwilliam district, south-western Cape: Seated human figures with yellow karosses. Eland.

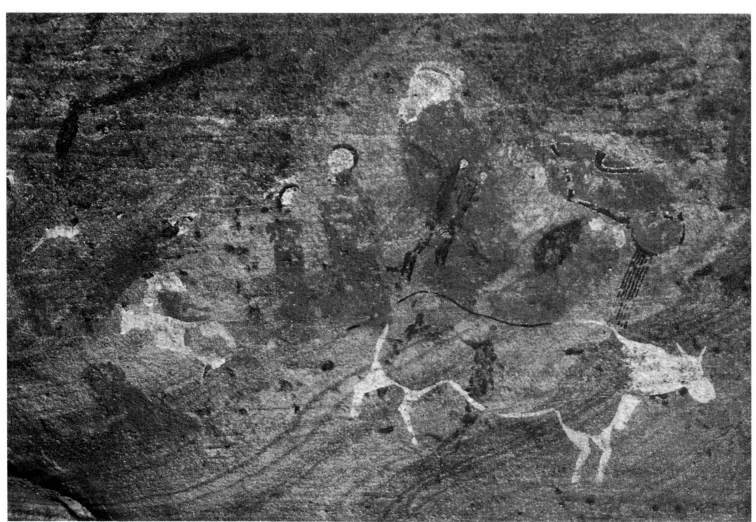

66

In the south-western Cape and the Little Karroo the superior pictures of the Formal School were followed by smaller, less sedate, more animated, hook-headed figures, mostly in maroon. To this period belong the pictures of fat-tailed sheep. The very few crude pictures of cattle, as well as pictures of Whites, horses and carts (Ill. 4.16; 4.17) and ships belong to the very last phase of rock art in these areas. It appears that the superior art must be related to the period before the cattle-owning Hottentots arrived. Yet the Hottentot-type pottery found in the painted shelters, as well as the pictures of sheep, the style of dress, the equipment and the physical appearance of very many of the people in the paintings, indicate that there must have been sheep-owning Hottentots in these parts at the time the paintings were made, whether or not they were the artists. Handprints, finger-dots and smears are features of the last phase of the superior art.

To some extent the Formal School extends into the eastern Cape and the Drakensberg areas, where it sometimes shares shelters with paintings of the Dynamic School. In the Albany district, below the mountains of the eastern Cape, there are shelters with paintings in the same hook-headed style as those in the south-western Cape and South West Africa. At Wilton, near Grahamstown, is a famous cave which is the type site for the Wilton Later Stone Age culture; in this cave the numerous paintings include creamy white (probably late) pictures of fat-tailed sheep, overlying faded red pictures of hook-heads.

The Cape Schematic School

The Schematic School of the Cape Province interior appears to be a final, crude expression of rock art associated with the so-called Smithfield B industry, Bushman-type pottery with typical grass tempering, and with Cape Bushmen who

4.13 Kriedoukrans, Clanwilliam district, south-western Cape: Faces in white.

4.14 Okapi shelter, Numas Plateau, Brandberg, South West Africa: Polychrome animal and red-haired men.

67

had lost almost all art tradition. The greatest concentration of these paintings is in the Kareeberge, in the Carnarvon area.

The paintings generally occur in shallow shelters along shale scarps and river cuttings. They are crude monochrome pictures, consisting almost entirely of designs drawn with the fingers – simple grid patterns, comb shapes, crosses and circles in red, black, white or yellow (Ill. 4.18). Finger-prints and finger-smears also occur, but handprints have not been found. Designs similar to these are to be found among the latest paintings in southern South West Africa and in the Tsodilo hills in north-western Botswana, as well as among late engravings. A very few crude pictures of animals occur among the paintings of the Schematic School.

4.15 Inankie cave, Matopo Hills, Rhodesia: Giraffe, human figures and strange shapes.

4.16 Stompiesfontein, Cold Bokkeveld, south-western Cape. Late pictures of Whites, horses and carts.

4.17 Stompiesfontein, Cold Bokkeveld, south-western Cape: Late pictures of Whites, horses and carts, in red.

Painted burial stones

A number of painted stones, 39 in all, have been discovered in archaeological deposits, mostly cave shell-middens along the southern Cape coast, but also in the Little Karroo and the Albany area of the eastern Cape. Unfortunately only a very few of these were scientifically excavated; otherwise we should have had many more crucial examples of direct association between paintings, Stone Age industries and human skeletal remains.

Many paintings on these stones are of human beings, but there are also some animal pictures, among them of buffalo, small and large antelopes, birds and a baboon, as well as pictures of a whale and dolphins. Black is the most common colour in these paintings.

Both the Dynamic and Formal schools are represented in these pictures. It would be expected that those of the Formal School would be the older, and with the limited dating evidence so far available, this appears to be the case.

A painted burial stone from the Matjes River shelter, on which are two large, red, human figures of the Formal School type, has been tentatively dated to about 5 600 years BP. It was probably associated with a Wilton industry and with a tall people of a hybrid Bush-Hottentot type. A stone from the Klasies River Mouth

4.18 Vlermuisgat cave, Carnarvon district, Cape Province: Designs.

4.19 Coldstream cave, Humansdorp district, southern Cape Province: Burial stone with pictures of hook-headed men.

70

cave on the Tsitsikamma coast, with black pictures of a man and four dolphins on it, probably belongs to the Dynamic School. It was associated with a crude Strandloper industry which was radiocarbon dated to about 2 300 years BP. A burial stone from Robberg, near Plettenberg Bay, with several small black human figures of the Dynamic School painted on it, has been dated to about 1 925 years BP. The most beautiful of the burial stones came from the Coldstream cave. On it are three hook-headed human figures in red, white and black. The central male figure has what seems to be an aquiline nose (Ill. 4.19). This is one of the best-preserved paintings of the Formal School, and it is a pity that so little is known of its associations: it was simply dug up, not scientifically excavated.

The paints

The pigments used by the rock artists were mainly earth pigments and charcoal ground into fine powder. Haematite, which includes red ochres and specularite, produces various reds, most popular among the rock artists; yellow ochre (limonite or hydrous iron oxide), iron pyrites and yellow shale produce yellows; gypsum, zinc oxide, kaolinic clay and lime give white; charcoal must have been used for black. The less common colours of the rock art – pink, khaki and orange – could have been obtained from mixtures of the above-mentioned pigments. Plant juices, such as berry juice, could also have provided colours. White and black seem to have lasted least well of all the colours.

Ancient haematite workings occur in southern Africa, and pieces of red ochre, as well as grinding stones stained with ochre, have frequently been found in painted shelters and other archaeological deposits. Haematite is still the favourite pigment for personal adornment among many Black peoples of southern Africa.

Sometimes the artists must have used the simple technique of drawing pictures on the rock surfaces with a red ochre or charcoal "crayon", but such paintings would not have survived for long. A good fluid medium would have been necessary for the more permanent pictures that are still there today. Very little indeed is known of the media that were used to make the paints. Animal fat has generally been suggested as the most likely medium. Other suggested media are blood, blood serum, egg, plant latex, urine, honey and gum. Sometimes the paint must have been quite fluid to have enabled the artists to paint the very fine lines found in some pictures. If a fat had been used it would have had to be fluid or kept warm. Ostrich and seal fat remain fairly fluid after rendering.

Chromatographic analysis of paint samples is said to have revealed, in practically all cases, amino acids from albuminous binding media, which could be egg, milk casein, blood or blood serum, animal glue or vegetable albumin. Fat does not contain albumin. According to the analyses, the medium in practically all the samples taken from rock paintings in southern Africa was probably blood or blood serum – yet blood soon turns dark, almost black! Clearly, much more research and experimentation are necessary to ascertain exactly what ingredients went into the paints.

An investigation has been made into the cosmetic and other paints known to have been used by Bushman and Hottentot peoples from historical times to the present day. This has revealed that fat was and still is the chief medium used for the paints. Occasionally water would be the medium. Other substances such as urine and plant juices were used in conjunction with the paints.

Very many paintings have disappeared in the course of time owing to the disintegration of the rocks and weathering of the pictures themselves. Sometimes mere faint blobs remain. Paintings that are well protected in shelters are usually well preserved, but even some of those exposed to the elements are remarkably clear. Weathering is not the only problem. Vandalism and animals rubbing against the painted rock faces have damaged and destroyed many paintings. Beyond legislation, which vandals ignore, and a few fences, which they break or climb, nothing really effective has yet been done by the authorities in South Africa to protect the rock art. In Rhodesia the position is happier. Apart from legislation and effective fences, with custodians at some of the main sites, the people have been won over by means of publicity and educational campaigns and they actively participate in protecting the rock art.

Age of the paintings

It is apparent that some pictures, especially in the Drakensberg areas, but also in the south-western Cape, were painted after the arrival of White settlers – that is, after 1652. Superpositions can indicate the order in which various styles of paintings were made, though it is not known whether the layers of paintings were separated by days, years or centuries. As has been pointed out above, radiocarbon dating is possible where painted stones or fragments of rocks with paintings are found in archaeological deposits. Painted rock slabs recently excavated in South West Africa came from a deposit dated by radiocarbon to over 27 000 BP. The dates which we have for painted burial stones range from about 5 600 years to about 1 900 years BP.

The paper chromatography method, which is valid only for about the last 1 800 years, has given 14 per cent of the South West African paintings an age of over 1 800 years, while 0,6 per cent were given an age of about 100 years. In the Drakensberg dates obtained by this method ranged from 200 ± 50 years to 800 ± 200 years BP.

Motivation

With careful research in a given area it is possible to determine which subjects, colours and so on the artists preferred. No amount of research will tell us all the reasons why the artists painted the pictures.

Some reasons are obvious: the scenes of battles, cattle raids, hunting and dancing seem to be the artists' records of specific or daily events. Sympathetic magic has been suggested as a motive for the painting of some of the pictures, but there is little to indicate that this was indeed so. Another suggestion is that some pictures may have formed part of initiation ceremonies and may have been associated with fertility rites. The strange creatures in the rock art (Ill. 4.20) may depict specific mythological creatures; some pictures may depict legends, but we shall never know for sure what legends.

There is no reason why some of the artists could not have painted just for the pleasure of doing so, or for decorating the walls of shelters.

The petroglyphs

Rock engravings in southern Africa are to be found mainly on the inland plateau along the edges of the Kalahari Desert, with an extension southwards into the

4.20 De Hoek, Oudtshoorn district, Little Karroo: Bird-like creatures in red.

72

4.21 Body painting, scarifications and beadwork have long been practised among many African peoples and all three forms of personal adornment are found among the living Bushmen.

semi-desert of the Karroo, and also along the eastern edge of the Namib Desert in South West Africa and southern Angola. There is a concentration of this rock art along the Vaal and Orange rivers.

Technically the petroglyphs consist of true engravings (that is lines scratched, carved or rubbed with a stone point) and peckings (produced by the pecking or hammering of dots with a stone hammer, or perhaps with a stone hammer and stone punch). With these two basic techniques a picture of an animal could be made with a single engraved outline, or as a silhouette consisting of an outline filled in with hatching or dotting, sometimes made to look more naturalistic by the addition of body patterns, eyes, ears, etc. These animal pictures were usually made in profile, often showing only two legs. In a very few instances, the artists showed the animals in attitudes other than standing. In the most advanced technique the entire inside part of a figure was worked down to a negative relief (Ill. 4.25) and even sometimes polished, a method often used to make naturalistic footprints.

Various animals are the main subjects in the engravings. Human figures are rare and they include men with quivers, bows and arrows (Ill. 4.26); in Griqualand West some male figures are shown infibulated. Animal footprints are common and sometimes occur in hundreds, particularly in northern South West Africa (Ill. 4.25) and at some sites in Griqualand West. Occasionally human footprints were made. There is also a pronounced abstract trend among the rock engravings, far more so than among the paintings. The designs consist of simple geometric figures such as circles, concentric circles, spoked circles, circle and dot patterns, etc., as well as crosses, star shapes, "ladders", honeycomb patterns, flower and leaf patterns, grids, insect-like "doodles" and single meandering lines.

4.22, 4.23 and **4.24** As trade beads have increasingly penetrated into Bushman society, more and more attractive designs have emerged in headdresses, necklaces, anklets, bangles and other forms of personal adornment. Often, the trade beads alternate with beads of ostrich-egg shell to produce the variety of combinations shown here.

In the Karroo and South West Africa the engravings are usually on koppies (or rocky hillocks) or on boulders scattered over the veld. In the Orange-Vaal river basin, they are often on rock floors, sometimes in river-beds.

It has been suggested that the true engravings are the oldest of the petroglyphs: they are found mainly in the northern Cape and south-western Transvaal. These were followed by deep peckings, shallow peckings and finally superficial scratchings, many of which are recent. The various degrees of patination of the petroglyphs – ranging from the same dark colour as the rocks on which they were made to almost white where the surface of the rock had been broken – indicate the relative ages of the pictures.

It is not known who made the bulk of the engravings. Surface lithic material found at numerous sites in the Orange-Vaal basin belongs to the Smithfield B industry, while surface material found at sites further west and in South West Africa belongs to Wilton industries. The very late, unpatinated engravings, often including letters of the alphabet, were made by latter-day herders and children. So far there have not been any excavations to reveal conclusively the association of petroglyphs with Stone Age material; such evidence, when it becomes available, may give an indication regarding the place of the petroglyphs in time.

Bushman art today

There is no longer any tradition or memory of painting or engraving on rocks among the surviving Bushmen. Drawings made by Bushmen a century ago for Dr W. H. I. Bleek, the philologist, and Miss Lucy Lloyd, his assitant, were disappointing, and modern researches have not revealed any particular aptitude for drawing among the Bushmen. This is hardly surprising: obviously not every Bushman was a rock artist, nor can talent be revealed when individuals are introduced to a form of expression for the first time. But the Bushmen do still

engrave designs and occasionally animal figures on ostrich-egg shells, sticks, bone knives and bone pipes. Some of these engravings resemble some of the engravings on the rocks, but the main reason for the similarity lies in the simplicity of these pictures and the limitations of the method. Today the pictures on the rocks are a priceless heritage that can never be renewed.

4.25 Twyfelfontein, northern part of South West Africa: The lion slab.

4.26 Groot Springbokoog, Vanwyksvlei, Cape Province: Hunters and eland.

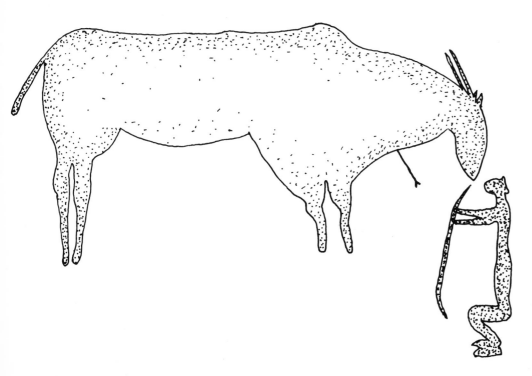

5
The Bushman in History

Alex R. Willcox

What is known of the Bushman in *prehistory*, involving amongst others questions of the time and place of his bodily differentiation, has been related in chapters 2 and 3. This chapter, therefore, begins with the first mention of the race in *history* – that is, in written record. First I must define the criteria by which the Bushman is recognised in historical descriptions. The names given to his people do not help. Sometimes they were lumped together with their fellow pastoral indigenes at the Cape as "Hottentots". They were also called "Sonquas" or "Soaquas", a term applied as well to some cattle-owning fishermen. Other names were applied to them, many opprobrious, such as "Ubiquas" (or "Obiquas"), a term applied indiscriminately to some Hottentot and Bushman cattle-thieves and murderers, and meaning, more or less, bandits.

If the Bushmen had a name for themselves more general than the clan or tribal names, it is not known. The Hottentots, who recognised them as people quite distinct from themselves, and with whom they were continually at war, called them *San*. The term "Bosjesmans" was first applied to them by the Dutch in 1682, and was later anglicized to "Bushmen". They might have been the people living to the south of Sofala and referred to as the "Wak-Wak" by Masudi, writing in the 10th century; if so, it is their first appearance in history.

The first certain historical mention of the people later to be called Bushmen was after the Dutch settlement at the Cape: in 1655 a party under J. Wintervogel encountered, about 50 *mijlen* north of Cape Town (nominally 230 statute miles, or 370 km, but probably much less), "a certain tribe, very low in stature, and very lean, entirely savage, without any huts, cattle, or anything in the world, clad in little skins". People conforming to this description were shortly afterwards encountered, always inland, in every part of the south-western Cape and, as exploration proceeded, in the eastern Cape and northwards beyond the Orange River.

"Bushman", therefore, as I shall use the term, means just what Wintervogel described: very small people having no cattle and therefore living by hunting and food-gathering. It is the synonym of San.

Using these criteria for identification, one finds that much information is available from the early records. The Bushmen were yellow-skinned, the men averaged about 1,47 m (4 feet 10 inches) in height; both sexes had physical peculiarities which need not be described here; they were armed with bows and poisoned arrows, rarely with wooden spears; and they spoke a language, or rather group of languages, distinct from that of the Hottentot, although sharing certain "clicks" with the latter. Professor Ernst Westphal of Cape Town has shown that some groups in the Kalahari, living by hunting and food-gathering, and therefore *economically* classified as Bushmen, speak languages he classifies as "Hottentot". They are somewhat taller and darker than the typical Bushman as described above, but the point is taken that linguistic criteria must be used with caution.

The first contact with the Bushmen – by Wintervogel's party – was peaceful. So were the next two encounters. When Danckaert's explorers met them near the Olifants River in 1660, they were indeed friendly, giving the travellers honey and guidance; and they were as helpful to Pieter Cruythoff's expedition passing through the same region in the following year.

The next report, however, tells a very different story. In 1677 three free burghers were reported murdered at the Breede River over the mountains of Hottentots Holland. The report came from a survivor of the massacre and from a certain Hottentot captain Claas, and the murderers were referred to as Obiquas dependent on Gonnema. But Gonnema, described by Cape Governor Johan Bax as the mischievous enemy of the Dutch East India Company, was definitely a Hot-

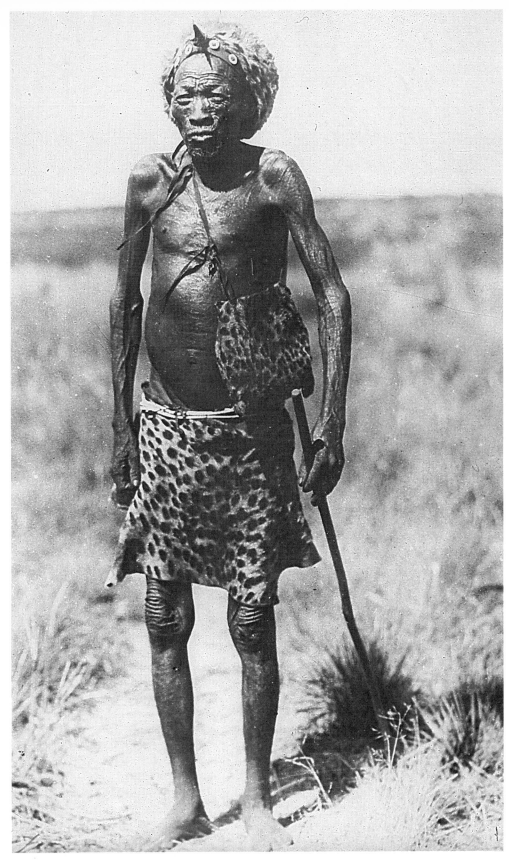

5.1 "... a certain tribe, very low in stature, and very lean, entirely savage, without any huts, cattle, or anything in the world, clad in little skins ..." (J. Wintervogel, 1655 – the first certain historical mention of the people later to be called Bushmen).

tentot chief, and the word "Obiqua", as already mentioned, had come to mean little more than "bandit". The assailants could as probably have been Hottentots, but if they were Bushmen the attack was no doubt provoked by the fact that the burghers were hunting "sea cows" (hippopotamuses) on their hunting ground – and without consent. This was an act of war, according to the Bushman code, which justified the killings. But to the White settlers, of course, it was plain murder, calling for ruthless reprisals. Thus do wars begin.

5.2 But they *did* have huts, often rough and temporary, of a kind that could be erected in a few hours. This one – and the family party inhabiting it – were encountered between Olifantskloof and Ghanzi in what was then the Bechuanaland Protectorate, in 1951.

A large expedition was dispatched to take vengeance – without success, for they could not find the enemy. Subsequent operations were entrusted largely to Hottentot "captains" friendly to the Company, including Captain Claas, whose character emerges from a later incident. In 1684 a party of burghers was attacked by people described as "Soncquas" by Commander Simon van der Stel, and as Obiquas in the original report; a burgher was killed. It is probably significant that the burghers were again *hunting* beyond the settled area. Captain Claas voluntarily undertook revenge and his *modus operandi* is best described in the words of Van der Stel's Resolution of Council.

"Having approached their kraals they (the Obiquas) sent to him three women, requesting him to renew and confirm the old friendship betwixt them; that he sent back a present of tobacco by three of his own Hottentots, and requested the captain of the said Obiquas to come to visit him in his kraal, which the said captain did on the following day, accompanied by ten of his people, and was there very kindly received and entertained by him, Claas, who killed a sheep for them; that on the next day, while still entertaining the said Obiquas, with every appearance of friendship, and making merry in their way, with dancing and beating the drum; he, on perceiving a favourable opportunity, ordered some of his people (speaking to them in Dutch) to seize the Obiqua's captain and his people, which being effected, he, Claas, asked them whether they were disposed to murder any more of the Dutch, and upon their answering yes, he instantly gave orders to kill the said Obiquas, which was instantly done, with the exception of three, who saved themselves by flight.

"This being taken into consideration, it was resolved to reward the said Claas for his faithful services, with two bunches of copper beads, a roll of Virginia tobacco of the weight of 20 lbs, an anker of anniseed arrack, 150 lbs rice, and a pair of coarse stockings."

From this time on hostile incidents between Whites and Bushmen become too frequent to recount in detail within the limits of my space. Only an outline can be given of what was virtually a war, and which continued, with increasing ferocity, for almost two centuries.

The causes of conflict were simple enough – complete incompatibility of the means of livelihood. When Whites first settled at the Cape in 1652, the Bushmen were already at war with the Hottentots, except for a few bands who had, it seems, formed a "client" relationship with them. It was the old story, hunter versus herder. In the drier parts of the western and south-western Cape, there is seldom enough grazing, and often not enough water sources, for both wild game and domestic stock. Competition was inevitable! The hunter, who was there first, naturally claimed priority and, according to his view, the right to kill any animal on his hunting territory. In any case, as the intrusions of the Hottentots, who also hunted, much reduced the game, he had no alternative but to prey on their cattle and sheep or give up his way of life.

The story was repeated almost exactly, as the Whites moved inland from the Cape, and again between Bushman and Negro. What was considered hunting by the Bushmen and cattle-thieving by the White men, occurred increasingly. And as the main purpose of the Company's station at the Cape was the supply of meat and other fresh foods for their ships, they were always short of cattle.

The year 1715 saw the beginning of the commando system as a mobile mounted volunteer force against an enemy equally mobile, by official sanction being given to a force of burgher militia to campaign against Bushmen. Previously such forces were composed of regular soldiers, with burghers, under an army officer. Now the commando elected its own officer, a man they were prepared to follow. Incidents grew ever more frequent as the White colonists penetrated further inland. From time to time the Administration at the Cape extended the boundary of the Colony by proclamation to include Bushman territory invaded by Whites.

In the 1750s the main front was along the Roggeveld and Nuweveld ranges of the eastern portion of the Stellenbosch district. Two commando attacks were made, resulting in the recovery of stolen cattle and the killing of over 100 Bushmen, at the cost of one burgher and two Hottentots killed. Another commando in 1758 recovered about 400 head of cattle and killed 56 Bushmen, with only one commando casualty. These accounts and others have a sad similarity, but a new, grim note is struck in the report of a commando of 1763 which, after shooting 26 Bushmen, rounded up 10 of their children and took them to be made farm servants, a euphemism for slaves, although they were not usually ill-treated. The boys made excellent cattle herders and *voorlopers*, were intelligent and honest, and such kidnappings became common thenceforward. If any treatment could have made Bushman resentment more bitter, this was it: they were and are intensely attached to their children.

From now it was war *à outrance,* with atrocities on both sides: the murder of a few Whites by Bushmen, and the killing of their herd-boys, sometimes most cruelly, on the one hand; and on the other the massacring by the commandos – especially by the Hottentot auxiliaries, their traditional foes – of Bushmen, regardless of age or sex. All that can be said in excuse for this savagery is that the Bushmen never surrendered, and that their seizure of cattle and sheep now went far beyond what could be justified by need. It was action against the enemy, and was the chief reason for the ruthless reprisals by the frontier colonists. Their livelihoods also were at stake.

The carnage continued. Adriaan van Jaarsveld's commando expeditions in 1770 and 1771 killed about 100 Bushmen and brought back many as "servants". Van Jaarsveld's usual method was to surround a kraal or cave and, at first light, fire into it, so that, in his words, "not a single one escaped". But in 1775 he tried a new method, which was described by Donald Moodie in *The Record* (1838-1841). Following thefts of cattle and the killing of a herder in the Sneeuberg, Van Jaarsveld took his force into the area. Encountering a single Bushman, he decided, again in his own words:

". . . to persuade this Bosman that we came as friends, and were merely travelling to the said river to shoot sea cows; we gave him a pipe and tobacco, and sent him to his companions, to tell them of our peaceful intentions, and also to come to us to show us the way to the said river; but we saw no more of the thief."

Two days later:

". . . we again came unexpectedly upon five robbers, and used the same words towards these prisoners (sic), as to the first robber; and as a mark of friendship we shot a sea cow for them; at the said Kop."

Van Jaarsveld then shot some "sea cows", left the carcases lying about, and sent messages to let the Bushmen of the district know they were there. He retired two hours' distance, knowing the Bushmen would come for the meal. Later he returned, and at dawn managed to slaughter 122 and take 21 prisoner.

In 1781 Van Jaarsveld was to use a similar stratagem against the Xhosa. Encountering a party of them, he scattered tobacco. Then, as the Xhosa, off their guard, were picking it up, he gave the order to fire on them.

If pretending friendship to an enemy to gain his trust and put him at a disadvantage against attack is treachery, then these are good examples. Claas the Hottentot, as has been related, did even worse, as those treacherously slain were guests at his feast. Dingane's murder of Piet Retief and his party, unarmed at his kraal in Natal, was as bad. I do not suggest that the Bushmen were "noble savages", but I can find no record of their ever descending to this execrable stratagem, nor of their ever failing to respond to a friendly approach, usually with help or guidance. Travellers such as W. J. Burchell and emissaries such as Jacobus Uys and John Shepstone often placed themselves in the power of "wild" Bushmen with a trust never abused.

There is no record either of the Bushmen ever descending to cannibalism, although there are many instances of this practice in the history of the Negroes. It is not unknown in the history, even recent history, of the Whites; but not in Africa, after a few occurrences among ship-wrecked Portuguese in the early 17th century.

In 1774, at the request of the colonists, Gottlieb Roedolf Opperman had been appointed by the Government as commandant to direct operations against the Bushmen. Although enjoined by the Government to "employ every possible means of entering into an amicable negotiation with them", three commandos took the field, one under Van Jaarsveld as related above. The final result was 503 Bushmen killed and 241 taken prisoner. Some of these were released, while others were distributed among the farmers. Another commando, in reprisal against further stock thefts and the murder of a shepherd, reported that "the moment the robbers perceived the Dutch, they charged; the Dutch however defended themselves bravely, and shot one hundred and eleven of the robbers." Fire-arms versus bows and arrows! Who were really the brave?

About 1790 the Bushmen, having become better organised and having acquired a few muskets, launched a counter-offensive along the Nuweveld and Sneeuberg ranges, causing the abandonment of many farms and about a hundred cattle-runs (established, of course, in Bushman territory). This was their last major effort in a war which, in the end, could have only one result. To continue the story in detail would be as tedious as it is saddening. There were, of course, a few local truces between Bushmen and farmers who observed the proprieties – who gave them some of the meat when they shot on their ground, and who did not interfere with their family life. Such was the case in the area between Colesberg and the Orange River when in 1803 the Governor, General J. W. Janssens, undertook an expedition to a point a short distance east of the confluence of the Orange and Seekoei ("sea cow") rivers; there some Bushmen showed courage and resource in saving from drowning one of the Governor's servants who had attempted to swim across the river. The next day Janssens's party visited a kraal of Bushmen pointed out to them by the field-cornet of the district. The Bushmen came to meet their visitors and showed no fear of them – a tribute, as the Governor noted, to the colonists of these parts.

The retreat had soon to be resumed, and in 1834 new enemies, the Griqua, attacked from the west and cleared the Bushmen from the area between the Orange and the Riet rivers. The last stand of the Bushmen in the Orange Free State was at Vaalbank Spruit, 13 km (8 miles) south of Winburg, in 1855. Henceforth in that region only a few remained – and those on sufferance, or in service on the farms.

J. M. Orpen, landdrost of Winburg and Harrismith, had to act against many cases of child stealing. He tells one story which illustrates the attitude of some Whites to the Bushmen in the north-eastern Orange Free State. It was told him by a *bywoner* while Orpen was a guest at his table. This man had been told by his farmer employer that there was an old Bushman thereabouts who was always saying that the farm really belonged to him. Hunting on the same farm, the *bywoner* shot a wildebeest, whereupon the Bushman suddenly turned up, no doubt to claim the share of the meat due to him by the custom of his people. Having helped to cut up the beast and load the best of it on to the hunter's horse, he was told he could take the offal. "Then," said Orpen's host, "when the Bushman turned and stooped over the offal, I took aim between the shoulders and shot him." Orpen dropped his knife and fork, said goodbye to the wife, and left the house.

I was myself told, as an amusing story, by a farmer in the southern Orange Free State, how a Bushman had been caught in the neighbourhood. Not daring to kill him (the law was beginning to be asserted), but being allowed to hold him for trial, his captors tied him to a tree in such a way that he was dead the next morning.

I do not wish to paint too black a picture: I have not the least doubt that such attitudes and such deeds were exceptional and that there were innumerable acts of kindness also to balance the picture, especially to the Bushman children, for the farmers' wives would not have tolerated their being ill-treated.

Meanwhile contact had long since been made between Bushmen and Bantu-speaking Negroes in the northern Cape, eastern Transvaal, Lesotho, Natal, Pondoland and the Transkei. Conflict broke out in the neighbourhood of Kuruman in the 1840s, and probably earlier, over cattle-thieving, and some Bushman clans were wiped out by the Tswana, who had by then acquired firearms. To the Negroes, with their devotion to cattle, there could have been no greater provocation than cattle-thieving. In other areas of contact the story is brighter. There is evidence that over a long period good relations were preserved by the Bushmen with both Nguni and Sotho. Trading occurred especially with the Xhosa and Pondo. The Bushmen, with their extraordinary knowledge of the flora, fauna and weather lore of their environment, became both the teachers and the rainmakers for the newcomers. There was, in all the contact areas, much intermarriage, the Thembu for instance being almost a hybrid people. In the eastern Transvaal, a workable co-existence was achieved between the Swazi and the Bushmen, of whom a small remnant live to this day in the vicinity of Lake Chrissie.

The happy relationship in the Transkei eventually broke down for the same causes as those mentioned above – cattle-thieving following infringements of hunting rights. Rarabe, a Xhosa chief, was fond of hunting and in about 1769

5.3 The Bushmen have an extraordinary knowledge of the flora, fauna and weather lore of their environment. Where new immigrants into their hunting areas live at peace with them, the Bushmen become both the teachers and the rainmakers for the newcomers.

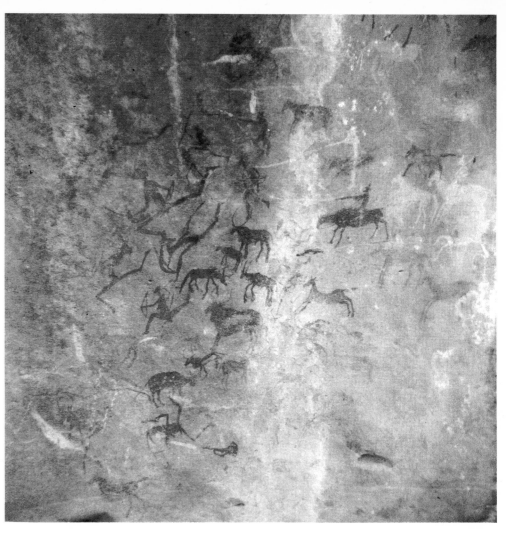

5.4 Part of a spirited scene from the Natal/Griqualand border. A commando has caught up with Bushmen driving off cattle. The farmers are shooting, one from the saddle, one dismounted.

invaded Bushman territory for this purpose. The Bushmen drove off and killed some of his cattle. The ensuing conflict was as merciless as in the northern Cape: Rarabe, using much the same methods, surrounded the caves of the Bushmen and killed all the occupants, even little children. Hunting Bushmen like animals, he cleared them from a large area near the Great Kei River.

In Natal, although the Nguni occupied large areas that had once been Bushman hunting grounds, there is no evidence of conflict in the process. The Bushmen retreated to the Drakensberg. With its abundance of game, habitable rock shelters and water, it was a terrain that suited them perfectly. Moreover, it was not coveted by the Bantu-speaking cattle-owners. Along the Bushman-Negro frontier, which from about the 16th century followed more or less the outer slope of the Little Drakensberg, there is no record or archaeological evidence of conflict until after the White men – the Voortrekkers – came to the interior of Natal in 1837. Thenceforth it was the old, sad story. White hunters made excursions into the remaining Bushman hunting grounds and killed much of the game. The Bushmen retaliated by sallying forth from their mountain redoubt, rounding up cattle and horses, driving them back into the Drakensberg, and thence sometimes south into Griqualand East (then known as Faku's country), or over the top of the 'berg into Lesotho. In both territories they had Bantu-speaking allies. If a commando could be raised in time, the marauders were chased, seldom with success. But if they were overtaken, there was the usual slaughter of men, and sometimes women, and the taking of children as "apprentices".

As in the case of the Cape Province the ferocity of the reprisals can be explained, if not excused, by the scale of the depredations. Cattle were taken in hundreds at a time and, if pursuit became too hot, were slaughtered one by one to discourage the pursuers. That this incensed the farmers beyond restraint, where only frontier law prevailed, can be readily understood.

Such raids, with variations in detail, continued for the next thirty years. Be-

82

5.5 From the point where the Natal, Griqualand East and Lesotho borders meet. Bushmen are riding stolen horses. A white foal follows its mother.

5.6 From a site near Underberg, we see part of a herd of cattle and horses being driven off. One of the horses has a rider.

83

tween 1840 and 1872 there were at least seventy Bushman cattle raids. Streams of complaints from the farmers poured in to the Administration in Pietermaritzburg, but the authorities acted tardily and ineffectually. Temporary military posts were established at Van Vuuren's farm in the Elandskop district in 1846, at the Bushmans River in the following year, and at Fort Nottingham in 1856. Still cattle were being taken from under the noses of the military, who, although mounted, very seldom caught up with the retreating raiders. The Bushmen had always the advantage of surprise and intimate knowledge of the country, and they had quickly learnt to ride the stolen horses, both for raiding and hunting.

As far as is known, it was Sir Theophilus Shepstone who thought of solving this problem, and another, which had become pressing, at one stroke. Large numbers of Negroes, driven out of Zululand by Chaka and his successors, were menacing the farmers from another quarter. Living space had to be found for them. Steps were taken from 1849 to establish "locations" for them along the Drakensberg, to form buffer zones between the Bushman haunts and the White-owned farms. The only effect seems to have been that the Bushmen raided the Blacks as well as the Whites, and soon were at loggerheads with them also.

The depredations of the Bushmen from the Drakensberg and the failure of the Government to prevent them or to punish the raiders was one of the principal reasons for the large-scale withdrawal of the Trekkers from Natal, leaving that area mainly to White settlers of other origin.

But for the Bushmen the addition of Nguni-speaking Negroes in Natal to their other enemies had its effect: by the late 1860s the Bushmen had fallen foul also of the tribes of northern Lesotho and were fighting on two fronts. It was combined action by Whites and Sotho which in 1869 finally liquidated the last organised Bushman band, killing their indomitable leader, Swayi. After that there were only a few minor forays from the 'berg, the last well-authenticated raid being in 1872.

A few small bands lingered on in the Drakensberg. The last to be seen was in 1878, where the Natal National Park is now established. On the Lesotho side of the border the Bushmen lasted somewhat longer, though not as independent groups. Many took refuge with the Phuthi chief Moorosi, until his defeat by Cape troops and volunteers, and his death, in 1879. Individual Bushmen remained on the farms in Natal and with friendly Sotho into the 20th century.

One of the young Bushmen captured by a commando, apprenticed to a farmer and given the name Sam, has a double claim to immortality. His skeleton is the only one existing of a "pure" Drakensberg Bushman (it is now in the University of Edinburgh) and he was the only Bushman ever to have been seen to make a painting by a trained observer.

Other skeletal remains found on the outer slopes of the Little 'berg – none has been found further into the mountains – are all of Negro with some Bush (or San) admixture. It is for this reason that the last physical descriptions of wild Bushmen are of particular interest. Although inadequate, they agree with one another and are consistent with the first descriptions of the San two centuries previously. The members of the last known band mentioned above were described as "strange weird looking creatures, hardly bigger than a child of ten". John Shepstone says of a band encountered in "Faku's country" that the tallest of the men was not more than 1,52 m (5 feet). A captured woman and two little girls seen on a farm by A. A. Anderson in 1863 were more fully described, but with plenty of racial prejudice:

"The woman was not old or young, of a yellowish white colour, a few little tufts of wool on the head; eyes she had, but the lids were so closed they were not to be seen, although she saw between them perfectly; no nose, only two orifices, through which she breathed, with thin projecting lips, and sharp chin, with broad cheekbones, her spine curved in the most extraordinary manner, consequently the stomach protruded in the same proportion, with thin, calfless legs, and with that wonderful formation peculiar to this Bushman tribe, and slightly developed in the Hottentot and Korannas. The two little girls – the eldest did not seem more than ten or twelve – were of the same type, the woman measured four feet one inch in height."

The men of the party, caught stealing sheep, had been shot and the females were the subject of a domestic argument, the farmer wanting to shoot them too, but his wife wishing to make servants of them.

84

5.7 Bushmen driving off cattle and horses.

5.8 In many hostile encounters between the Bushmen, on the one hand, and Whites, Blacks and Khoikhoi, on the other, it sometimes happened that while the Bushman males were killed, the women and children were taken as servants or serfs to the farms of the newcomers – such as the woman and children seen on a farm by A. A. Anderson in 1863.

Towards the end the Bushmen were no longer strictly Stone Age people, since they were using iron for knives and arrow points and had managed to steal a few muskets; but otherwise they were still Stone Age hunters even though their quarry included cattle and sheep. The latter, when stolen, were kept alive only as meat "on the hoof". Enough of the horses were kept as mounts, and they had some dogs to aid hunting.

Thus, by near genocide, ended two hundred years of war. "They fought to the last man" has become a cliché, but it is very nearly true of Bushman resistance. Lest the world condemn too much, let the fate of the North American Indians and the Australian aborigines be also remembered, and that a process of extermination not dissimilar has been in progress until recently against the Indians of Brazil.

During the whole long war only two serious attempts were made at negotiated peace. One, at the suggestion of that admirable man, Floris Visser, and accepted by the Governor, Lord Macartney, was to offer the Bushmen of the Roggeveld and Bokkeveld gifts of cattle and sheep, a district to be allocated to them as their own (ironical this!) and an assurance that their children would not be taken away from them on any pretext whatsoever. The transaction took place in 1798 and was honoured by the recipients of the stock. It failed because the Bushmen were not sufficiently organised for a general agreement to be possible. Other groups continued their marauding and even plundered those who had made peace.

The second attempt, also offering cattle, sheep and a location, was by the Natal administration in 1846, in what later became Griqualand East. The offer, made by a party led by Jacobus Uys, with John Shepstone as interpreter, was refused, the Bushmen saying, in effect, that the life of the hunter was the only one for them.

Another effort at contact also failed. Greatly helped by the same Floris Visser, Johannes Jacobus Kicherer and William Edwards attempted to establish a mission to the Bushmen on the Sak River. It was a half-hearted effort by men racially prejudiced, and it failed partly because the missionaries did not learn the Bushman

5.9 The children of the Bushmen were often orphaned, or at least left with only one parent, during the period of over two centuries of conflict between the Bushmen and other peoples encroaching relentlessly on their traditional hunting and gathering territories.

5.10 White men wearing knee breeches buttoned up on the outside and jackets with two rows of buttons in the style of the beginning of the 19th century. This painting is from a site on the bank of the Caledon River a few miles north of its junction with the Orange River. It may represent Colonel Richard Collins's expedition that reached the Orange River at this point in 1809. Note the muskets and powder horns. The cattle and sheep may be later paintings.

language. The few people who were persuaded to build huts at the station turned out to be not Bushmen, but Hottentots, and – it is to be feared – were out more for material gifts than salvation.

The only solution would have been to have left the Bushmen a very large area of their territory for themselves alone, and to have approached them as far as necessary only through people who knew their language and culture. But this would have been an attitude ahead of its time.

The art of the Bushmen forms the subject of another chapter of this book. Paintings of Whites, their horses and cattle and other subjects that can be historically dated show that the artists continued their work right up to the time they ceased to be a free people. Some of the latest work, depicting horses for example, is as fine as the earlier work, though executed by people at the limit of their endurance.

The examples illustrating this chapter are chosen for their historical interest. Ill. 5.10, showing Whites with their muskets and powder horns, is from a site on the bank of the Caledon River a few miles north of its junction with the Orange River. There are cattle and sheep also, but these may be later paintings. C. S. Orpen, brother of J. M. Orpen, mentioned above, described the paintings in 1885. He was told that they were there when the farmers moved into the area in 1835 and he thought that the dress of the figures – knee breeches buttoned up the outside, and jackets with two rows of buttons – pointed to the beginning of the 19th century at the latest. He suggested that the men represented were Colonel Robert Jacob Gordon and his party, who reached the confluence of the two rivers in 1777. Gordon's party did not cross the Orange River, however, and it is not recorded that he met Bushmen near his camp who might have painted the strangers from memory.

But when the next expedition, led by Colonel Richard Collins, reached the south bank at this point in 1809, they were visited by Bushmen from the northern bank. It is therefore rather more likely that it is Collins's men who are depicted here. Expert study of the dress (which is probably military) and accoutrements shown might decide the point.

6
An Epitaph to the Bushmen

M. D. W. Jeffreys†

6.1 "... The greatest friendliness is the rule, and all share alike in the resources of the group ... Food-gatherers are noted for their hospitality. Strangers are welcomed, and are given due share of the food and shelter that their hosts possess ..."

The culture of the Bushmen of South Africa is known to anthropologists as that of the food-gatherer. People of such a culture neither cultivate the soil nor herd stock. The following characteristics are for the most part applicable to food-gatherers everywhere, from the Eskimoes of the Arctic to the Bushmen of the Kalahari, and form a background that enables one to understand the bravery displayed by the Bushmen.

W. J. Perry wrote: "The predominant grouping is that of small bands of relatives. Each group has its own hunting grounds, about which it moves, making temporary settlements here and there. It would appear that each group is equal to every other group ... They are basically monogamous and the union is for life ... The family group is united by ties of affection. Usually the utmost harmony prevails within it ... They avoid family quarrels. The greatest friendliness is the rule, and all share alike in the resources of the group ... Food-gatherers are noted for their hospitality. Strangers are welcomed, and are given due share of the food and shelter that their hosts possess. Territoriality is strongly developed among food-gatherers. Should their area be infringed by neighbouring groups, or by strangers, they are quick to retaliate, often even taking the life of the offender. A guest, so long as he does not attempt to infringe this rigid rule, is welcome. Another amiable characteristic of primitive people is their transparent honesty ... The last and most striking character of the food-gatherer is that, so long as he is left undisturbed by outside influence, he rarely indulges in violent behaviour. Within the family group all is peaceful. His emotions are apt to be uncontrolled, but violence usually only appears as a reaction to violence."

Against this generalised description of the behaviour of virtually all food-gatherers, let us see what contemporary early records report about the South African Bushmen.

G. W. Stow reported that Bushmen exhibited a strong attachment to the place of their birth, that their hospitality to strangers was noteworthy and their unselfishness in the division of food outstanding, that their love of freedom showed in the self-sacrifice and devotion with which they attempted to rescue their wives and children from a life of bondage, which they abhorred, and that their unflinching bravery was unparalleled in the recorded history of man.

As these were illiterate people, only a few accounts of their remarkable bravery have come down to us, written more or less at the same time as the events they describe – and, moreover, written generally by inveterate enemies of the Bushmen.

Acts of bravery by Bushmen may be grouped into three main categories, namely: defence of their territory, or territoriality; defence of the group, or altruism; and defence of their freedom.

Territoriality

Nowhere has "man's inhumanity to man" been more vilely displayed than in Bushmanland, against these misunderstood people. Nowhere in the world has such widespread, indomitable courage per square kilometre of territory been displayed as in Bushmanland, the immemorial territory of the Bushmen, inherited and occupied continuously by them, to the exclusion of all others until recent times, for many thousands of years. When such territory is usurped, the group's means of subsistence and hence its existence are threatened. Such a menace prompts a rising of the group in defence of food and territory.

It was in defence of such rights, of hearth and home, that these little people, the

88

original "harmless people", displayed heroic bravery that has nowhere in the annals of recorded history been surpassed.

The territory of the Bushmen was invaded by many peoples. Among them were the Boers, armed with their "roers" or long guns. The Scottish-born 1820 Settler poet, Thomas Pringle, refers to such weapons, saying how he loved to ride afar in the desert "with the death-fraught firelock in my hand – the only law of the Desert Land".* How true this description was! For the Bushmen, "hunted like wild beasts whenever they were found wandering over the plains which they had inherited from their fathers, their extinction became a mere matter of time in an unequal struggle between the primitive bow and arrow . . . and the deadly gun in the hands of the invaders. Whenever there was cover they tenaciously clung to their favourite haunts and when attacked, fearlessly and courageously defended their rock citadels."

Even when the Bushmen were driven from their ancient homes, a remnant would return. G. W. Stow gives a poignant account of such a pathetic return. An aged Bushman couple were discovered by him in the Jammerberg. Although all the rest of the Bushman tribe had been annihilated, the old man and his wife still clung to their ancestral haunts. When Stow showed them copies he had made of Bushman paintings, the woman started to sing the old songs that the paintings recalled. Her husband besought her: "Don't! Don't sing those old songs. I can't bear it. It makes my heart too sad." Stow's comment was: "One is not prepared to meet with such a display of genuine feeling as this among a people who have been looked upon and treated as such untamably vicious animals as this doomed race is said to be. It was proof that 'all the world's akin' and was certainly a Bushman edition of 'John Anderson, my Jo, John'."

*From "Afar in the Desert" by Thomas Pringle (1824), republished in *Poems Illustrative of South Africa: African Sketches: Part one* by Thomas Pringle, edited by John Robert Wahl, Cape Town, G. Struik (Pty.) Ltd., 1970 – Ed.

6.2 ". . . The last and most striking character of the food-gatherer is that, so long as he is left undisturbed by outside influence, he rarely indulges in violent behaviour. Within the family group all is peaceful . . ." A family group seated before a hut in the central Kalahari.

89

6.3 . . . The old woman started to sing the songs that the rock paintings recalled, songs of a long-forgotten day before the rest of the clan was annihilated . . . until her husband exhorted her to stop because "It makes my heart too sad." A poignant moment recorded by G. W. Stow in an interview with an aged couple who had clung to their ancestral haunts.

6.4 From an early age Bushman children play with miniature bows and arrows. They learn by trial and error the techniques that they will later put to good effect when they are old enough to accompany their fathers on the hunt.

The accounts of Bushman bravery that are to follow reflect the general attitude of food-gatherers towards invaders of their territory. "All the available evidence . . . with regard to the vindictiveness of the Bushmen proves that it was not part of their natural character, but rather a developed feeling which gradually took possession of their hearts: it was the outcrop of desperation and despair" – desperation and despair at being robbed of the land of their forefathers and of the means of their livelihood.

The missionary Dr John Philip, writing in 1828, reported that members of a Boer commando told how they had attacked a group of 25 Bushmen. "The engagement lasted nine hours and though three different offers were made to spare their lives if they surrendered, these offers were rejected. The Bushmen continued to defend themselves till 17 were killed and the others, though wounded, did not attempt to escape till they saw their leader fall."

There are many other instances of such bravery among the Bushmen. Kousop, a Bushman leader of his band, resentful of his land being confiscated by Boers, determined to wage a war of reprisal to the bitter end. "No inducement could prevail on him or his people to cease from the depredations they carried on against the intruding Boers . . . His invariable answer was, 'Restore my land, and I will cease from troubling you. Give me back the land of my fathers, and then there shall be peace.' " The reaction of the Boers was to send an armed commando against Kousop, who "defended himself desperately; but his determined courage availed him nought. He and his people perished to a man . . . not a soul survived."

The defence of the mountain pass at Thermopylae comes to mind, but whereas at the battle of Thermopylae the combatants were evenly matched in bodily size and weapons, in the many encounters between settler and Bushman the midget Bushman armed with his puny bow and short-ranging arrow unflinchingly faced the settlers with their far-ranging, death-fraught firelocks. Yet the same brave human spirit that burned in the unconquerable Greeks at Thermopylae flared in the gallant little Bushmen. In both instances there were no survivors.

The great difference between Greek and Bushman history is that there was only one Thermopylae, but many settler-Bushman encounters ended in there being no Bushman survivors.

The Romans had an epitaph for such unknown heroes: *Dulce et decorum est pro patria mori*. No such epitaph commemorates the unsurpassed bravery of the little Bushmen – except, possibly, an obscure remark published more than a hundred years ago. "The Bushman is a dangerous foe, as he never surrenders, but armed with his contemptible looking, though often fatal weapons, fights to the last, preferring death to capture."

Altruism

Bushman bravery in defence of the group is repeatedly chronicled. An early example was reported in 1847. On being captured by a white settler force, a group of Bushmen would not betray the whereabouts of their band. This report runs: ". . . we constantly find the Bushmen misleading the Dutch, and on one occasion in 1774, two of these resolute mountaineers submitted to every species of torture, and eventually resigned themselves to death rather than betray to the commando the secret hiding place of their group".

The missionary John Philip recorded a similar case. Seven Bushmen were captured by a commando and were told that their lives would be spared if they would lead the commando to where the other members of their tribe were hidden; otherwise they would be put to death. The Bushmen, after leading the commando astray for about an hour, sat down and refused to move. When no answer could be obtained from them, and as their determination remained inflexible, their captors slew them on the spot. As these Bushmen were fully aware of the consequences of their resolve, the conduct was an instance of altruism unsurpassed in ancient or modern history. Christianity has a motto for such bravery: "Greater love hath no man than this . . ."

We erect monuments to our "immortal dead". The grave in Westminster Abbey to the Unknown Soldier is a perpetual reminder. But no single beacon

6.5 Keen-eyed and ever alert, the Bushman is in tune with his surroundings. Approaching benefits – like rain or game – and impending dangers – like hostile foes and trespassers on his territory – move him swiftly to the appropriate responses.

6.6 Often in his past the Bushman has had to use his bow and poisoned arrow to defend his territory and his life against those who sought to encroach upon the former and to endanger the latter.

6.7 Incredible acts of bravery occurred in the numerous fights of the Stone Age Bushmen with the challengers to his land and life. A 200 Years' War resulted in the virtual extinction of the Bushman in all parts of southern Africa except for the few refuge areas where he still survives.

stands in mournful solitude on some deserted crag or lonely hill, in silent acknowledgement of the unexampled bravery of these little men.

Freedom

To choose death rather than to surrender into chains and slavery was another feature of Bushman character. Thus, when surrounded and borne down by a host of enemies, "the solitary Bushman seldom or never asked for mercy from his hated foes. Wounded and bleeding as he might be, he continued obstinately fighting to the last. Shot through an arm, he would instantly use his knee or foot to enable him to draw his bow with the one remaining uninjured. If his last arrow was gone, he still struggled on as best he might, until finding death remorselessly upon him, he hastened to cover his head that no enemy might see the expression of death agony upon his face."

In our culture one recalls the episode of Sir Francis Drake, surrounded by his compatriots, dying on the deck of the little *Revenge,* ringed by hostile battleships. Yet his spirit rang through his exhortation to his master gunner to sink the *Revenge:* "Sink her, split her in twain, fall in the hand of God not into the hands of Spain."

A little Bushman in similar perilous circumstances reacted similarly – for all the world's akin: "He belonged to a clan in the Sneeuwberg mountains which had been cut off by a Boer commando among the rocks of a projecting shoulder of a great precipice. Here these retreating Bushmen turned at bay. Their enemies were on one side, a yawning gulf without any chance of escape on the other. A dire but hopeless struggle for life commenced. One after another they fell under the hail of bullets with which their adversaries assailed them. The dead and dying were heaped upon the dizzy projecting ledge, many in their death throes rolled and fell over among the crags and fissures in the depths which environed them. Still they resisted, and still they fell, until one remained: and yet, with the bloody heap of dead around him and the mangled bodies of his comrades on the rocks below, he seemed as undaunted as when surrounded by the entire band of his brave companions. Posting himself on the very outermost point of the projecting rocks, with sheer precipices of nearly a couple of hundred feet on either side of him, he defied his pursuers, and amid the bullets which showered around him he appeared to

6.8 In the Kalahari Desert, the Bushmen found relative peace and security, perhaps because this was the one part of the sub-continent that, until recently, nobody else wanted. Warfare with other groups does not seem to have featured in the history of the Bushmen here. A smiling Bushman youth in the borderland between Botswana and South West Africa.

have a charmed life and plied his arrows with unerring aim whenever his enemies incautiously exposed themselves.

"His last arrow was on the string. A slight feeling of compassion seemed at length to animate the hostile multitude that hemmed him in. They called to him that his life would be spared if he would surrender. He let fly his last arrow in scorn at the speaker, as he replied that 'a chief knows how to die, but never to surrender . . .' Then with a wild shout of bitter defiance . . . he leaped headlong into the deep abyss and was dashed to pieces on the rocks beneath."

The lonely figure of the little Bushman, poised on that high mountain crag, recalls another lonely figure, one who stood on Pisgah's silent mount and gazed wistfully at the Promised Land, banned to him, and who now lies in an unknown grave. His name lives on, but what of that other brave, courageous little figure, poised high on a mountain crag, gazing over *his* banished land, and himself vanishing into it by hurling his brave little body down the depths to certain death? Can it be that the startled cry that gave him life as he drew his first breath on earth caused Mother Earth to take him back into her bosom when she heard his death cry echoing in the high empyreum of his ancient mountain home?

7
Ecology of a Contemporary San People

Richard Borshay Lee

Perhaps the most remarkable thing about the San is the fact of their survival. In Botswana, hundreds of Bushmen are hunting and gathering for a living with bows and poisoned arrows. Elsewhere in the country there are thousands more who have taken to agriculture and stock-raising only within the last generation.

Mr and Mrs Laurence K. Marshall initiated a renaissance in Bushman studies in 1951 when they began their researches among the 600 full-time hunting and gathering !Kung Bushmen around the Nyae Nyae area of South West Africa, or Namibia. At the same time, Professor Phillip V. Tobias and the Kalahari Research Committee of the Witwatersrand University were initiating a series of investigations into the physical anthropology of the Bushmen. Since 1953 new studies have been made by many of the authors contributing to this volume.

In recent years the style of Bushman research has been transformed from a salvage operation to the study of on-going social and economic systems. This new research has overthrown many of the traditional views of the Bushmen and has played a part in developing a more accurate picture of the hunting and gathering way of life in general – a way of life that was, until 10 000 years ago, the universal mode of human organisation.

Among the last of the hunting and gathering !Kung Bushmen are the 1 600 scattered at waterholes in north-western Botswana between the Kavango swamps and the South West Africa (Namibia) border and around Lake Ngami. The largest and most isolated population in 1963-1965 was the 466 !Kung in the Dobe area, a line of permanent waterholes around the Aha mountains.

The peoples of the Dobe area

The Dobe area has retained its character as a hunting and gathering stronghold because of its geographic isolation and the unsuitability of its soils and rainfall for agriculture. The eight waterholes are surrounded by a belt of waterless, uninhabited country which varies in width from 30-50 km (20 to 30 miles) on the north and west to 100-160 km (60 to 100 miles) on the south and east. The area was unknown to outsiders until the 1880s, when White hunters and Tswana pastoralists began to make summer hunting trips to the interior. In 1925 a small colony of Herero cattle herders settled at !Kangwa, but it was not until nine years later that the British colonial administration made its first official tour of inspection. The Dobe area was relatively peaceful, and since it required no "pacification", little attention was paid to it. In 1946, however, a !Kung Bushman murdered a Negro. This resulted in the appointment in 1948 of a Tswana headman, Mr Isak Utuhile, who administered justice at his tribal court at !Kangwa.

During 1954 the character of the country changed markedly as a large number of Hereros with several thousand head of cattle entered from the east, having been driven out of the Kavango swamp margin by an outbreak of tsetse fly. Until this date the Dobe area had been in close contact with the Nyae Nyae area 64 km (40 miles) to the west. Visiting and intermarriage between the two populations of Bushmen were common, and many of the Dobe area residents had originally emigrated from Nyae Nyae. Most of the incoming Herero pressed through the Dobe area and built their cattle posts throughout the Nyae Nyae area. The South African government put an end to this, and for the first time international politics became a reality to the Dobe !Kung. The border was surveyed and demarcated, and the Herero were forced to move all their cattle back behind the Botswana frontier. Today the Bushmen share their waterholes with some 340 Hereros and Tswanas, and several thousand head of cattle, goats, donkeys and horses.

7.1 A temporary Bushman camp in a nut grove in the Dobe area of Botswana.

The pastoralists live in small, permanent hamlets of three to ten well-built mud huts arranged in a semicircle around the central kraals, where the livestock are penned at night. To some of the hamlets are attached small camps of Bushmen who divide their time between the usual round of hunting and gathering activities and helping the Herero or Tswana cattle-owners with herding and milking, for which they receive a daily ration of soured milk, the basic staple of the pastoral diet. Agriculture plays only a minor role in the economy of the Herero. With a highly variable annual rainfall varying from 150 mm (6 inches) to over 1 000 mm (40 inches), cultivation is a risky proposition, and crops might be harvested only one year in three.

The majority of the Bushmen (72 per cent at the time of the 1964 census) live in independent camps, 0,5 to 1 km (roughly $\frac{1}{4}$ to $\frac{1}{2}$ mile) from the nearest hamlet. The camps consist of a ring of grass huts around a central plaza and dancing ground. These are temporarily occupied for three to five months each winter, while the members carry out the complete round of subsistence activities. During the summer months the camps are abandoned as the population moves up-country to enjoy the resources of the rainy season water points. After the rains, when the group returns to the permanent waterholes, a new winter camp is built at a different site.

The relations between the Bushmen and their neighbours are friendly. The Hereros are generous, making a point of giving milk, meat or tobacco to the Bushmen when they come to pay a visit. The Blacks have a healthy respect for the fierce reputation of the Bushmen, and they remember the days when stock theft was a common occurrence. One of the older Tswana residents told me: "I always give tobacco to the !Kung. If you don't, you never can tell when you'll get a poisoned arrow shot at you."

The principal economic relation is the oral contract in which a young Bushman enters the service of a Herero household as a cow-herd. During the one or two

95

7.2 A permanent Bushman camp in the Dobe area.

years of his contract, the young man shares his meals with the family and is provided with clothing and the use of a donkey or a horse. At the end of the period, he receives in payment a donkey or a goat, or if he has done particularly well, a cow. Cash wages were introduced only in the late 1960s. After marriage, the young man usually returns to the camps and takes up hunting as a full-time occupation, leaving his cow or goat in the herd of his employer. Many of the younger men and women have experimented with agriculture at some point in the past, but because of the unpredictable rainfall, few have succeeded.

In addition, thirteen of the !Kung women have married Blacks and are raising their children as Hereros or Tswanas. A few of the women have adopted the characteristic Victorian dress of Herero women.

Although the Tswana are numerically few in the Dobe area, their cultural influence has been more profound than that of any other outside group. Their relationship with the Bushmen extends back almost eighty years. All matters concerning government, modern technology and migrant labour are dealt with in

7.3 Ten per cent of the population is over 60 years of age. The aged hold a respected position. They are the leaders of the camps, the collective owners of the water-holes, and the repositories of traditional ritual-medical skills.

the Setswana language. The major contribution of the Tswana to Bushman life from the point of view of Bushmen and Tswana alike is *molao*, the bringing of the law. Even since the founding of the tribal court at !Kangwa in 1948, the Bushmen have increasingly preferred to make use of the Tswana headman's arbitration to resolve conflicts.

Knowledge of the outside world has come slowly to the Dobe area. Few of the Bushmen were aware in 1964 that they were citizens of the then Bechuanaland Protectorate, and none of the people whom I asked had ever heard of "Africa". In recent years, however, this picture has changed drastically.

Population

The breakdown of the population by age and sex is shown in a table on page 98. The first point to be noted is the high percentage of old people: 10 per cent of the population (46 individuals) is over 60 years of age. This should contradict the widely held notion that the hunter's life is so rigorous that people rarely live beyond the age of 45. The data suggest that Bushmen who survive childhood may have at least as good a change of surviving to old age as the average member of tribal and peasant societies.

Among the !Kung the aged hold a respected position; they are the leaders of the camps, the collective owners of the waterholes, and the repositories of traditional ritual-medical skills. Senilicide is rare, and we have observed old people being

7.4 A grandmother and child using an imported iron pot and a traditional mortar and pestle – Dobe area, Botswana.

supported by their descendants long after their productive years have passed. Similarly young people are not pressed into the food quest at an early age. Adolescents are expected to provide a share of the food only after they are married, and it is not uncommon to see healthy, active teenagers moving from camp to camp on visits while their older relatives provide food for them.

The Bushman population of Dobe by age and sex (November 1964)

Age	Males	Females	Total
Old (60 years and over)	17 (7,5%)	29 (11,9%)	46 (9,9%)
Adult (15 to 59 years)	141 (63,5%)	138 (56,8%)	279 (59,9%)
Young (birth to 14 years)	65 (29,0%)	76 (31,3%)	141 (30,2%)
All ages	223 (100%)	243 (100%)	466 (100%)

Dependency ratio (the number of young and old per 100 adults) = 67
Child dependency ratio (the number of young per 100 adults) = 51

The factors that produce this favourable demographic picture are difficult to define. There is some indication that the average interval between successive births is four or five years. This long spacing limits the number of pregnancies a woman may undergo during her reproductive span. The nomadic life of the Bushmen requires that children under the age of five be carried by the mother while she is out gathering food and during group moves. A mother with two-year spacing of births will find at the end of four years that she has a four-year-old, a two-year-old and a newborn to carry. On the other hand, a woman whose births are spaced five years apart will have only one child to carry at a time. Contraception, infanticide, infant mortality and hormonal mechanisms affecting lactation and ovulation are some factors that may contribute to the spacing of births.

Habitat and climate

The Dobe area is part of a level, sandy plain stretching from the South West African escarpment in the west to the Kavango swamp in the east. The mean elevation is about 1 000 m (3 300 feet) above sea level. The main topographic feature is a series of fixed dunes running parallel to each other, 8 to 80 km (5 to 50 miles) in length and oriented roughly east-west. In the spaces between the dunes are parallel basins or *molapos*. This remarkably uniform pattern is interrupted by several rock outcrops and pans, and in places the landscape is incised by dry river courses that expose the bedrock.

At the lowest elevations, in the exposed beds of limestone, are eight permanent waterholes. With a highly variable annual rainfall, there are no permanent rivers through the area, but during exceptionally heavy rains the low-lying regions are subject to flooding. Later the flooded areas are reduced to scattered large pools or pans which may hold water for up to six months after the rains have stopped. All the rainfall is absorbed by the deep sand long before it reaches the Kavango drainage system.

The Dobe area supports a particularly rich vegetation characterised by broad-leaved trees and shrubs on the dunes and flanks, and acacias and other thorny species in the molapos and river courses. There are twenty species of excellent shade trees, some growing to over 15 m (50 feet) in height. Mature open woodlands with abundant deep shade are more common than are the sparsely wooded, open grassy plains that characterise most of the Kalahari Desert.

Apart from edible species, the habitat provides the Bushmen with an unlimited supply of shade and firewood and a wide variety of fine hardwoods for making weapons, tools and domestic articles.

The climate is characterised by hot summers with a four-month rainy season and by moderate winters without rainfall. The Bushmen divide the year into five seasons:

1. *!huma* (spring rains). The Bushman year begins in October or November with the onset of the first rains. These are light convectional thunderstorms which

have the effect of triggering growth in plants and reproduction in animals. Overnight the landscape is transformed from a parched, dry state to one of lush greenery. The Bushmen take advantage of the water that collects in the hollows of trees by leaving their winter camps around the permanent waterholes and establishing temporary camps in the mongongo nut forests.

2. *bara* (main summer rains). From December to March the heaviest rains fall, bringing with them a season of plenty. In years when flooding occurs, migratory ducks and geese flock to the pans in great numbers while elephants, buffaloes and other wet-country fauna migrate from the swamps into the Dobe area. This is also the period when the major summer plant foods (fruits, berries, melons and leafy greens) make their appearance. There is standing water at many points in the hinterland and the Bushmen abandon the permanent wells to live up-country.

3. ≠*obe* (autumn). A brief autumn occurs in April or May, after the rains have ceased but before the onset of cold weather. As the seasonal water points dry out, the Bushmen converge on the main summer pans, which may continue to hold water right into the winter. There is plenty of food, for the nut harvest is mature and there is still an abundance of summer berries and melons.

4. *!gum* (winter). The cold, dry season extends from the end of May through to August. It is heralded by a sharp drop in nightly temperatures. The days are crisp and clear and the temperature warms up to 24-27° C (75-81° F). The Bushmen fall back on permanent waterholes or, in exceptionally rainy years, on the largest summer waters, where they build new camps, well stocked with firewood to burn through the nights. Mongongo nuts and a variety of roots and tubers comprise the staples. The fine weather and good tracking conditions encourage hunting and snaring. In time, plant foods become increasingly scarce in an ever-widening radius around the permanent waterholes.

7.6 Digging bulbs at the end of the rains: this is usually woman's work.

5. *!ga* (spring dry season). From late August to the first rains in October is the most unattractive time of the year. Although the humidity remains low, the days are exceedingly hot, with highs ranging from 35-43 °C (95-109 °F) in the shade. Working is difficult and good foods are plentiful only at considerable distances from the camps. In this season the Bushmen use the widest variety of plant food species. Fibrous, unattractive roots are dug and eaten without enthusiasm. Hunting is hard work, but the men may go out often, out of boredom with the drab diet more than anything else. It is a time of waiting for the rains to come.

Health

Because of the relatively high altitude and dry climate, the Dobe area is free from many of the infectious diseases that are endemic in tropical Africa. There is no bilharzia or sleeping sickness, although both are found in the swamps 145 km (90 miles) to the east. The dry, sandy soils and five species of dung beetles solve many public health problems for the Bushmen. The incidence of parasitic infection appears to be low. Gonorrhoea, introduced by men returning from the mines, is the major epidemic disease among the adults. Tuberculosis, rheumatic fever, leprosy, malaria and trachoma are also present. Colds and chronic sniffles affect the children through the cold winter months.

Fauna

Because of the broken nature of the vegetation cover, the area does not support the large herds of migratory plains game that are found on the open stretches of the southern Kalahari. Wildebeest, for example, seen in herds of 5 000 to 10 000 in the Central Kalahari Game Reserve, are seen in herds of only 10 to 20 in the Dobe area. There has been a diminution of game in the north-western Kalahari over the past fifty years. Rhinoceros, hippopotamus and springbok have disappeared completely, while zebra are now rarely seen. Buffalo and elephant were formerly numerous, but now are only occasional summer visitors.

Of the forty species of resident larger mammals, the most prominent are kudu, wildebeest and gemsbok (oryx). Giraffe, eland, roan antelope and hartebeest are also present. Of particular importance to the Bushmen as game are warthog, antbear, porcupine, steenbok, duiker and spring-hare.

The major African predators are all represented in the area, including lion,

100

leopard, cheetah, wild dog and two species of hyena. The smaller carnivores include caracal, wildcat, genet, jackal and several species of mongoose.

Unprovoked attacks by wild animals on Bushmen are extremely rare. The people do not regard the bush as threatening or hostile. They sleep in the open without fires when necessary and make no provision to protect or fortify their living sites. The most common threat to Bushman homes, in fact, comes from Herero cattle which periodically blunder into camp to browse on the grass huts.

Bird life is remarkably abundant and varied. Some eighty species have been recorded. Ostriches are still common and continue to provide the !Kung with a supply of ostrich-egg shells as water containers and as material for making beads. Only eight species of birds are systematically hunted by the Dobe Bushmen for food: guinea-fowl, francolin (two species), korhaan (bustard), kori bustard, sand-grouse, Cape turtle dove and the red-billed teal.

Some twenty-four species of reptiles and amphibians are known and named by the Bushmen, including five poisonous snakes. Only two reptiles are of any importance as food: the rock python and the large leopard tortoise.

Fish are not present in the Dobe area, but aquatic species such as terrapins, leeches, clams and snails are found in isolated waterholes, indicating that at some time in the past the area was connected to a river system by flowing water.

Of invertebrates there is an abundance: scorpions, spiders, ticks, centipedes and millipedes, as well as at least seventy species of insects known to the Bushmen. The most important are the mantises (about which there is a body of myths), bees (highly prized for their honey), flying ants and click beetles (dietary delicacies) and poison beetles (the sources of Bushman arrow poison).

Almost 500 species of local plants and animals are known and named by the Bushmen. Of these, the Bushmen find some use for 150 species of plants and 100 species of animals. From their virtually exhaustive knowledge of the environment they are self-sufficient – with a single exception. The only item the Dobe area does not provide is iron.

Subsistence ecology

The "hunting and gathering way of life" has assumed a misleading connotation in the ethnographic literature. Especially in reference to the Bushmen, the term has come to imply a random, precarious existence, one of searching for food and eking out a living of odds and ends. Service, for example, writes of the !Kung Bushmen:

"In utter contrast to the Pygmies of the Ituri forest, the !Kung are a hungry people, their habits oriented around a constant struggle for food and water. Vegetable foods are rare most of the year, as is grass and water that would attract game. The most usual game hunted is a small antelope, birds, rodents, snakes, insects, lizards and the difficult ostrich. Foods gathered include mostly roots and seeds, and in the northern areas fruits and nuts." (1966, pp. 100-101)

This description bears almost no resemblance to the condition of the !Kung Bushmen of the Dobe area. The hunting and gathering Dobe Bushmen have a reliable subsistence, based on a systematic exploitation of abundant food resources. Very little of their food-getting is left to chance. Their knowledge of the local environment, of the habits of game and of the growth phases of food plants is virtually exhaustive. The people know where the food is at each season of the year and how to get it. They do not allow themselves to get into difficult situations, and even during the time of scarcity at the end of the dry season gatherers never come home empty-handed.

What makes their security of life possible? First, they depend primarily on vegetable foods, and these are abundant, predictable and surprisingly nutritious. Game animals, by contrast, are scarce and unpredictable and the meat is only of secondary importance in the diet. A second factor is the intelligence and sophistication that informs their exploitation of the food resources. And a third factor is the principle of generalised reciprocity that pervades the social life of the Bushmen. Food is shared throughout the camp in such a way that everyone receives an equitable share. This principle extends as well to the relations between camps; local food shortages are always balanced out through the redistribution of population in the visiting network.

7.7 A mongongo nut grove provides an ideal setting for a temporary Bushman encampment.

The resource base

The foundation of Bushman subsistence is the over 100 species of edible plants of the Dobe area. These include 30 species of roots and bulbs, 30 species of berries and fruits, and an assortment of melons, nuts, leafy greens and edible gums. The most important of the food plants is //"xa, the mongongo or mangetti nut *(Ricinodendron rautanenii)*. This superabundant staple yields both an edible fruit and a kernel. The latter has a caloric content of 600 calories per 100 grams and a protein content of 27 per cent, a level of nutritional value that ranks it with the richest cultivated foods. Thousands of kilograms of these nuts are consumed each year by the Bushmen, yet thousands more rot on the ground for want of eating.

Another staple is ≠m, the baobab fruit *(Adansonia digitata)*. It yields a delectable and refreshing powdery fruit rich in vitamin C, calcium and magnesium, and a kernel which compares favourably in calories and proteins to domesticated nuts.

The sour plum, //gwe *(Ximenia caffra)*, is a delicious tart fruit that enjoys a two-month season in December and January, when thousands are harvested. The flesh of the fruit is high in thiamin and carotene.

The marula nut, *gai (Sclerocarya caffra)*, less common than the mongongo nut, yields an inner kernel which is even more nutritious than the mongongo. The nut contains 31 per cent protein and extremely high concentrations of calcium, magnesium, phosphorus, sodium and potassium.

The mongongo and other nut species, the baobab and marula are particularly important, since they contain high levels of vegetable proteins of good quality and fats that substitute for meat when game is scarce. Not all Bushman foods are attractive, however. Some larger roots and melons have a decidedly bitter taste

102

and a high proportion of roughage. These the Bushmen eat only when more desirable foods are depleted.

The vegetable foods are sufficiently plentiful for most of the year that the !Kung can afford to be selective. They tend to eat only the most attractive foods available at a given season and bypass the less desirable ones. Over the course of a year, only twenty-three species of plants make up about 90 per cent of the vegetable diet by weight, and one species, the mongongo nut, accounts for at least half of the total.

Game resources are less abundant and less predictable than plants. Meat provides from 20 to 50 per cent of the diet by weight, depending on the season and the number of men hunting in the camp. The general diminution of game in the north-western Kalahari has not led to the collapse of the hunting way of life, however, for the hunters have developed their techniques for capturing smaller mammals, and the meat from these kills serves to supplement a diet based primarily on vegetable sources.

At some camps, for short periods, the amount of game brought in may be much higher. In December 1964, for example, a camp with four hunters killed twenty-nine animals over a seventeen-day period.

The big antelopes – kudu, wildebeest and gemsbok – are regularly hunted with poisoned arrows, but a hunter feels he has done well if he kills as many as six of these in a year. In addition, warthogs are stalked with hunting dogs. The owner of a well-trained pack of four or five dogs can count on twelve to fifteen of these animals a year. Duiker and steenbok, small antelopes weighing 9 to 18 kg (20 to 40 lbs), are next in importance. These are taken with dogs, trapped in rope snares, or, more rarely, shot with poisoned arrows. In the birth season (December to March), the young are often run down on foot or brought down with throwing clubs.

An unorthodox but highly effective hunting technique is the probing of underground burrows. Four important species are taken this way. The spring-hare is killed with a flexible pole of 4 m (14 feet) with a metal hook at the end. These nocturnal animals sleep in long, narrow burrows by day. The hunter finds an occupied burrow, probes it with the pole until he has hooked his prey, and then excavates the soft sand until he can retrieve the animal. The large African porcupine (18 kg, or 40 lbs) and the ant-bear (up to 63 kg, or 140 lbs) are also underground dwellers. When an occupied burrow is found, the hunters close off the exits and build a fire at the mouth until the half-asphyxiated animal tries to break out, whereupon they finish it off with spears and clubs. Warthogs also are killed in this way when they have run to ground. There are moments of high

7.8 A mother and her children crack and eat mongongo nuts in front of their hut. This is the most important of the one hundred species of food plants in the Dobe area.

excitement here, and when the prey bursts through the flames, dogs and occasionally men are injured in the fracas. The underground species are highly desired because they are very fat, and animal fat is one of the scarcest elements in the Bushman diet.

The game birds – guinea-fowl, francolin and bustard – are captured in ingenious snares when the opportunity arises, as are small mammals such as hares, bat-eared foxes, mongooses, genets and aard-wolves. Occasionally the dogs flush these animals out of the bush and are allowed to eat them. When there is no other meat in the camp, however, the people themselves eat these.

The big leopard tortoise, weighing up to 3,6 kg (almost 8 lbs), is a great favourite and is easily collected by men, women and children. It is baked in the shell and can feed a family of four. The non-poisonous rock python also makes a good meal. By and large, however, the snakes, insects and lizards that Service (1962) says are the staples of the Bushman diet are despised by the Dobe Bushmen.

In all, 220 species of animals are known and named by the Dobe Bushmen. Of these, 54 species are classified as edible, but only 17 species are systematically hunted. These, in order of importance, are:

1 warthog	7 spring-hare	12 francolin ⎫ two species
2 kudu	8 guinea-fowl	13 francolin ⎭
3 duiker	9 porcupine	14 korhaan
4 steenbok	10 leopard tortoise	15 hare
5 gemsbok	11 ant-bear	16 rock python
6 wildebeest		17 flying ants

These 17 species make up over 90 per cent of the animal diet by weight.

The organisation of subsistence

The camp, *chu/o,* is the basic residential unit and the focus of subsistence activities. It consists of a circle of grass structures with doors facing inwards around a central plaza 7 to 30 m (25 to 100 feet) in diameter. The constituent social units are nuclear families that exploit a common range and share in the products of individual subsistence efforts.

The organisation of work is simple. Members move out of camp each day individually or in small groups to work through the surrounding range, and return in the evening to pool the collected resources. The sexes are almost always segregated in food-getting activities. Women go out in groups of three to five with a well-defined objective of which species they want to collect. They move to the species area, fill their karosses, and return to the camp, gathering other species along the way to add variety to the evening meal. They are home by mid- or late afternoon and never stay out overnight.

Hunting is a more individualistic activity. Men prefer to hunt alone or in pairs. Game drives are not practised, and the men see no advantage in putting larger hunting parties into the field. The essence of successful hunting is to cover ground. The density of game is so low that it is necessary to cut a wide swath in a march of 13 to 24 km (8 to 15 miles) through the bush in order to come into contact with fresh *spoor,* or track. The day's hunting is rather open-ended. A man starts with a good lead which determines the opening direction of the march. This may be a reported sighting of fresh kudu spoor or a plan to check up on recently occupied ant-bear burrows. Dreams and divination may also give a hunter his lead. But luck plays a major part. Men are willing and even delighted to give up the opening lead if a better opportunity presents itself. If nothing turns up, the hunter will usually fill his bag with roots or nuts in order to have something to bring home. In a typical run of days in July 1964, I found that men averaged one kill for every four man-days of hunting.

The men rarely stay out overnight. Even if they have shot an animal in the afternoon, they break off tracking and return to the main camp to sleep. Their arrow poison works effectively but slowly, and if the arrow has been well placed, the hunter is reasonably sure that his prey will die during the night. At dawn the next day the hunter makes up a carrying party of two to five men and women and

7.9 A permanent camp in less hospitable terrain.

sets out to track the animal to the place where it has died. It is frequently necessary to drive off lions and hyenas that have gathered in the night before the meat can be butchered and brought home. Kills are sometimes lost to the carnivores in this way, but this is a risk the Bushmen accept. One hunter pointed out that even if he stayed with the prey all night, he would still have to leave it exposed to scavengers when he returned to camp to bring back the carrying party.

In the Dobe area the men consistently confined their hunting to within a day's walk of their camps. Long hunting expeditions, such as the four-day giraffe hunt depicted in John Marshall's film *The Hunters* (1956), were rarely observed in the Dobe area, where the men appear to get enough meat close to home.

Within the range men travel more widely than women. Each evening there is a thorough "debriefing" around the campfire, as the people relate in detail the latest news of rainfall, the ripening of fruit and food plants and the movements of game. Visitors arriving from other camps add to the discussion, relating what they have observed along the way. In this manner the members of the camp are kept fully informed about what their environment has to offer.

Records kept by us of the daily activities of individuals show that very little time is actually devoted to the food quest. In July 1964 the women of the Dobe camp put in only two or three days of work per week. The men tended to work more, but their schedule was uneven. A man might hunt three days in a row and then do no hunting for ten days or two weeks. Since hunting is an unpredictable business and subject to magical control, hunters may experience a run of bad luck and stop hunting for weeks or months at a stretch. Part of the explanation of this stop-and-go rhythm may be that, after a run of successful hunting, during which he has played host at several meat distributions, the hunter stops hunting in order to enjoy some reciprocal favours. For example, ≠oma, the best hunter of the Dobe camp, stopped hunting for three months in 1963. He explained that his hunting power was "cold" and that the game "refused" him. He stayed in camp awaiting inspiration while his wife and kinsmen provided food for him. In 1964 his luck returned and he started killing warthogs at the rate of three per month.

The activity diary of the Dobe camp in July 1964 showed that of the eleven men of hunting age in residence, four did no hunting at all, while the other seven worked an average of three or four days per week. In 78 man-days of hunting, 18 kills were made yielding about 200 kg (450 lbs) of edible meat. Their efforts produced a daily share of about 250 g (8 oz) of meat for each man, woman and child in the camp.

Food distribution

The net result of individual food-getting is that there is always something to eat in the camp. Food is the property of the man or woman who gets it, yet somehow every member of a camp participates in the evening meal, even on days when only a few members have been out collecting. Every evening the Bushman camp is the scene of quiet activity: fires are built up, food is put on to cook, and small portions of foods, both cooked and raw, are passed from fire to fire. Children are called over to a neighbouring fire to have a bite of this or that, or to take a handful over to their parents. The men gather at one of the fires to discuss the day's events and, as roasted roots are rolled out of the hot ashes, they stay on for supper.

The sharing of meat is more formally organised than the sharing of vegetable foods. The owner of the meat – usually, but not always, the hunter who killed the game – is responsible for butchering and distributing the meat.

The style of distribution varies according to the size of the kill. The smallest game, weighing less than 4,5 kg (10 lbs), such as spring-hare, hare, game birds, tortoises and young duikers and steenbok, is butchered, cooked and eaten by the hunter's immediate family and by anyone who joins them at their fire.

Game of medium size, such as adult steenbok and duikers, porcupines and young warthogs weighing 9 to 18 kg (20 to 40 lbs), is usually butchered and cooked by the hunter's family, and portions of the cooked food are distributed throughout the camp.

Larger game, weighing 45 to 180 kg (100 to 400 lbs), such as ant-bear, warthog, kudu, wildebeest and gemsbok, is butchered and divided into three portions: roughly one-fifth remains with the family, one-fifth is cut into strips for drying into biltong, and three-fifths are distributed to closely related households in the camp. This latter portion then undergoes a secondary distribution to more distantly related households and to visitors. Each family then cooks part of its allotment at the family fire. On subsequent days, when news of the kill reaches neighbouring camps, visitors arrive to join in and eat the fresh meat and to receive five or six dried strips to take home with them.

The primary division of meat is carried out with care. The hunter, especially if he is young, calls in older men to advise him, or he may even turn a whole carcass over to his father or father-in-law for division. Due attention is paid to the taboos of each of the recipients, to the size of the family of each recipient and to the number of other obligations they in turn may have to fulfill, and also to current alignments and divisions within the camp. This may involve subtle distinctions: for example, if the owner is currently bickering with a brother-in-law, he may tacitly express his disagreement by giving him a slightly less desirable cut or by calling over his spouse to accept the family's portion.

By the end of the fourth day the animal is finished, having been consumed by as many as sixty different people. I never observed hunters set aside a "surplus" of meat for later consumption, although Mrs Lorna Marshall says that the Nyae Nyae hunters do. There are two good reasons for this seeming prodigality. The first is that meat spoils quickly in the desert, and even carefully dried biltong is often contaminated after 72 hours. The second and crucial reason is that withholding a portion of one's meat would immediately draw the hostility of one's neighbours. On the other hand, the total distribution of meat draws their good feelings, that later on will make one a favoured guest at the neighbours' distributions. Mrs Marshall writes:

"The !Kung are quite conscious of the value of meat sharing and they talk about it, especially about the benefit of mutual obligations it entails . . . To keep meat without sharing is one of the things that is just not done." (1961, p. 241)

Group structure

The !Kung commonly live in camps that number from ten to thirty individuals, but the composition of these camps changes from month to month and from day to day.

Inter-camp visiting is the main source of this fluctuation, but each year about 15 per cent of the population makes a permanent residential shift from one camp to another. Another 35 per cent divide their time equally between periods of residence at two or three different camps, both in and out of the Dobe area.

The camps of the Dobe !Kung are not "bands" as understood by some anthropologists, for they do not consist of a core of males related through the male line. But neither is the camp a random assortment of unrelated individuals whom adverse circumstances have thrown together. What the !Kung camp is, in essence, is a group of kinsmen and affines, or relations by marriage, who have found that they can live and work together well. Under this flexible principle of organisation, brothers may be united or divided and fathers and sons may live together or apart. Furthermore, through the visiting network an individual may, during the course of his life, live for a time at many waterholes, since establishing residence at one camp does not require one to relinquish a claim to any other.

The constant circulation of population makes it appear at first that there is no stable basis of residential life and that the !Kung are a mobile people who can live anywhere and with anyone, but in no one place for very long.

The !Kung living arrangements *do* have a stable basis, however, although the underlying principles can be discerned only after lengthy field study. At the centre of each camp is a "core" of siblings – both brothers and sisters – and their offspring of both sexes, who share a claim to the ownership of their waterhole. These owners, or K"*ausi,* are generally recognised as the "hosts" whom one approaches when visiting a given waterhole.

The K"ausi are simply the people who have lived at the waterhole longer than any others. The camps associated with the waterhole are built up gradually by the addition of in-marrying spouses of the core siblings. These spouses in turn may bring in *their* siblings and their spouses, so that the basic genealogical structure of the camp assumes the form of a "chain" of spouses and siblings radiating from the core, as shown in Ill. 7.10. Other means by which the camp is built up are by the incorporation of whole families through primary marriages and of partial families through secondary marriages. At a given time the camp is composed largely of persons related by primary ties: almost every member has a parent, a child, a sibling or a spouse to link him to the core.

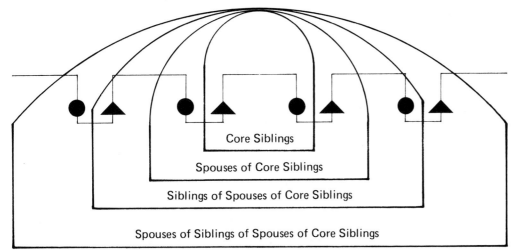

Core Siblings

Spouses of Core Siblings

Siblings of Spouses of Core Siblings

Spouses of Siblings of Spouses of Core Siblings

7.10 A Bushman camp develops from a core of residents composed of siblings of both sexes. To this core there are added spouses, then siblings of spouses, and so on.

The core units of camps are composed of siblings of both sexes. An analysis of twelve camps showed that a brother and sister formed the core in four cases, two sisters and one brother in two cases, and two brothers and one sister in one case. In addition, four camps had a core composed of two sisters, and one was composed of two brothers. These combinations are to be expected in a strongly bilateral society such as the !Kung. Thus, it is futile to try to establish whether the !Kung have matrilocal or patrilocal residence arrangements.

The causes of the high turnover may be found in demographic factors. Given the small family size and the likelihood of disparities of sex ratios, it is extremely improbable that a family would be able to maintain its numbers at a viable level if it had to depend solely on natural replacement. For example, if the rule of residence were strictly patrilocal, a waterhole group with all daughters would be quickly put out of business, while a waterhole group with a preponderance of male offspring would have far more hunters on hand than the limited game could support.

A far more adaptive way of maintaining group size and of distributing population with reference to resources is to allow many different avenues of group affiliation. The flexible group structure of Dobe is the result. The !Kung do not resort to elaborate fictions to bring living arrangements on the ground into line with an ideal model. They simply leave group and geographic boundaries open and allow the most effective subsistence units to emerge anew in each generation.

Kinship and the name relation

If the !Kung had to rely on genealogical reckoning alone, their kin universe would be severely circumscribed. Their genealogical knowledge is shallow; only one or two generations beyond the oldest ascendants are known, and they rapidly lose track of cousins beyond the second degree. This primary kinship system, however, is only the start for an elaborate development of imaginary kinship based on the common possession of personal names. There is a limited repertoire of personal names among the !Kung: only 35 men's names and 34 women's names were in use in the Dobe area in 1964. All names are sex-specific and there are no surnames. Personal names are transmitted from grandparent to grandchild according to strict rules of precedence. There are no "new" names, and the current repertoire appears to have been handed down over many generations. A first-born male is named after his father's father, and a first-born female after her father's mother. The second-born of each sex is named after the maternal grandparents. If further children are born, they are named after siblings of their parents or more distant relatives. A parent may never name a child after himself.

This is only a bare introduction to the complexities of !Kung naming rules. Readers desiring to go further into the matter should consult Lorna Marshall's classic paper "The Kin Terminology System of the !Kung Bushmen" (1957).

Their naming system enables the !Kung to extend primary kinship ties far beyond the boundaries of personal genealogical kindreds. In fact, the thousands of !Kung-language speakers are connected by name relations into a network of imaginary or fictive kinship that extends all the way from Angola in the north to Ghanzi 800 km (500 miles) to the south in central Botswana. The basic principle is that bearers of the same name have a special affectionate relation with one another. They use the kin terms "old name-young name" regardless of the actual biological connection, and even in cases where there is no traceable connection at all.

Marriage

The far-reaching ties made possible by the name relation are of particular importance in the arrangement of marriages. The !Kung Bushmen are unusual among hunter-gatherers in that they extend the incest taboo collaterally and forbid marriages between actual cousins. This prohibition sends a young man (or woman) far afield when seeking a spouse.

A young man has a wide range of potential spouses to choose from. In addition to his immediate female relatives as far as second cousins, a man may *not* marry a girl with the same name as his mother, his sister or, in the case of a second marriage, the same name as his daughter or his mother-in-law. Similarly, a girl may not marry a man whose name is the same as that of her father, her brother, her son or her father-in-law. All others not excluded by reason of blood or name-sharing kinship are potential spouses if they are of a suitable age.

Men marry between the ages of twenty and thirty, usually after they have served a period as cattle-herds for the Herero. Girls marry around the time of menarche, which tends to occur late, between the ages of fourteen and sixteen. Parents try to arrange a match while their children are still young, and one of the more pleasant topics discussed during inter-camp visiting is *gau !xom*, or betrothal. Most of these arrangements go by the board, however, since the adolescents of both sexes often have ideas of their own. In current practice, there is a period of unstable marriage when young people may have several temporary liaisons before settling down with a lifelong partner.

The qualities a girl's parents look for in a son-in-law are hunting ability and a pleasant, non-aggressive personality. In order to prove himself, the young husband may serve a period of "bride service" in the camp of his wife's parents. However, with the fluidity of group structure, the young couple may spend as much as half of their time living elsewhere.

In 1964, to take but one example, only 5 per cent of the marriages in the Dobe area were polygamous. There were six cases of polygyny (and only one man had three wives) and one polyandrous household. Several factors would seem to

favour a higher incidence of polygyny. There is no lack of surplus women; in 1964 thirty-five divorcees and widows (16 per cent of all women over fifteen years) were living without husbands. Also, the economic burden of a second wife is not great, since the women provide over half of the food for the household. The major obstacle seems to be the attitude of the wives themselves. Many men say that they desire a second wife, but fail to take one for fear of incurring the wrath of their present wife. Married women threaten to leave their husbands if they bring a second wife into the household; and if a man does, in spite of his wife's objections, she may make life miserable for the junior wife and the husband alike. A marriage to two sisters has the best chance of success, since the girls have grown up in a close co-operative relation: three of the six polygynous unions were of this form.

Divorce is common in the early years of adult life. Arranged marriages often fail to prove durable, although the young couple may eventually reunite after a period of travelling around in temporary liaisons. Divorce in both young and older adults is initiated as frequently by the women as by the men. A wife may pack up and go if

7.11 A Bushman mother and children in the Dobe District.

109

the husband is adulterous, if he beats her, or if he insists upon taking a second wife. Divorce is a simple matter, since there is no community of property and no bride wealth to dispute. Children always remain in the "custody" of their mother. In general, divorce does not leave the same quality of bitterness among the !Kung that it often does in Western society. Ex-spouses usually maintain extremely cordial relations and may even continue to live in the same camp after one or both have re-married.

After the age of thirty almost all San settle down to a stable union which lasts until the death of one of the spouses. These unions survive the frequent temporary separations of husband and wife in the visiting network and even such trying circumstances as adultery by either partner, and long periods of hunting inactivity by the husbands. For those who seek it, the Bushman social system offers ample opportunity for sexual experimentation in early adulthood, and this latitude undoubtedly contributes to the stability of marriage in later years.

The management of conflict

Verbal disputes are the common currency of camp life. The !Kung must surely be among the most talkative people in the world. The buzz of conversation is a constant background to the camp's activities: there is an endless flow of talk about gathering, hunting, the weather, food distribution, gift-giving and scandal.

A good proportion of this talk in even the happiest of camps verges on argument. People argue about improper food division, about breaches of etiquette, and about failure to reciprocate hospitality and gift-giving. The language is peppered with far-fetched analogy and hyperbole. Cases are built up out of an individual's past bad behaviour, and ancient conflicts are rehashed in minute detail! Almost all

7.12 The !Kung must surely be among the most talkative people in the world. The buzz of conversation is a constant background to the camp's activities: there is an endless flow of talk about gathering, hunting, the weather, food distribution, gift-giving and scandal. And there is story-telling, as among this group of males in a permanent camp.

the arguments are about specific individuals. The most frequent accusations heard are of pride, arrogance, laziness and selfishness. As tempers mount the language and the charges become more and more extravagant.

These disputes are puzzling for their apparent lack of clear-cut outcomes. They flare up and die down without either party giving ground. The bubble of tension is often burst by a joke, which reduces the entire camp, including the disputants, to helpless laughter. One is astonished to see two men chatting amicably together who only a few minutes before had been shouting abuse at each other. To a certain extent verbal battles appear to be a game played principally for the fun of laughing about it afterwards.

Not all conflicts are dissipated so rapidly. More rancorous disputes may require the intervention of peacemakers to restore good relations, but several days later one party – or both – packs up and leaves the camp. Much of the coming and going observed in Bushman camps can be traced to a recent history of strained relations. When an argument is too serious to be dissipated by rough good humour, it is far simpler to split the camp than to stay together and fight it out. One old man explained it this way: "In the case of arguments in the camp, we sit down and talk it out, and bring in others who know more to listen. But with people like myself who don't want trouble, we will just pack up and go away."

The Bushmen recognise three levels of conflict: talking (n≠wa), fighting (nh!aie) and killing (n!waakwe). They appear to delight in the first level and engage in it at every opportunity. But their dread of the second and third levels is extreme. The word "n!waakwe" means literally to "kill one another". Fighting as well is to be feared, since the act of homicide is well within the means of all adult men, whose poisoned arrows are always close at hand.

The Bushmen are perhaps unusual among human societies in that they attach no value to fighting. They have no ideal of honour or of brave, aggressive masculinity. There are no culturally accepted outlets for physical violence, no wrestling matches, no games of strength, and no ordeals or duels in which a man can "prove" himself.

The extreme fear of violence among the !Kung by and large appears entirely justified: there have been some nasty "punch-ups" in the past and the !Kung have a reputation among their neighbours as fierce fighters. At least twenty-two homicides occurred among the !Kung during the period 1920-1955. The recent introduction of Tswana legal institutions has undoubtedly played an important part in controlling fighting. Today serious disputes are usually brought to the attention of the Tswana headman. In one recent case of adultery the aggrieved husband asked a neighbouring Herero: "Are you going to take this matter over, or shall I do what is in my heart to do?" The Herero man, of course, interceded and brought the principals to court. My impression is that the Tswana court has proved very successful because the Bushmen have been relieved to have an outside agent take the heavy responsibility of resolving conflicts out of their hands.

The economic basis of !Kung society

Until the mid-1960s, the !Kung Bushmen of Dobe continued to live as hunters and gatherers without cash, trading posts, wage labour or markets. One valuable result for the anthropologist was the opportunity to observe how ecological adaptation, social structure and ideology articulate in a dynamic, ongoing system.

In the first place our study has shown that, at least in the Dobe area, the hunting and gathering way of life is not as rigorous and demanding as it is often made out to be. If we are to understand these societies, we have to go beyond the overly simple argument that hunters are poor because the harsh environment and the crude technology does not allow anything better.

A number of features appear to set the Bushmen and other hunter-gatherers apart from tribal and centralised societies. An important one is their radically different conception of the relation between man and his environment. Among agricultural and pastoral peoples, wealth is amassed from nature by careful husbandry and improvement of land, livestock, homesteads and durable goods. The Bushmen, by contrast, make no sharp division between the resources of the natural environment and social wealth. The unimproved land itself is the means of production. Since it is owned by no one exclusively, it is available to everyone who can make use of it. The Bushmen do not amass a surplus, because they conceive of the environment itself as their storehouse. The necessities of the hunter's life are in the bush, no less surely than those of the agriculturalists are in the cultivated ground. The Bushmen know everything there is to know about what their environment has to offer. This knowledge is, in effect, a form of control over nature: it has been developed over many generations in response to every conceivable variation in climatic conditions. The Bushmen are not experimenters introducing new crops or domesticated animal species into an unknown habitat. Their adaptation is a conservative one, based on naturally occurring plant and animal species that have been genetically adapted to desert conditions.

Because they know what to expect from the environment, they see little point in bringing food and raw materials to camp before they are actually needed. The food collected by the members of a camp is distributed and consumed without delay within the boundaries of the camp, or by the camp's immediate neighbours. There is no "setting aside" of part of the production for consumption at a later date, or for distribution to more distant points. This lack of "surplus" requires a constant level of work to be maintained throughout the year. Such uniformity of effort stands in sharp contrast to agricultural societies, in which intense periods of work (planting and harvesting) are followed by periods of relative inactivity. The actual amount of time devoted by Bushmen to the food quest is modest, amounting to about twelve to nineteen hours of subsistence effort per adult per week, or about 600-1 000 hours a year, a lower level of work than has been observed in some agricultural societies.

The Bushmen make a relatively small investment in what may be called the capital sector of their economy. Every adult manufactures and maintains a basic set of utensils considered essential to the tasks of daily life. Lorna Marshall compiled an exhaustive catalogue of the material culture in use among the Nyae Nyae !Kung, a list that comprises only ninety-four items in all. With the exception of iron, beads and pots obtained from the Blacks, all the items of material culture, necessities and luxuries alike, are easily manufactured from locally available materials. Building a house for a rainy-season camp is a day's work; shelters for the dry-season camps are thrown up in a morning. The all-important digging stick can be whittled in an hour, and will last the user for several months. A complete set of bow, arrows and quiver takes somewhat longer to make: a man assembles the materials over a period of weeks in the course of normal activities, and then spends three or four days manufacturing the kit. These weapons will then have a useful lifetime of several years.

Because of the ease with which articles can be made during the abundant leisure time, there is no lack of duplicate items. These are put into circulation through the gift-giving network, called *hxaro*. If an individual receives a valued item such as a necklace of ostrich-egg shell beads, a thumb piano or a finely carved pipe, he keeps it for several months and then passes it on to a trading partner. Months or even years later his trading partner reciprocates with a similar item. The net effect is to maintain a constant circulation of goods and an equal distribution of wealth among the members of the society. Particularly active participants in the hxaro network are not richer than others in the sense of possessing a greater share of the world's goods. Rather, they are those who have a greater than average number of trading partners and thus a more rapid turnover of goods. Nobody keeps hxaro goods for very long.

This lack of wealth accumulation, even though the means for it – free time and raw materials – are at hand, arises from the requirements of the nomadic life. For people who move around a lot and do not keep pack animals, it would be sheer folly to amass more goods than can be carried when the group moves. Portability is the major design feature of the items themselves. The total weight of an individual's personal property is less than 11 kg (25 lbs) and it can easily be carried from place to place. When a family is packing, it is remarkable to see all of their wordly possessions – weapons, cooking utensils, water containers, medicines, cosmetics, pipes, musical instruments, children's toys and beads – disappear into a pair of leather sacks the size of overnight bags.

The immediacy of food consumption, the modest investment in capital goods,

and the lack of wealth disparities all contribute to the distinctive style of Bushman social relations. With personal property so easily portable, it is no problem for people to move as often as they do. There is a similar lack of investment in fixed facilities such as village sites, storage places and fenced enclosures. When parties come into conflict it is simpler to part company rather than remain together and resolve differences through adjudication or fighting.

It has become a commonplace in the anthropological and popular literature to regard the hunters and gatherers as living a life of constant struggle against a harsh environment. The nomadic round, the paucity of material goods, and the lack of food surpluses of these people are taken as *prima facie* evidence of the dreadful conditions endured by man in the state of nature. That the hunter's life is difficult is self-evident, the argument runs, for if it were not, surely the hunters would be able to settle down, lay in food reserves, and generally have the leisure time to "build culture".

Data on the !Kung Bushmen of Dobe contradict this view. The people of the Dobe area are full-time hunters and gatherers in an unattractive semi-desert environment, yet they appear to work less and live longer than do some peoples with more advanced economic systems. Their subsistence requirements are satisfied by a modest input of labour, of the order of two or three days of work per adult per week. This level of effort is sufficient to support a large proportion of non-productive young and old people. There is plenty of time to develop the public life of the community. Ritual curing dances with their elaborate trance performances are frequently held, bringing together fifty or more participants from kilometres around. At some waterholes these all-night dances occur as often as two or three times a week.

The Bushmen do not have to struggle amongst themselves over food resources. Their attitudes toward ownership are flexible and their living groups open, offering a wide latitude for individuals to choose congenial surroundings. Because the members of the society are not divided into close-knit territorial groupings defending what they have against outsiders, a major source of conflicts is removed. It is possible to keep conflicts, both within and between groups, to a minimum by fission. This feature alone sets the !Kung apart from more technologically developed societies whose very survival depends on their ability to maintain internal order and to control real estate – at the family, tribal and national levels.

It is precisely this feature that has been and is the fatal flaw in the hunting and gathering way of life, and not its nomadic style and low productivity. In encounters with more aggressive societies, the hunting peoples have always come out second best and have tended to give up their land base and move away to avoid or end conflicts with agricultural, pastoral or industrial peoples. The fact that the hunters of today are largely confined to unattractive marginal areas or to rural slums should not blind us to the fact that the hunting and gathering way of life was a remarkably stable and successful one.

8
The Biology of the San

Ronald Singer

Human populations are never static in their biological make-up, and even over quite short periods they evince those changes that are termed evolution. The agencies and conditions which influence the rate and direction of evolutionary change are now well defined. The paramount agent is natural selection, acting on both existing hereditary variation and on novel variation (such as gene mutation). Selection in favour of a particular character (for example, in relation to disease or climatic stress) will in time alter the genetic constitution of the population. A high degree of isolation (geographical or social, or both) and small size of population (favouring genetic "drift") are factors which may speed up the spread of adaptive change. On the other hand, there may be mixing between two or more distinctive populations, as a result of conquest or contact (for example, trade, migration), and this is a powerful factor in changing the genetic constitution.

The ever-continuing, ever-present process of evolution is extremely complex and its ramifications cannot be considered here. One aspect, though, indicating the interaction of the above mechanisms, could interest us. It should be remembered that for tens of thousands of prehistoric years mankind probably existed, just like the Bushmen of today, as small groups or bands of scavengers and hunter-gatherers. Some bands were isolated for varying periods of time, but others always came into contact with each other in their instinctive quest for economic survival, thereby spreading their genes and developing the remarkably wide variability and phenomenal plasticity (both physical and cultural) of our species. In small populations of this sort potentially favourable genic alleles (those versions of a gene capable of occupying the same site on a chromosome) may accidentally be lost, while disadvantageous alleles may persist. Under these circumstances, evolutionary changes in small groups may even proceed against the direction of natural selection pressure.

As a hunter-gatherer population, the Bushmen represent a primitive cultural society which, like other rare hunter-gatherer communities in the world, are now steadily "disappearing" into neighbouring populations with agricultural and industrial cultures. Do the San constitute a unique race? With whom do they share morphological, genetic, physiological and cultural characteristics? How do their social values and behaviour affect their biological constitution? If they are a "fossilised" population, culturally speaking, can we determine their ancestral relationships with the other indigenes of southern Africa, the Hottentots (or Khoikhoi) and the Bantu-speaking Negroes (or simply "southern Negroes")? In order to answer these questions, a few preliminary generalisations on race and race formation are necessary.

The term "race" has become politically explosive and generally disreputable, and many scientists prefer to avoid it. There is even some doubt about its applicability and suitability in referring to subspecies of animals in general. The neutral word "population" is preferable when reference is made to variations in and between groupings of people. These may have a particular geographic distribution, constitute a functional or political unit such as a nation, tribe or clan, speak a particular language, and share a common social structure and one or more religions.

For scores of millennia people have been milling over the surface of the earth. Africa has been a vast shifting sand of human mobility providing ample opportunities, over and over again, for multiple hybridisation processes, and also, of course, for hybridisation with peoples beyond the confines of the continent both by land and sea. Hence, it should not be surprising that the historic populations of southern Africa represent a genetic mixture, albeit not uniform in make-up. This is the background for the refutation of the artificial, and often politically inspired, concept of "pure races". Consequently in Africa it is possible to find a group of populations which claim a common origin and share features of culture and language, but yet are far from constituting a biological unit. The Fulani are one example. On the other hand, the Malagasy of Madagascar constitute a distinct, non-African cultural and linguistic (Malayo-Polynesian) unity, and yet historic and biological evidence indicates a large African Negro component in their ancestry.

Detailed genetic studies of large samples of populations are needed to verify such loose and outdated statements (which may be theoretically plausible) as: "The Bantu type in Africa arose from the cross of Bushman and Negro, with infiltrations at intervals of 'Caucasian' blood from the Nile Valley". We shall attempt to stick to facts and theorize only when we have to. In the first place, the definition of "Bushman" has just recently become somewhat clarified. For centuries laymen – travellers, missionaries, civil servants and others – have written about Bushmen, and very often it is obvious that Bushmen and Hottentots have been confused with each other, leading to misunderstanding and error. Secondly, we are not very sure of the precise number and distribution of modern Bushman groups, how they are interrelated, their degrees of admixture with other populations, or their affinities in early historic times. Thirdly, detailed, controlled, scientific investigations have been conducted only over a period of less than fifty years.

Therefore, in order to describe "the biology of the San" one must not only have an overview of the total *population*, but also consider the meaning of gradients and variants within the population, with reference to ancient and recent mixtures with neighbouring contact populations. It is thus important to understand that such a description seeks out the averages of the distinctive traits and features, as well as those indicating kinship within and outside the *present* population. Population comparisons should be based on as many independent traits as possible, to minimise the risk of mistaking a few chance resemblances for signs of relationship.

The Khoisan "click" languages, used as a cultural distinction, may be useful in determining biological affinity in the local setting, at least south of the Zambezi River.

It is important to note that the distribution of Bushmen, widespread even now despite centuries of oppressive forces limiting their movements, has resulted in varying degrees of contact with southern Negroes and Hottentots. A good example of contact with Negroes is that of the Angola !Kung, while the Heikum in South West Africa mostly speak a Nama dialect, and culturally and physically have been influenced by the Nama and Bergdama.

Anatomical features of the San (Bushmen)

The small stature, woolly and often "peppercorn" hair and yellowish brown skin of the San (Bushmen) have often been taken as evidence of an affinity with the Pygmy peoples of the equatorial forests of Central Africa. But, other than their having a few "African" genes in common, there is no reason to consider them as being closely related or of recent common stock.

As in most physical traits within populations, the height of the San varies from group to group and between sexes. Recorded measurements indicate a range of about 140 cm (55 inches) to about 170 cm (67 inches) for males, with an average of about 157 cm (62 inches), while females are generally a few centimetres shorter. The upper level of the male heights overlaps the lower measurements for neighbouring southern Negroes, and the northern and central Bushmen are generally taller than the southern, reflecting a greater degree of admixture with these Negroes. Measurements taken a century ago are usually smaller than those more recently observed. To some extent the apparent implication of this – that earlier Bushmen tended to be of smaller stature – is artificial: early investigators selected for study the smaller Bushmen as being more "pure". A trend for increasing height recently documented among the San results from a number of factors, the two most obvious being improved nutrition due to more Bushmen "settling" near southern Negro and White farms and villages, and increasing admixture with the

8.1 Mother with child in the Ghanzi district of north-western Botswana. The "peppercorn" distribution of hair is well seen when it is short, as in this young San baby. Note also the tiny ears, the marked protrusion of the back of the head (occipital bossing) and the diamond shape of the mother's face.

new neighbours. In general, one can state that the San vary from short to medium, while neighbouring Negroes range from medium to tall. The Khoikhoi tend to fall between the two populations, with the larger number tending towards the medium-tall range.

For decades anthropologists used a technique of measuring skin colour in populations whereby a standard set of colours was placed against the skin and the nearest match noted. This highly subjective and inaccurate method was recently supplanted by the reflectance spectrophotometer. This instrument is capable of measuring many wavelengths of light by means of different filters; it is standard-

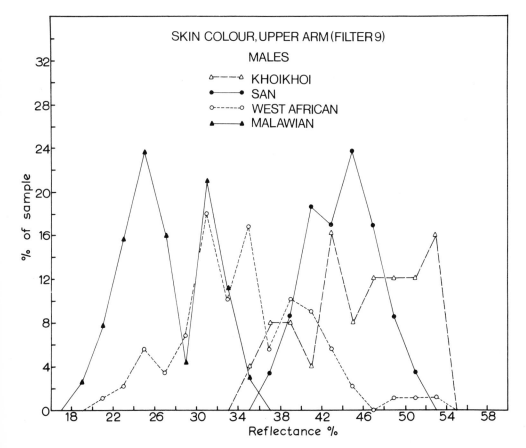

8.2 Graph showing data obtained by reflectance spectrophotometry of skin colours of groups of Khoikhoi, San, West Africans and Malawians. The lighter the skin, the higher the reflectance. We see that the San, as well as the Khoikhoi, have high reflectances, with peaks on the right side of the figure; whereas the Malawi and West African samples have low reflectances with peaks on the left side of the figure. This confirms what the eye shows – that the Khoisan peoples are lighter-skinned than the Negro or Black Africans.

117

ised against a white control. It has been shown, in a fairly extensive study, that the Khoisan skin colour is clearly distinguishable from that of southern Negroes, and that the so-called "black" Bushmen (or Mbarakwengo) are distinguishable from both Negroes and "yellow" Bushmen. The palest groups are the Cape Coloured and Rehoboth hybrid population, in which a White element is clearly detectable. Furthermore, it was found that tanning may contribute considerably to variation in the skin colour of Africans, which may explain why Negroid peoples of the African savannahs are notably darker than those in neighbouring forest environments. One of the tests separated the Khoikhoi somewhat from the San and Negroes, which may be another feature pointing towards isolative differences between these populations. This study also illustrates (Ill. 8.2) the gradation in the spectrum from the light yellow-skinned Khoikhoi (or Hottentots), overlapping with San (or Bushmen) and West Africans, who in turn overlap the rather black Malawians.

It will be shown later that the San and Khoikhoi peoples are genetically, at least, part of the African Negro mosaic, with a long history of differentiation, or micro-evolution. The skin colour investigations, then, should lead us to consider widening the spectrum of "black" Africa to include the light yellow-skinned Khoisan populations. Because our knowledge of the modes and intensities of selective forces is so scanty, we cannot explain why the serological, or blood group, pattern should be so similar between southern Negro, San and Khoikhoi, while in genetically more complex characters, such as skin colour and other physical traits, the differences are marked.

Interestingly enough, as in the case of stature, studies have shown that the San tribes that have been exposed most to Negro contact – that is the northern and eastern groups – are darkest in colour. An as yet unexplained phenomenon is the early formation of deep wrinkles and folds of the Bushman skin, especially in the exposed face. This loss of elasticity is often associated with the absence (or loss) of fat in the skin, giving relatively young people a wizened, "leatherbottle" appearance. However, young persons (below forty years) may have smooth, well-nourished skins. It is likely that the phenomenon is related to exposure to sun and desert glare, and possibly also to constant closeness to open fires, but the physiological mechanisms involved are not obvious.

As in some other African peoples, the San body shows a remarkable tendency to be hairless. It is only on the scalp and sometimes on the eyebrows that the hair is thick – and even on the scalp, occasionally, tightly spiralled hair tufts are separated from one another by patches of skin apparently bare, but with a normal distribution of hair follicles. The adult hunter-gatherer Bushman does not shave, yet a moustache or beard are most uncommon, and when present are usually rudimentary. Armpit hair is hardly obvious, or may even be absent, while pubic hair is sparse. The hair is always dark, and becomes grey only in very old people. On the other hand, baldness is very rare. Head hair can grow fairly long, but one does not see San men or women with their hair long, that is shoulder-length, even when the hair is of the "woolly" type and is teased out.

Compared to the size of the whole head, the San's flattish face is relatively small (Ill. 8.3). This tends to be more obvious in juveniles and teenagers. It appears that the brain case grows more rapidly to adult size than does the face – or conversely, that facial growth is slower. This is one of many San features that have been referred to, rather loosely, as "paedomorphism", or the retention of infantile proportions in the adult. The use of this phrase has become somewhat distorted and confused. Naturally, not *every* Bushman has a small face, but it is a common characteristic and may have been more universal in the distant past. It highlights an essential principle differentiating San from Khoikhoi populations, namely smallness or a tendency towards diminution in the size of a number of features, possibly reflecting the over-all diminished size of the skeleton. For example, the San tend to have small ear-lobes (or none at all), small mastoids, and small jawbones; also smaller teeth, narrower bony orbits and smaller cheek-bones than the Khoikhoi. However, there is considerable overlap between members of the populations, and in some cases it is not possible dogmatically to distinguish a particular individual as belonging to either one or the other population. This is what one expects in populations that derive from common ancestral stocks and

8.3 The face of the San is generally flattish and low, though broad across the angular cheek-bones. This man is G cou Q'Conta and he lives in the vicinity of the Tsodilo Hills in the far northwest of Botswana where rock paintings are to be found.

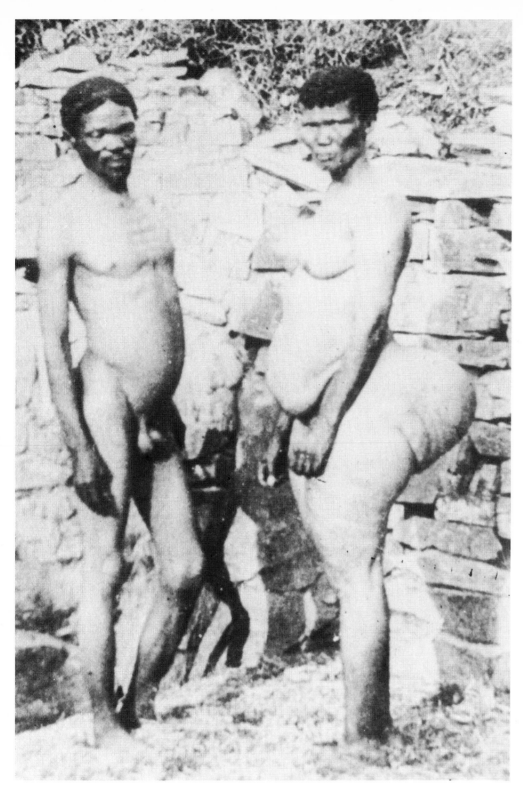

that, after periods of separation and isolation, come together at various times to remingle their genes.

There are many popular myths about Bushmen (and Hottentots). One is that, because of their small stature, yellow skins and narrow, occasionally oblique or sloping eye-slits, they are of Mongolian origin. Reference is made also to an epicanthic eye-fold, sometimes mis-called a "Mongolian fold", that passes down from the upper eyelid along and beyond the nasal side or inner angle of the eye. Bushmen, like Khoikhoi, do have skin folds over their upper eyelid, usually in the middle and outer parts of the eye. Occasionally a medial or inner fold is present (usually before puberty), but it is not a typical "Mongolian" fold, neither do their blood groups and other genetic characteristics suggest any Asian relationships or origins.

Steatopygia

Probably the most outstanding and unique physical characteristics of the San are the presence in the females of steatopygia and of elongated labia minora or nymphae (the so-called "Hottentot apron" or tablier). Both are more commonly found among Khoikhoi women.

Steatopygia presents as a localised accumulation of fat or fatty-fibrous tissue high over the buttocks, and it may be a particularly marked feature even when the woman is otherwise not obese. Occasionally, and especially in generally obese women, there is another large deposit of fat on the outer side of the thighs, which is called steatomeria. Rock paintings that are many centuries and possibly thousands of years old show that members of ancient populations in southern Africa that must be directly ancestral to the Khoisan people exhibited this condition (Ill. 8.5). Steatopygia was recorded by travellers as early as the 16th century, and it has been noted and theorised on in the scientific literature since the latter part of the 18th century (Ill. 8.6, 8.7). Although many hypotheses about its significance have been proposed, few worthwhile studies have actually been made on the condition. Another myth that is noted in publications even to this day is that steatopygia is associated with an accentuated forward curvature of the lumbar spine, or lumbar lordosis. However, our X-ray studies have shown that no lordosis is present: in fact, the lumbar curvature is even somewhat less than that observed in some other populations. Another common belief is that steatopygia is found in males. I believe that this is not true except in possibly abnormal conditions. For example, I noted it in one San male who also had gynaecomastia, or enlargement of the breasts; he probably had an endocrine anomaly. Generally speaking, Bushman males have well-developed gluteal (buttock) muscles, probably resulting from their hunting activities. When a male has a prominent, muscular rump and stands in the typical, normal extended-hip posture (see below) with his belly pushed forward, he may give the impression of having steatopygia, but this is purely in the eye of the beholder.

Most of the surface of our bodies has an underlying blanket of fat that provides insulation, protection from injury, serves as a caloric reservoir and, under appropriate hormonal control, assumes contours of high value as sexual stimuli. This fat forms a distinctive layer that can be measured by various techniques, including calipers and radiographs, and its structure can be assayed by chemical means. It is well recognised that fat tends to accumulate in certain parts of the body more than in others; these "storage depots" are found in such places as the abdominal wall, hips, arms and inner thighs of both sexes, and in the female breasts (more than in those of males). Increasing fatness may contribute to ageing, but it is not necessarily a response to advancing age. The fat pattern, or relative thickness of fat on different parts of the body, in older individuals appears to differ from that in younger adults. When fat additions occur with age, certain sites are favoured, and the old adage that "men run to belly . . ." holds true. Generally speaking women carry more fat on, and less in, their smaller frames than men. Twin studies have shown that fat deposition and growth patterns are to a larger extent determined by the genetic constitution than by purely environmental factors.

Steatopygia is rarely manifest prior to puberty, whereafter it progresses gradually (Ill. 8.4, 8.8). The localisation seems more obvious in older women, especially if they have lost subcutaneous fat elsewhere. It has been suggested that the degree of fatty accumulation over the buttocks bears a direct relationship to the availability or the scarcity of food, the buttocks developing to a great size during plentiful periods and rapidly diminishing during lean ones. This is not confirmed by our observations, but controlled experiments with quantitative analyses are required to corroborate this. Nevertheless, we observed that when women lose weight rapidly, as in tuberculosis, the steatopygous deposit is the last to go. Among the Khoikhoi women a fat bottom is considered a sign of good health.

Despite the interest in steatopygia by European scientists recorded over a period of 150 years, only three autopsy dissections have been done, and in these records virtually nothing was added to our knowledge. The third dissection, in 1924, made almost a century after the first, was performed on the putrefied body of a Bushman woman sent from South West Africa to Vienna in a pork barrel, the voyage lasting four months! Little was left for study.

8.5 Rock painting showing numerous females with steatopygia. The painting is at Camp Siding, Tylden, Cape Province.

Our X-ray studies confirm our impression that the fat is lumped more above the level of the sacrum, over the upper part of the gluteal muscles, than below the sacrum. In other populations fat is usually deposited over the upper border of the hip bones and in the fold or crease below the bottom where it meets the thigh. The steatopygous deposit is not flabby (or "jelly-like", as described by early travellers), but of a softish, rubbery consistency and typically shelf-like, projecting rather straight back from the lower part of the back and tending to be angulated at the apex, or furthest point (Ill. 8.4 and 8.8). In older women the whole mass tends to sag and become underslung, as it were, which is the result of a general loss of elasticity of the supporting tissues. The fibro-fatty mass is strongly attached to the upper, outer ends of the femurs, or thigh bones.

Our studies on the chemical composition of the deposit demonstrated that between pre- and post-menopausal females there were no differences in any of the major fatty acids. This suggests that the female sex hormone, oestrogen, has no apparent influence on the composition of the deposit. Between males and females

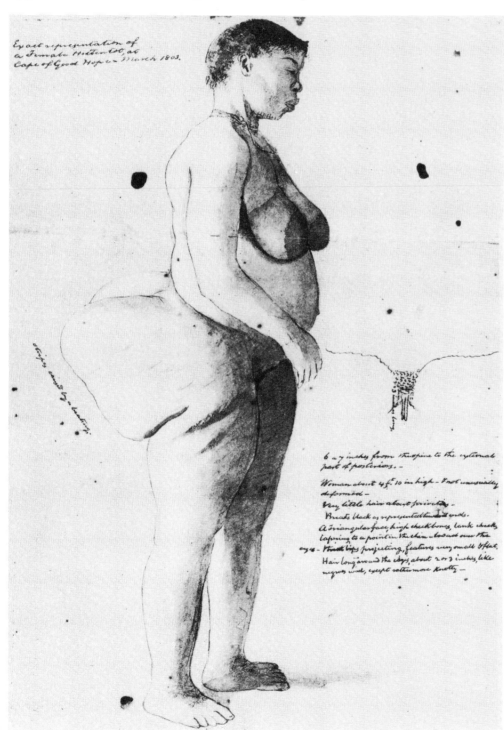

8.6 Sketch of a Khoikhoi woman with steatopygia, made in Cape Town in 1803. The notes specify her height as 4 feet 10 inches (147,3 cm), the buttocks as projecting 6 to 7 inches (approx. 15 to 18 cm) from the spinal column. There are also details on hair, breasts, etc., with a sketch of the genitals and a note on the sparseness of the pubic hair.

8.7 The first accurate drawing to scale of steatopygia, executed by the famed French Captain of Engineers and architect, Louis Michel Thibault, in 1801. He resided at the Cape of Good Hope for some years from the 1790s onward. The watercolour drawing was presented to the East India Marine Society. Together with Ill. 8.6 and others, it is now in the Peabody Museum at Salem, Massachusetts.

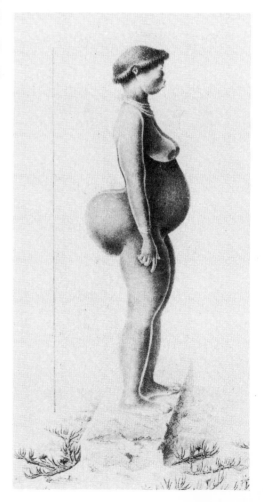

there are statistically significant differences in the fatty-acid composition of the buttocks region. However, these sex differences are no greater than those found in populations without steatopygia. This tends to disprove one possible view on steatopygia, namely that it results from a greater metabolic turnover in the steatopygous female: for if this view were correct, one would expect that male-female differences in a steatopygous population (like the San) would be greater than in a people lacking steatopygia. The facts do not support this inference. If then steatopygia does not reflect a greater metabolic turnover, involving fat, this may indicate that the deposit is not entirely fatty tissue: it may consist of a fair amount of fibrous connective tissue.

One may well ask: "Why do San and Khoikhoi women have this steatopygia?" The answer is simply that we don't know. In 1918 a Harvard professor suggested that the large buttocks may be a part of the Bushman woman's glamorous attraction, and that sexual selection maintained the phenomenon in the population. This idea of artificial selection was based on certain cultural characteristics of some African Negroid tribes. Among many Negroes, obesity was – and is – considered beautiful and a sign of strength. Girls of marriageable age sometimes go into "fattening houses", where they are put upon special diets in order to acquire corpulence – quite the reverse of their westernised sisters! Just a century ago, it was reported that the Somali chose their wives by arranging women in line, and by picking out the ones who project farthest to the rear. In a society where busts are always exposed and probably of little stimulation to males, this reported practice is probably no different in concept from the portrayals of exposed breasts in magazines and movies to excite the westernised male.

If steatopygia was maintained by sexual selection (and it is highly dubious that sexual selection has played a dominant role in human evolution over a long period), the cultural trait would seem to have disappeared, because our careful investigations failed to locate a preference by Bushman and Hottentot males for steatopygous females. However, the important biological consideration is the mode of origin (mutation) and physiological significance of the phenomenon, rather than its mode of maintenance. Its persistence over hundreds and probably thousands of years seems to indicate a natural selective advantage to the possessor. Its mode of inheritance is not yet clear.

Because male Bushmen do the hunting, they are more exposed to danger and are for this reason alone more liable to earlier death than women. There are no

8.8 Side view of a Bushman woman ("Anako"), showing extent and angulation of steatopygia. Note her small, flat face and the gaps between her hair spirals.

8.9 and **8.10** A position of squatting on the haunches with tightly flexed knees and thighs, the bottom just off the ground, can be maintained effortlessly for long periods. Bushmen squatting in the central Kalahari.

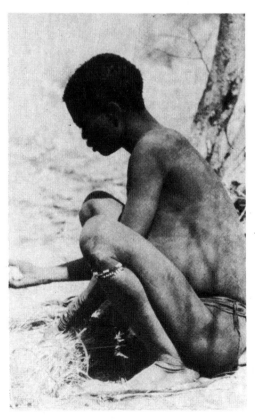

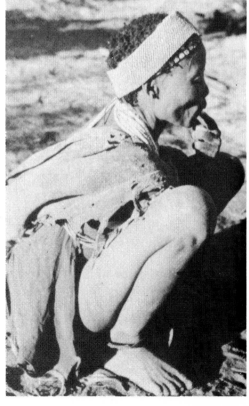

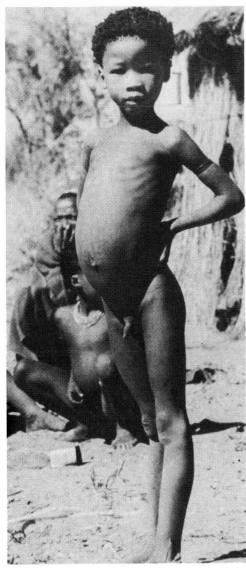

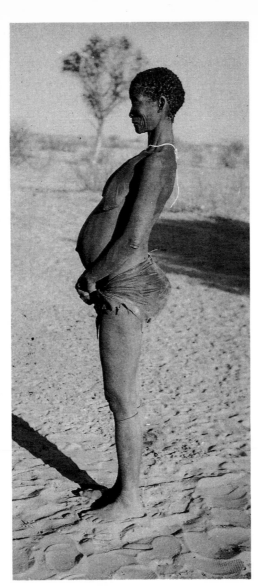

8.11 Young !Kung Bushman boy in "African physiological stance". Note the squatting posture of the boy behind him.

8.12 A Nharo lady in the Ghanzi district of north-western Botswana. She stands in the "African physiological stance": the belly is protuberant, the steatopygia moderate, the knees and hips almost hyper-extended.

adequate statistics on longevity among male and female San, but among the Khoikhoi we found that women tend to outlive males. About whether or not their fat deposits are of survival value under severe nutritional stress, one cannot yet venture an opinion, but it is interesting that steatopygia occurs in a higher percentage of post-menopausal Khoikhoi women than of women in their 'thirties and 'forties. It may just be that in simple societies, uncomplicated by the stresses of urbanisation and advanced technology, fat plays a role in survival, rather than being a contributing factor to early death as in complex, highly competitive societies.

Steatopygia is not evenly distributed among San groups. For example, during an investigation in 1952, prominent buttocks were rarely observed among about 700 fairly well-nourished females in the Kavango region of South West Africa.

There is also something special about the fact that although steatopygia is expressed in females, the incidence among the Cape Coloured is very low (this is a population of a couple of millions that has in the course of about 300 years "hybridised" essentially from Khoikhoi and White gene pools). Why is such a dominant physical feature that has survived for so long suddenly lost within a few generations after this admixture?

Reference has been made above to the apparent forward curvature of the lumbar spine, not only in steatopygous women, but also in other women, men and children. This impression is gained because of at least two major characteristics. Among the San, many Khoikhoi and tribal southern Negroes, we have observed two positions of "rest". A position of squatting on the haunches with tightly flexed knees and thighs, the bottom just off the ground, can be maintained effortlessly for long periods. The second position is a stance where the knees and hips are almost hyper-extended (Ill. 8.4 and 8.11). In the latter position, which I call the "African physiological stance, or position of rest", and when the belly is protuberant, compensatory positioning of the trunk produces the *effect* of an accentuated lumbar curvature (Ill. 8.12). Couple this with steatopygia or developed gluteal muscles, and one can understand how the eye mistakes the "curved" appearance of the lower back for a lordosis. These postures are adopted from early childhood onwards (Ill. 8.11).

Attempts have been made to correlate steatopygia with climate and with habits of hibernation and of aestivation, or dormancy during summer or the dry season. It has been ventured that localisation of the fat blanket in a single large storage depot allows the female to control heat loss better under physiological stress such as pregnancy. But one can find as many cons as pros for these (and other) arguments, especially in the absence of any controlled experiments. Some of these speculations are based on theoretical comparisons with fat-tailed mouse lemurs that subsist on their fat during hibernation, and also with fat-tailed sheep, fat-rumped sheep, humped cattle and humped camels. However, most of these comparisons are really romanticisms without factual bases.

At the turn of the century a theory was outlined that survived many generations of textbooks. In parts of Europe, statuettes were found in association with the upper Palaeolithic Aurignacian culture and with skeletal remains often referred to as those of Cro-Magnon Man, in caves decorated by engravings and paintings. Some of these statuettes were carvings of fat nude women, the most famous being the Venus of Willendorf, on the left bank of the Danube near Krems (Ill. 8.13). Others were discovered in Belgium, Moravia and southern European areas. Carvings on the walls of caves were found also at Laussel in France. It was believed that these figurines closely resembled steatopygous Bushman females. This belief was linked with the rock art and with the fact that some of the early European skeletons were reputed to resemble Bushmen, especially those said to belong to the Grimaldi race found at Menton, on the Mediterranean coast of southern France. It was thus concluded that during Aurignacian times there existed at least two races in Europe, one of which was closely allied to the Bushmen, and that modern Bushmen are migrant descendants of these Cro-Magnons. Irrespective of the arguments against the validity of this theory, the Aurignacian figurines are not steatopygous, but just generally hyper-obese women!

8.13 Sketch of an Aurignacian figurine, the Venus of Willendorf. Carved in oolitic limestone, and originally painted with red ochre, it is 11 cm in height and comes from Willendorf on the Danube.

The tablier or "Hottentot apron"

Another unusual characteristic found among San women, and to a greater extent again among Khoikhoi, is the "Hottentot apron" or tablier, the elongated or hypertrophied labia minora, also called longinymph and macronymphae. At puberty, or shortly after, a significant proportion of girls display an enlargement of the labia minora, which commence to extend beyond the outer labia majora. They do not undergo turgescence (swelling) during menstruation or intercourse, but during childbirth they swell considerably, become painful and remain swollen for about ten days after parturition. With each pregnancy they increase in length, up to as much as 10 cm, or 4 inches. Again, as in steatopygia, no histological or other examination has yet been done on these tissues, and no good reason can be ascribed to the presence of this anatomical "peculiarity" – which, of course, is quite normal for Khoisan females. There is no absolute correlation between the presence or absence of the tablier and the presence or absence of steatopygia.

Although one small study reports the presence of the tablier in some southern Negro women in a Johannesburg hospital, elongation of the labia is not a common trait among Negro women. The significance of this unusual observation among a small group is yet to be assessed as the report indicates that the tablier is no longer than about 2 cm. However, it is not surprising that a small percentage of Negro females in South Africa or South West Africa do display some degree of labial elongation. Already in 1719 the remarkable Peter Kolb quoted Thévenot to prove that the tablier was found also among Negro and Egyptian women, while in 1911 Shrubsall wrote: "I am assured in the most explicit manner that in the Transvaal, among the Ba-Klangwe – one of the various Thonga clans living along the East Coast – not only are the women longinymph, but that an *intombi*, or maid, not possessing these appendages would be repudiated as a wife, and the *lobola* or purchase money returned.'' A century ago it was reported that even before the 16th century this phenomenon was known: ''Negro and Abyssinian women are so much incommodated by it that it is found necessary to remove these excrescences by the use of the knife or by cauterisation''.

Another myth to be buried is that the elongated labia are produced by artificial means – stretching by hand or with weights or other mechanisms. There is not a shred of evidence that artificial genital deformation is practised either by the San or by the Khoikhoi. The phenomenon is a genetic trait acted on by unknown (possibly endocrine) factors at puberty and exacerbated by childbirth.

Blood groups and other genetic characters

During the past twenty-five years many studies have been carried out on the blood chemistry of San and other African indigenes. These have greatly clarified the genetic affinities of the populations and have provided us with new insights into their evolutionary patterns. In 1963 J. S. Weiner and I pointed out that Bushmen, Hottentots and South African Negro populations are very similar in nearly all the genetic characters we considered then: ''Bushmen and Hottentots . . . both share with the Bantu those genes which are characteristic of Negro Africa generally and that are not found outside Africa south of the Sahara to any significant extent.''

At the same time we should note that San and Khoikhoi diverge in some respects from Negroes. Thus they possess in common a number of features that are largely absent in Negro peoples. This is the justification on biological grounds for classifying them under the common term ''Khoisan''. The ''Khoisan'' characters include the relatively light skin colour, the occurrence of steatopygia, the relatively short stature, the occasional presence of an inner eye fold.

Recently information has been published about some other gene markers of haemoglobin and blood serum which seem unique to the San and serve to separate them genetically from even the closely related Khoikhoi. We must be wary, though, of reading too much into the presence or absence of a particular gene allele. A considerable amount of work is still required before we can piece together the mosaic of the San gene system and before we can draw far-reaching conclusions concerning their ancestry.

Health and nutrition

In a 1952 investigation of the health and nutrition of about 100 Heikum *(Hai//num)* and 1 250 !Kung Bushmen in the Okavango River region, some interesting information was obtained concerning their relationship to the environment.

Despite the high prevalence of tropical disease, the state of nutrition was reasonable. No obese Bushmen were seen, but women of childbearing age appeared to be fatter than men of comparable age. Anaemia was rare. Angina and sudden death from possible coronary heart disease was not unknown, but high blood pressures were not found. Respiratory diseases were quite common.

A protuberant abdomen was a common and striking feature, even in children, and their abdominal muscles were noted to be very lax (see also the remarks on the ''African physiological stance'' above).

About one in ten people had enlarged livers, but no explanation for this was elicited. It was found that the proportion of people with large livers increased, the greater the distance from the river. Half the !Kung Bushmen had enlarged spleens, which was almost certainly the result of malaria infection. In this case the proportion of large spleens decreased, the greater the distance of the groups from the Okavango River (the source of the malaria). Another cause of the splenomegaly was the presence of schistosomiasis, or bilharzia.

Trachoma was present in 12 per cent of 324 examined, and other eye diseases were prevalent. The teeth of the whole group were in poor condition.

Bushmen obtain excellent protein supplementation from their extensive use of wild vegetation. The use of pulp made from nuts and beans as a milk substitute in the post-weaning life of the infant avoids the serious protein malnutrition

8.14 A group of southern Kalahari San photographed in the 1930s. There is evidence that there has been an increase in the average height of the San since that time.

(kwashiorkor) which results from the use of maize *pap* in populations through the rest of Negro Africa (and elsewhere).

In another recent investigation on 105 !Kung Bushmen on the fringes of the Kalahari Desert in Botswana, 97 were found free of cardiac abnormalities. The 97 were examined and tested with the electrocardiogram: hypertension and ischaemic heart disease, so common in other societies, were found to be absent.

Silberbauer has observed that the diet of the /*gwi* Bushmen is predominantly vegetable, and even at the peak of their hunting activity meat does not make up more than 40 per cent of their intake. They are principally dependant on much the same food as are the game animals themselves, and their energy and activities through the seasons are closely related to those of the animals. When the animals are weak and in poor condition, the Bushmen are also listless and soon tire, and are therefore unable to take advantage of the poor condition of the animals to hunt them more easily and in greater numbers. At such times the bands break up into their constituent families of husband, wife and children, or extended families of a couple and their married daughter and her husband. The units live apart and come together when the food supply can support a greater population density.

Many of the cultural traits must affect the biology of the population. A hunter-gatherer economy requires virtually unrestricted use of large tracts of country. At least during historic times, the increasing encroachment of pastoralists, cultivators and settlers must have affected tribal and clan size, which contributed to changes in the ranges of the local and total gene pool. Naturally, increasing contact with different cultures threatened the survival of the Bushmen, resulting in numerous clashes, with loss of men and the absorption of women and men as slaves into the conquering groups.

Among the /gwi, girls marry at an early age, between their seventh and ninth

126

year, to a suitor about seven years older. There is a long probationary period, and if there is incompatibility the husband merely moves away and the marriage is annulled. Sexual intercourse commences only after the first couple of years of marriage, when the girl's breasts begin to develop. If she is slow to mature, the husband indicates his impatience, and he may take a widow or divorcee as a temporary concubine until his wife is old enough. Among other groups, marriage usually occurs only after puberty.

The average number of children born alive to a woman is three, spaced at intervals of from 4 to 6 years. There are few reliable figures on birth rates, abnormalities, abortions, etc. In the 1952 investigation in the Kavango region among the !Kung it was estimated that the neonatal death rate was 50 per cent. In a crude sense small, spaced families serve the economic needs of the small hunting

8.15 A Bushman mother feeds her baby on the breast for about four years – and even longer. A young mother at Sonop Koppies in the northern part of the central Kalahari.

127

8.16 A rare case of twins that have been allowed to survive – in a society that generally regards twin births as unlucky and perhaps as challenging the mother's supply of milk beyond its normal capacity. This mother and her twins, both happily feeding on the breast, were located by P. V. Tobias at Sonop Koppies in the Ghanzi district during the July 1959 expedition of the Kalahari Research Committee.

groups, who are not then restricted in movement by many pregnant women or by having to feed many mouths of small children who do not contribute to the economy.

The !Kung also limit their population by infanticide. A woman goes into the veld to give birth either alone or with her mother. If she decides not to keep the baby, it probably never breathes. A mother breast-feeds her baby for about four years (and even longer), and she is not considered to have enough milk to feed two infants simultaneously. Consequently it seems that the logic of survival is that, if another pregnancy occurs during this period, it must be sacrificed: one child can survive, but both would die if they had to be breast-fed.

Hunter-gatherers are always on the move. A journey of 100 to 160 km (about 60 to 100 miles) is not unusual. A child of about seven is expected to walk about 25 km (15 miles) per day along with the adults, and needs strong legs and stamina.

A really difficult childbirth may mean the death of both the mother and child. If a woman dies during or shortly after birth, some other woman may suckle and rear the child, but more often than not the child is buried alive with its mother, especially among the more isolated, or "wilder", bands. Twin births are said to be very rare. Among the Auen and Heikum (Hai//num) one of the twins is invariably killed by being buried alive by the mother or one of her attendants immediately after birth. If the children are of opposite sexes, it is always the boy who is killed in this way. Among the !Kung, both are buried alive at birth, for it is believed that they bring ill-luck on the parents. It is obvious that such practices, over long periods of time, will tend to rid populations of twin-producing genes, explaining why twinning is as rare as it is now.

Abortion is known to have been induced by treading on the body of a pregnant woman, and it appears to have been practised mainly on unmarried women.

After a child is born, the umbilical cord is not tied, but cut with a knife or with the sharp edge of a reed. If there is much bleeding, a plaster of mud and leaves is

128

placed on the baby's abdomen – which could, of course, serve as a good source of infection and ultimately death.

Bodily mutilations are recognised in populations throughout the world. Even in "civilised" societies, women pierce their ears, for example, to be able to wear beautifying objects. Throughout Africa numerous practices were, and still are, known. Artificial deformation, such as the filing and chipping of teeth, the removal of teeth and body scarification, is well known. Bushmen still practice the latter, and sometimes, though very seldom, sever a finger joint, as a rule that of one of the little fingers. Although earlier writers noted it in some men and women, as well as in children, it is not universally found. The joint is removed during childhood. There have been various explanations for the custom. One informant stated that the joint is cut off with a reed before the child sucks at all, and that the motive underlying the custom is that the child should live to grow up: a form of Spartanism? Other writers add that the operation is performed only on a child whose predecessor has died young, and is intended to protect it from a similar fate. Naturally infection may have taken its toll here too.

In the light of these and other customs, as well as of the high infant mortality caused by natural hardships and the strenuous conditions of San life, relatively few children survive and families are thus small. In the over-all picture, the balance of natural selection has probably, despite high mortality rates, favoured the survival of such small groups in a hunter-gatherer economy.

Another factor limiting the number of children born to a population is the length of the reproductive life of adults. Bushmen are known to age rapidly and not many reach an age of more than 45 to 50 years.

Marriage customs aid in multiplying the genes and increasing the variability of the gene pools. Although monogamy is the general rule, polygamy is not forbidden. Among the northern tribes marriage is forbidden within the band, so that a man must seek his bride from another band. Widows generally remarry, and the second husband is responsible for his new wife's children. Brothers and sisters must avoid each other's company when grown up, as must mother-in-law and son-in-law.

Tied intimately into the biology of the modern populations are the important data derived from careful, controlled excavations of occupation sites of the past 50 000 years such as are being conducted in the Cape Province by R. Klein, H. Deacon, R. Singer and A. Wymer. These are to be correlated with R. J. Mason's excavations in the Transvaal, so that eventually reasonable extrapolations may be made between living and fossil populations. In a sense, we are trying to un-scramble an omelette: we have sorted out some of the ingredients, but it is more difficult to analyse the timing and sequence of the constituent unions. Towards this, the data from many disciplines – archaeology, palaeontology, ecology, serology and chemistry, genetics, etc. – are needed. We have fitted together some of the pieces of the biology of the San and related indigenous populations, but there are still more gaps in our knowledge than solid facts.

The data obtained by the author and studies referred to in this chapter were supported by grants from the United States Public Health Service (GM 10, 113); the United States National Science Foundation for Anthropological Research; the Boise Fund of Oxford University, U.K.; and the Abbott Fund of the University of Chicago.

9
Early Socialization in the !xõ Bushmen

Irenäus Eibl-Eibesfeldt

In recent times several theories concerning the behaviour of hunters and gatherers have been advanced:

1 Hunters and gatherers live in open, fluctuating societies and are not territorial; one author even spoke of a nomadic style of life as being the original pattern of man.

2 Hunters and gatherers exhibit a peaceful nature.

3 They are permissive in their education and therefore children do not experience frustration. (According to W. Schmidbauer, "the much discussed anti-authoritarian education" of our times reveals itself to be in part a return to palaeolithic practices.)

4 Since hunters and gatherers are allegedly non-aggressive, it was concluded that this accords with the nature of man, since man after all lived for the greater part of his development at this economic level. Competitiveness, territoriality, possessiveness and aggressiveness came with the Agricultural Revolution, reaching their climax in the modern industrial societies.

More or less explicit statements of this nature can be found in the writings of many authorities (such as H. Helmut, M. D. Sahlins, R. B. Lee, H. V. Vallois and J. Woodburn). To back these statements, recent observations were quoted, in particular on Bushmen and Hadza. H. J. Heinz and I have discussed the subject and presented evidence for Bushman territoriality. This was based on personal observations, as well as on the older literature. Indeed, only the gross neglect of earlier researches, coupled with observations on strongly acculturated (pacified) groups, could have led to such unbalanced views. It seems as if research strategies were guided by wishful thinking as to what the nature of man should be like!

As to the peaceful nature of the Bushmen, it was found that the cultural ideal is a peaceful one indeed. However, it is achieved by a process of education.

During four visits to the !xo Bushmen near Takatswane and one visit to the !Kung in South West Africa, I had the opportunity to document unstaged social interactions by film and to observe and analyse the patterns of interaction in detail. This Bushman documentation project is still in progress. About fifty film units have been published in the Film Archive for Human Ethology of the Max Planck Society. The project is conducted by H. J. Heinz and the author. It is my great pleasure to thank my friend Heinz for introducing me to the Bushman group where he has worked for fourteen years. A summary of my observations on early patterns of aggression and their socialization is presented here.

Early manifestations of aggressive behaviour

Already at an age of one year, Bushman babies show remarkably adaptive patterns of physical aggression. Aggressive acts are released by a few standard situations.

Robbing objects: If another child is in possession of an object which a baby desires, the baby tries to grasp it, often slapping, scratching or pushing the other child over. Robbing the other of an object is one of the very basic interactions between children. Indeed, I have found this to be a universal trait.

Defence of objects: When a child tries to grasp an object in the possession of another, the object is defended and often retaliation occurs. The unsuccessful robber is pushed over, scratched or slapped. Pushing, scratching and directing at the opponent blows from above are the first functional patterns of fighting to occur (Ill. 9.1, a-f).

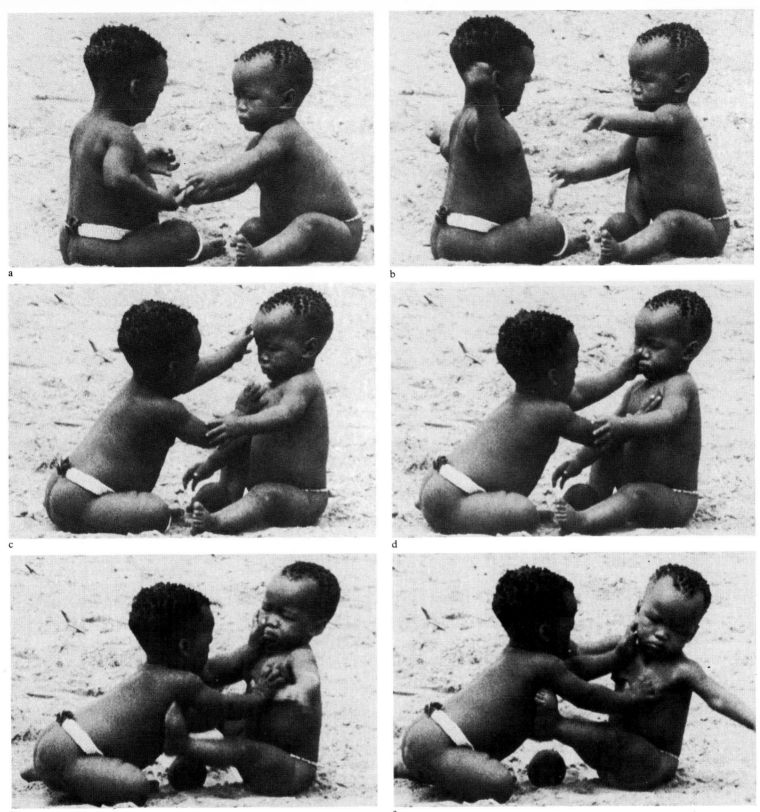

a b c d e f

Defence of a place: A baby of approximately one year of age starts to defend the place where it plays, as well as the place at its mother's breast. Between siblings sharp rivalries can be observed. South of Tsumkwe I filmed a !Kung mother with two sons. One was approximately a year, the other 3½ to 4 years old. The baby defended its place at its mother's breast, directing kicks and throwing objects at the other (Ill. 9.2, a and b). The older brother tried to scratch and hit his younger brother (Ill. 9.3, a-c) and if there was an opportunity he took away his toys, often just to tease him, since he threw the robbed objects away. The more intolerant was the younger one, who really frustrated his older brother. The older one often cried in fury and despair, since the mother prevented any retaliation.

9.1 a-f: Attempt to rob another child of an object and defence of the object. The actors are a !xõ Bushman boy, age 11 months, and a girl (right), approximately 8-9 months. The girl attempts to grasp the object which the boy (left) holds. The boy withdraws the object and then attacks in turn, pushing the girl over and scratching her. *(From a 16 mm film taken by the author)*

131

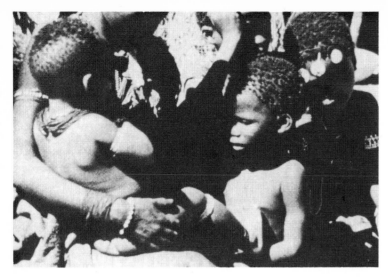

9.2 Sibling rivalry between two !Kung boys. The younger, approximately 10 months of age, kicks the older brother, 3½-4 years. The child defends its mother as its most important possession. This bond is probably the oldest, most highly valued property of man. If anyone interferes and threatens the bond between two individuals, aggressive behaviour is aroused, and jealousy as the subjective correlate. Our cross-cultural studies show this to be a universal phenomenon. *(From a 16 mm film taken by the author)*

Sometimes a mother, when fondling another mother's baby, puts the baby on the breast. If her own child is older, it tolerates this, but demonstrates by its behaviour that it is the "owner" (Ill. 9.4, a-c).

Reaction to strangers (fear of and hostility towards strangers) : At an age of eight to ten months Bushman children show a pronounced fear of strangers. They turn away and run toward their mother when approached, sometimes even when looked at or spoken to. Often they start to cry (Ill. 9.5, a-c). With increasing age the reaction to strangers changes in quality. Instead of fleeing, the child attacks on the approach of a stranger, especially if his reference person (for example, his father) is close (Ill. 9.6, a and b).

This xenophobia is found universally and does not necessarily stem from unpleasant experiences with strangers. At a certain age, due to a process of maturation, children respond to some signals of their fellow men with fear. Personal acquaintance blocks the fear-releasing value of these signals, but not completely. An ambivalence of approach and withdrawal responses characterizes man's reactions even towards familiar persons. Amongst others the eyes are perceived with ambivalence. A stare is threatening. On the other hand, one has to look at a companion in order to document readiness for contact. The conflict is solved by interspersed cut-offs, which can be observed in any conversation. On this basic disposition rests our inclination to live in closed, individualized groups and to reject strangers. This reaction towards strangers seems to be a basic inborn human characteristic. The human "enemy pattern" of thinking (strange = enemy, familiar = friend) seems to be rooted in this disposition.

Unprovoked playful aggression : It is a fairly common sight to see a Bushman baby running around with a stick in one hand beating playmates and adults. Since I have never observed that babies were instructed to do this, and since the same stereotyped pattern of beating with an object has been reported in chimpanzees, it could be an inborn response. This response is universal.

Aggression control and early socialization
The reaction of older children and adults to the types of aggressive interactions just described differs according to the situation. Robbing of objects is not tolerated. The most common reaction is to separate the fighting babies by removing them. A baby or toddler is rarely slapped. Verbal admonishing and cursing, however, are fairly common. If an older sibling takes an object from her baby sibling, then the mother will take the object and return it to the smaller child.

Rivalry between siblings is carefully watched by the mother, whose main concern is to keep the rivals apart, for example, by forming a barrier with her hand between them. According to our standards, she often acts unjustly, since she clearly favours the younger child, being more protective towards it. If the younger, however, intends to throw an object at his sibling rival, then the mother

132

intervenes by taking the object and initiating a game with it (Ill. 9.7, a-f). Distraction is a favourite means of educating young children.

The parents' reaction towards the baby's response to strangers is remarkable in several ways. First of all the baby is comforted. Indeed, the mother or father utters friendly words, even about the stranger. But the behaviour is clearly ambivalent. Babies are often teased by verbally reinforcing the fear of strangers ("He will take you away!"). In addition, real threats using the stranger to scare the child are made as a means to discipline the child. This follows the pattern: If you do not do this, or if you continue to behave like this, then the stranger will come and take you away. Again it is fascinating to see that the enemy pattern is universally used in the education of children. I have observed it in Waika Indians, Papuans and Balinese, as well as Europeans. This certainly serves to reinforce the existing stranger avoidance pattern.

Playful aggression is tolerated and even reinforced by laughter. Very often one sees a small boy of one year of age hitting with a branch his father or elder siblings (Ill. 9.8). The bystanders as well as the "victim" laugh and the small child exhibits the expression of "relaxed, open-mouth face", uttering rhythmical gasping sounds. Older children sometimes resent being attacked. They take the stick away and may show intentions to punish the child physically, but they are generally strongly inhibited.

When a boy has reached the age of two, however, his beatings are no longer

9.3 (top row) : Sibling rivalry. The actors are the same as in Ill. 9.2. The older brother attempts to scratch the younger. The mother intervenes with her hand, holding him back. Thus frustrated, he starts to cry. (From a 16 mm film taken by the author)

9.4 (centre row): A !xõ woman nurses a baby of another mother. Her son watches, then grasps the other breast and drinks too, thus demonstrating ownership. (From a 16 mm film taken by the author)

9.5 (bottom row) : Reaction to strangers: Fear of a stranger in a boy of 10-11 months.

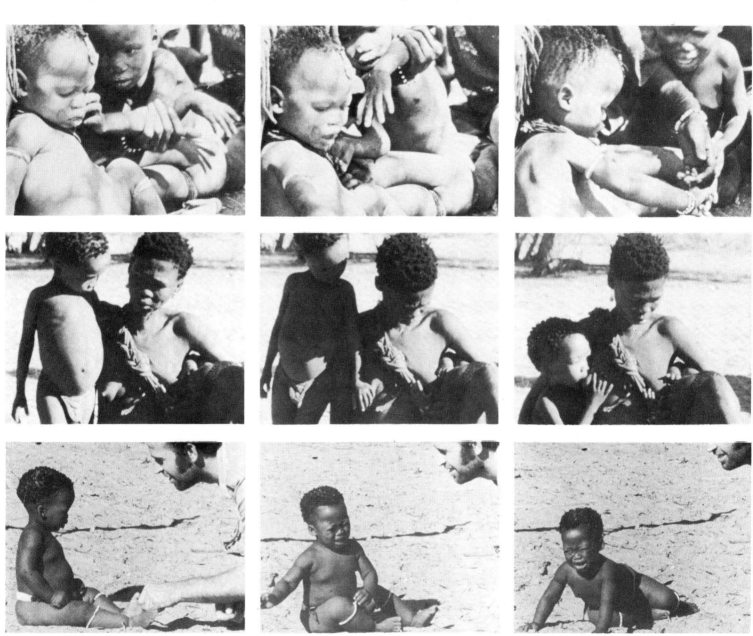

133

9.6 Repulsion of a stranger by the same boy, one year later; he threatens the stranger with a raised arm, hitting towards him. *(From a 16 mm film taken by the author)*

tolerated. Even his father will admonish him. At this age, aggression ceases to be reinforced by tolerance. I have not observed thus far any incitement to aggression from elder playmates or adults. Not even revenge for an insult is encouraged by the group. This is in total contrast to other ethnic groups. Waika Indians, for example, regularly incite their children to act aggressively and to respond with a counter-attack if hurt by somebody. Even very small children are taught to take revenge, the offender sometimes being held.

Aggression and its control in the play groups of children

Within the play groups of children, aggressive interactions can frequently be observed (Ill. 9.9). Children rob each other of melons, they tease each other, wrestle, slap each other, etc. Although many of these acts can be classified as playful, by the fact that no spacing, subordination or cut-off behaviour results, in a fair number of cases the interaction ends with the withdrawal of one partner or with clear submission and crying. For example, in one play session of 191 minutes I observed 166 aggressive acts (slapping, kicking, spitting, throwing sand and the like). In 10 cases one party, as a result of the interaction, started to cry and

9.7 Sibling rivalry in the !Kung Bushmen. (The participants are the same as in Ill. 9.2 and 9.3.) The younger in the foreground threatens his older brother with a stone (a). The mother intervenes by inviting him to give her the stone, to which he agrees (b). She shows him how to play with it on the ground (c) and the boy imitates her (d) and afterwards invites his mother, in turn, by offering her the stone (e). He gets it back shortly after and continues to play (f). *(Since the film was taken with a mirror lens, the photographs show a mirror image. From a 16 mm film taken by the author.)*

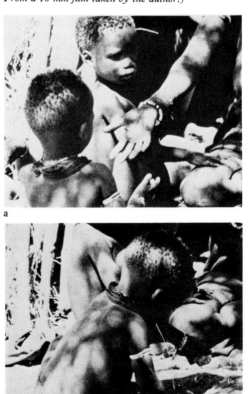

a   b   c

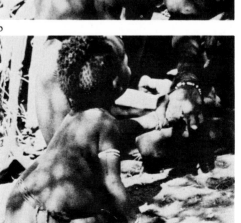

d   e   f

withdrew. Some expressive movements are found to be universal, for example, the threat stare and the pattern of submission by lowering the head, cutting off eye contact and pouting (Ill. 9.10).

Conflicts are solved within the play groups, mostly without interference from adults. Often older children intervene, comfort the insulted and punish the attacker verbally and physically. In the !xo group it was observed that the oldest girl dominated the group, initiating games and intervening when the harmony of the group was endangered by aggression from younger playmates. She herself put up aggressive displays, particularly in the mornings, when she joined the group of children already playing. She would kick the melon ball out of the hand of a playing child. In my interpretation, this demonstrative aggression served to keep her high-ranking position, a prerequisite for her power to control and subdue the aggression of others.

Within the play groups, children collect experiences with aggression and learn to control it. Older children at the same time instruct the younger in group games, in particular numerous dancing games, by which the group is bonded. Other rituals that counteract aggression are those of sharing. It is no exaggeration to say that the socialization of the older child takes place in the play group.

The role of punishment in education

We have mentioned that older children punish playmates for aggressive misconduct. They also occasionally punish a child who does not join in a collective game or disrupts its flow by unskilled behaviour. In general, to be laughed at, ridiculed and mocked by the group exerts enough conformity pressure and acts as a very effective educational device. Such interventions are seen fairly often.

I rarely saw adult persons punishing children. They scold them for misconduct, but physical punishment is rare. However, I did observe a few instances. Once a little girl of approximately seven refused to follow her mother into the field. The mother cursed and dragged the child roughly along the ground by one hand. But since the girl just did not want to come with her, she left her behind. After a while the father of the girl arrived and started cursing and pulling her by one arm, as the mother had done. Now the girl finally got up and poutingly followed her mother.

On another occasion a little girl of four years of age defaecated in the vicinity of a hut. Her little brother followed her and took a mouthful. Mother and grand-

9.8 Playful aggression in a !xõ boy approximately 11 months of age. The "playface expression" (relaxed, open-mouth display) is a universal pattern of expression for which homologies in infrahuman primates can be traced. (*Photograph by the author*)

135

9.9 Two examples of aggressive interactions in !xõ children. (a) Girl throwing a stick at a boy. (b) Girl directing a threat-stare at another girl (left). *(From a 16 mm film taken by the author)*

9.10 Pouting: !xõ girl, with down-turned head, eye-contact cut off and pouting of the lips. *(From a 16 mm film taken by the author)*

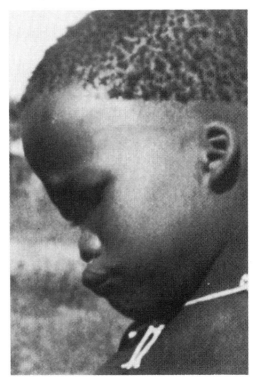

mother rushed to the rescue and, while cleaning the baby's mouth, both scolded the girl; the mother slapped the girl for not looking after her brother and a few moments later the grandmother slapped her too.

When another girl robbed a morsel from a small boy, a man approached, took the morsel away, slapped her and returned it to the boy. When a small boy followed another boy, threatening him with one of our glass bottles, several adults started to shout. One took the bottle away and slapped the offender.

Once a boy of six years robbed a baby girl of a biscuit we had given her. Two older boys pursued and beat him, whereupon the offender withdrew into a hut. After about five minutes he appeared again. Seeing him, the mother of the baby girl rushed at him, caught him, broke a twig from a nearby bush and beat him until he managed to escape. It was the only time that I witnessed real beating and not just a few slappings.

On another occasion, I heard of a girl of about fifteen years of age who was heavily beaten by her father and her elder sister for having intercourse with too many different boys. Although the Bushmen are fairly liberal in sexual matters, open promiscuity is not tolerated. This severe punishment did indeed inhibit the girl's sexual activity.

In sum, the proposition that man in his original state is devoid of aggression does not hold up to close examination. Among the Bushmen, as among other peoples investigated, the study of ontogeny, or individual development, reveals that aggressive acts develop in a functional way without apparent instruction.

136

10
The Languages of the Bushmen

Anthony Traill

The languages of the Bushmen have been classified traditionally as members of the Khoisan language family. Their linguistic relatives would therefore include various Hottentot languages, such as *Nama* (spoken in South West Africa and western Botswana), *!ora* (Korana, now almost extinct), *Xri* or *Xiri* (Griqua, also almost extinct), two languages about which we know very little, namely *Sandawe* and *Hadza* of Tanzania, and *Kwadi*, a recently discovered language of Angola, apparently spoken by only three people!

What are the languages of the Bushmen like?
Our knowledge of the languages of the Bushmen, past and present, is mostly very incomplete and is based on extremely sketchy and inadequate accounts. Everything we know about the extinct Bushman language of Lesotho, for instance, is contained in a four-page list of vocabulary and some twenty phrases. Clicks are not represented at all in the orthography used! In other cases strange prejudices seem to affect the judgement of the observer: the person who felt that the speech of the Bushmen was reminiscent more of the barks and grunts of baboons than of true language could hardly be expected to write a decent grammar for the Bushman language. At a more sophisticated level one finds claims about the mind of the Bushman, its needs and the effect of these on his language: a Bushman doesn't need abstract nouns or complex sentences (it is said by some) because his thinking is concrete and simple! Yet our studies have shown that Bushman languages do have complex sentences. Or (others assert) he needs well-developed tenses and moods: these are characteristic of all "savage" languages. At the same time another investigator will report of the Bushman language he is studying that it has no distinctions of tense and mood!

What we can be sure about, however, is the amazing linguistic diversity amongst these languages. We shall examine some of these features directly, but before doing so we must explore the feature most commonly associated with the Bushman languages, namely the extensive use that is made of the click consonants.

Some aspects of phonetic structure

Those clicks
The Bushman and Hottentot languages are not unique in the linguistic use of clicks. Both Zulu and Xhosa make fairly wide use of these sounds, while Southern Sotho and Swati employ them to a marginal extent. But the clicks in these Bantu languages were borrowed from Hottentot and Bushman languages and are definitely not original Bantu stock. So the Bushmen and Hottentots can claim a linguistic "first" in this respect: they are the original click users, and this makes them a subject of intense interest to phoneticians and linguists. In addition to clicks, these languages have many other complexities of pronunciation involving both consonants and vowels.

Six distinct clicks have been reported, but the maximum number found in any one language is five. It is virtually impossible to convey in simple terms what these sounds are like, so we shall have to use diagrams to assist us. In Ill. 10.1 are three diagrams showing sections through the mouth and throat. Clearly shown are the palate, the tongue, upper and lower teeth and lips. The section profiles represent three distinct positions of the speech organs for the production of the various clicks.

10.1 The Bushman languages are marked by a variety of clicks. In order to produce different clicks, the relative positions of the lips, the tongue and the palate must be varied. In each diagram two points, A and B, are shown. Clicks are produced by rarefying the air trapped between the points A and B. This is achieved by hollowing the body of the tongue. Point B is the same in each case: the back of the tongue is applied to the soft palate. However, point A is made to vary in order to produce different forms of click. In the first diagram, A is where the two lips are in contact; in the second figure, the position of A is achieved by the tip of the tongue being placed against the palate immediately behind the upper front teeth; in the third, A is where the tip of the tongue is applied to the hard palate where it rises sharply to form the roof of the mouth.

Clicks are produced by rarefying the air trapped between the two points A and B. This is achieved by hollowing the body of the tongue. The point B is articulated with the back of the tongue on the soft palate in all three positions.

In (a) the front position is effected by bringing the two lips into contact; this gives the *bilabial click*, written ⊙. Its sound-effect is very much like that of a kiss. This click is found only in the so-called Southern languages.

Position A in (b) is brought about by placing the tip of the tongue against the part of the palate immediately behind the upper teeth. Three distinct clicks are produced at this point: the clicks written as /, ≠ and //. They differ as follows: / has suction reminiscent of cleaning one's upper teeth by sucking air through them (this click is written in comics as *tsk!*) ; ≠ has no suction at all and has a sharp flat sound; // is made by sucking air in laterally along the molar teeth and resembles / in having friction. It is the noise one uses to spur on a horse.

Point A in (c) is articulated by the tip of the tongue against the hard palate at the point where it rises sharply to the roof of the mouth. The two clicks produced here are written ! and ///. While ! is described as having a sharp "popping" sound, /// creates the effect of suction or scraping. This latter click is not common.

All the Khoisan languages have the four clicks /, //, ≠ and !, whilst the Southern ones have ⊙ in addition. Each click has a number of distinctive accompaniments (referred to as the *effluxes* of the click), and these yield between 20 and 85 distinct click segments for different languages. The data in Table 1 use / to illustrate some of the effluxes found in *!xõ*, a Southern language of Botswana.

10.2 The variety of Bushman languages is immense and the maximum range of human vocal possibilities is exploited to the full.

Efflux	!xõ word	English
plain	/a	go
voiced	/gã	work (vb)
nasal	/na	see
fricative	/xã	dance (vb)
ejected	/kʔa	hand (n)
aspirated	/ʰa	build
prevoiced	g/ʰu	tail
glottal	/ʔã	fire
preglottal and nasal	ʔ/ŋa	suit (vb)

Table 1 Some !xõ click effluxes

Some of these effluxes combine on a single click, yielding a system that is staggering in its phonetic complexity. Different effluxes have been reported for *!xũ*, but it seems that no language exceeds the phonetic complexity of !xõ. A language like Nama, for instance, has only four clicks and five effluxes, yielding a much simpler system of only 20 click variants. Other Central languages, however, show slightly greater complexity than this.

Well over 70 per cent of words in Bushman languages begin with a click consonant. Although we lack precise figures for most of these languages, this figure is undoubtedly much higher for many of them. It is of great interest to note, however, that the grammatical particles in the language are clickless. Since these particles occur very frequently in all sentences, their effect is to "dilute" slightly the number of clicks in any sentence.

Vowel colourings

The vowels of these languages are also notable for their complex colourings. It is undoubtedly these vowel quantities to which early observers reacted so strongly, talking of "ghastly aspiration" or "strange croaking sounds". Not all languages exploit these vowel qualities as fully as some. Again !xõ illustrates what is probably the greatest complexity of these phenomena (Table 2).

Vowel colouring	*!xõ word*	*English*
plain	ka	"to"
nasalised	kã	relative pronoun
breathy	ka^h	"cheat"
pressed	qa̰	"yesterday"

Table 2 The various vowel colourings in !xõ. They may combine with each other to produce seven vowel colours for each of the five vowels.

Nama and !ora distinguish only plain and nasalised vowels. On the other hand, /gwi, also a "Hottentot" language, has plain, nasalised and pressed vowels. It is not clear what these discrepancies in phonetic complexity between the members of the Central group might mean.

Tone languages

As an additional feature, all of these languages are *tone languages*. That means roughly that different words may have identical vowels and consonants but be distinguished by their tone alone. In !xõ, for example, *ka* with a low tone is the mark of the passive voice, while *ka* with a higher tone marks conditionality; *u*^h with a low tone means "they", while with a slightly higher tone it means "you" (plural). In Nharo *te* with a low tone means "me", with a higher tone "to come up". In !xũ, successively lowering the tone on the word *!xo* will change the meaning from "unlucky" to "elephant" to "pipe".

Phonetic complexity

From the phonetic point of view, these are *the world's most complex languages*. To speak one of them fluently is to exploit human phonetic ability to the full. We have no idea how this complexity arose, and it is unlikely that we shall ever know. Speculation that these languages are phonetically complex *because* they are primitive is in the nature of a circular argument, while a recent suggestion that clicks are a hangover of our supposed chimpanzee past can most charitably be regarded as eccentric.

Aspects of grammatical structure

In the minds of many people, a technologically simple culture implies a "primitive language", and this in turn implies a language without grammar, or at best one with "very little" grammar. But even if one could make sense of these prejudgements, a careful study of the languages of the Bushmen provides no support for them. The sort of linguistic diversity we explored earlier is manifest as well in the grammatical systems of these languages, so it is not possible to provide a general "grammar of the Bushman languages", nor indeed is it possible to refer to "typical" characteristics, since they do not exist.

Take for example the way in which nouns are classified in Nharo (Central), !xõ (Southern) and !xũ (Northern). In Nharo nouns have masculine, feminine or common gender and three numbers, namely singular, dual (that is, two of) and plural (that is, three or more), all of which are signalled by suffixes. For example:

Singular	kweba	man	kwesa	woman	kwe	person
Dual	kwetšəra	two men	kwešəra	two women	kwekhara	two people
Plural	kwe//kwa	men	kweši	women	kwene	people

The masculine and feminine suffixes -ba and -sa signify more than just "maleness" and "femaleness": the masculine suffix conveys the notions of strength,

10.3 The diversity of vowel colourings, the variety of clicks and their distinctive accompaniments (or effluxes), coupled with the fact that the Bushman tongues are tone languages, make these the world's most complex languages from a phonetic point of view! Yet children learn them readily without any formal schooling.

10.4 Body language, too, is well developed among the San. They have a rich variety of gestures and manual signals.

tallness or slenderness, while the feminine suffix adds the notions of smallness, weakness or roundness:

hi – plant   hiba – tree   hisa – a broad, low bush

In !xõ a totally different classification is found. Nouns are classified in three different ways:

(i) into five harmonic classes
(ii) into singular and plural
(iii) into three pronominal classes

Let us examine these individually.

The principle of phonetic harmony in its broadest sense is that there be a similarity of sounds over a given stretch, either within a word or over a longer stretch. In the case of !xõ the stretch involves many words, and certain linguistic forms within the stretch are made to sound like a governing noun. Examples will help to clarify this:

140

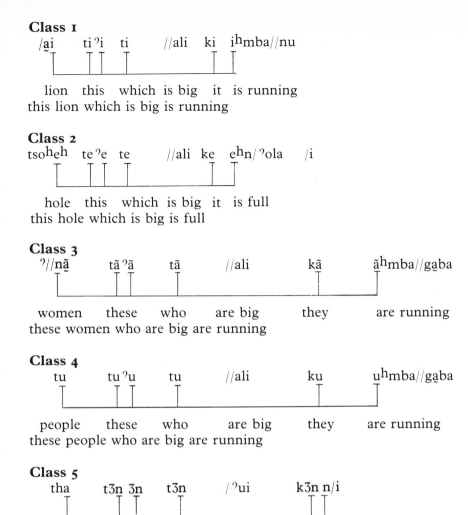

Class 1

/ai   ti'i ti   //ali ki iʰmba//nu

lion this which is big it is running

this lion which is big is running

Class 2

tsoʰeʰ te'e te   //ali ke eʰn/'ola /i

hole this which is big it is full

this hole which is big is full

Class 3

'//nã   tã'ã tã   //ali   kã   ãʰmba//gạba

women these who are big they are running

these women who are big are running

Class 4

tu   tu'u tu   //ali   ku   uʰmba//gạba

people these who are big they are running

these people who are big are running

Class 5

tha   t3n 3n t3n   /'ui   k3n n/i

thing this which is small is here

this thing which is small is here

One can see the harmonies clearly in most of these sentences; in each the initial noun governs the harmonic changes in the demonstratives, relative pronouns and the verbal pronoun. Every !xõ noun belongs to a harmonic class.

Secondly, Classes 1, 2, 3 and 5 may be singular *or* plural; Class 4 is always plural. (The concept of duality that we saw for Nharo is marked in !xõ by the suffix ≠*num*, meaning "two".) Thus this classification cuts across the harmonic one.

Thirdly, pronouns in certain positions in sentences "agree" with the antecedent noun, *not* according to the harmonic principle, but according to whether that noun denotes something living or non-living. If it is living and singular, the pronoun will be *e*; if it is living and plural, it will be *u*; if it is non-living and either singular or plural, it is *n*. Wives, by the way, count as non-living in !xõ.

In !xũ (Northern), nouns are classified into a number of grammatical classes, but bear no mark of the class to which they belong! The way in which a noun reveals its class is through the possessive and demonstrative pronouns that agree with it. In this respect !xũ resembles English, but the basis for the classes is radically different. Whereas in English we are interested in gender and number, !xũ concentrates more on the difference between living things and non-living things and on number. As is to be expected with human languages, such classifications are never perfect, and one finds snakes among sand, wind, shade and heaven, and a loafer amongst bows, wagons, cooking pots and teeth!

This sort of diversity extends to all aspects of the grammars of these languages. It is worth noting that the harmonic system of nominal classification for !xõ is unique and is not a feature of any other language.

Coming to plural formation, we find that there are not only many differences between the languages, but also great irregularity within a single language. Some examples are given in Table 3.

	/xam (Southern)	!xũ (Northern)	!xõ (Southern)
person	tu	žu	ta
people	tutu	žu	tu
man	!ui	!ʔhwã	taa̱a
men	!uiten	n//a̱e	//xã
child	!oa	daʔama	⊙a
children	!auken	deʔebi	⊙ani
woman	/aiti	dz'heu	taqae
women	/agen	dz'heusi	ʔ//ŋã̱
lion	//ha	n!'hei	/a̱i
lions	//ha	n!hei	/a̱bate

Table 3 The variety of plural formation in three languages

It is claimed that /xam has between 50 and 60 different ways of forming plurals. One writer on !xũ asserts that definite rules for the formation of plurals simply cannot be provided. Still, a language will tend to favour one formation, and we find not only that more plurals are formed in that manner, but also that new words such as borrowings will take that form. In /xam, reduplication of the noun stem appears to be the most general rule; in !xõ it is the adding of the suffix -te, and in !xũ of the suffix -si.

A fascinating aspect of number, involving a distinction between collective and distributive plurality, is found in !xõ and ≠hõa. For example, if one says ci guu-'a in the ≠hõa language, its English translation would be "they have fallen" (for example, from a tree). However, if one says ci ki-guu-'a, the addition of the particle ki conveys that "they" must have been in different trees! In English the distinction would have to be rendered by circumlocution, something like: they fell, each one from its tree; or: each one fell from the tree it was in. In !xõ the collective-distributive distinction requires the use of completely different words: if one were putting ostrich eggshell bead necklaces into a bag one at a time, one would !gaʔama them (distributive), but if one shoved a whole bunch of necklaces into the bag at one time one would u̱na them. To remove them one at a time would be to ≠nama them (distributive); to do so in one fell swoop would be to ʔ≠na̱na them. In these languages it is essential to make your meaning clear by selecting the appropriate verb. It is easy to imagine the unwary English speaker of !xõ producing inanities like "pour the water distributively" or "take out the sand distributively" (that is, one grain at a time)!

An interesting and unusual construction is found in at least /xam and !xõ and involves the distinction between alienable and inalienable possessions. Certain nouns are regarded as permanently part of something or someone. For example, body parts do not come and go like material possessions and will therefore require a different possessive construction. In /xam the alienable possessive is marked by the particle ka, while in !xõ it is marked by the harmonising particle / + vowel. The following examples are from !xõ.

Alienable		*Inalienable*	
my pipe	n/i!xu	my hand	n/kʔa
his goats	eʰ/u pulute	his head	eʰ/nʒn
the lion's meat	/a̱i/e ⊙aje	the lion's eye	/a̱i !ʔũi

The possessive used in nominal constructions like "his departure" or "the king's assassination" are treated as alienable possessives in !xõ: eʰ/asasa ("his going") and !xa̱a̱ /i qai ("the chief's killing").

In many cases in !xõ this distinction is conveyed not by possessive construction, but in distinct nouns. For example:

blood in my body	is	!na̱m – inalienable
blood spilt	is	!na̱ – "alienated"
a tail on an animal	is	/ão – inalienable
a tail cut off it	is	g/ʰu – "alienated"

142

These distinctions are apparently not found in the other languages.

One could never do justice in the space available to the wide range of grammatical processes found in these languages. We have examined just a few to show the great differences that exist at this level of linguistic structure, and one could easily multiply these. It is worth stressing that the frequent claims one finds that these languages have very little syntax have never been substantiated by careful research. It is plain that many investigators have been tempted into saying this because the *translations* they provide of linguistic texts from these languages *look as if* they have none. Below is a short text from a fable in /nuʰki (Southern) with a literal and a free translation.

/nuʰki text	Literal translation	Free translation
//gai c3n sija !kae	wolf come run girl	The wolf came
//kei/ka hacɔcʔem	he make love girl	running to the girl
//kei/ka. a//gai cɔn //ga	wolf go return home	and he made love to
//haru.		her. The wolf then
		went and returned home.

Is /nuʰki strange or is the literal translation strange? Is it the mind of the /nuʰki speaker that is uninterested in syntax or was the translator incompetent? The /nuʰki speaker produced the text on the left; it means what appears in the free translation. The literal translation has a dubious status, yet it is translations like these that have led investigators to characterise the language of the Bushman as "primitive", "simple", constructed only for efficient talk about hunting, love affairs, building a hut or searching for water!

The Khoisan "language family"

The Khoisan languages are subdivided into Northern, Central and Southern languages. The Northern languages such as !xũ are found in the north-western regions of Botswana, South West Africa and southern Angola. The Central languages are distributed roughly through central Botswana, westwards from about 27° E longitude and north of 24° S latitude into South West Africa; they include Nama, Kxoe, /gwi, //gana, Nharo. Sandawe probably belongs here as an extremely distant relative; the position of Hadza is unclear. Many of the Southern languages are now extinct; the surviving languages in this group are found in south-western Botswana, the southern Kalahari Desert (Gemsbok Park area) and at Lothair in the eastern Transvaal. The extinct languages were spoken in the Cape Province, the Orange Free State, Lesotho and Natal. This Southern subgroup includes !xõ, /xam, /nuʰki and //xegwi.

There have been attempts to establish linguistic connections between the Khoisan language family and other language families, such as the Nilo-Saharan (once called Hamitic) languages of North Africa and even the Indo-European languages, but these efforts have been unsuccessful. The traditional Khoisan family is therefore linguistically unique.

Recently, however, the traditional view has been challenged and it has been claimed that there is no valid basis for recognising a Khoisan language family. It is argued that the linguistic evidence points instead to there being four totally unrelated language groups instead of what has been traditionally regarded as the Khoisan family of languages. These suggested categories of languages are as follows:

Group A: the old Central languages, including Nama, /gwi, Nharo, etc.;
Group B: the old Northern languages, including !xũ;
Group C: the more northern of the old Southern languages, that is !xõ and its related dialects;
Group D: the remaining Southern languages, of which /nuʰki of the Kalahari Gemsbok Park and //xegwi of Lothair are extant.

Before we examine the kind of evidence that has led to these conflicting views, we should note a point of agreement between them. It is that some Bushmen speak

10.5 The exact relationships among the various Bushman languages is not at all clear. Even in far-off Tanzania, the Sandawe speak a click language probably distantly related to the Central group of Khoisan tongues. Some of these fascinating and enigmatic languages are spoken today by fewer than a dozen speakers!

a Hottentot language, namely those in the Central group, or Group A. But if this is so, then it is not at all obvious how we should answer the question: "What is a Bushman language?" Clearly the term Bushman does not coincide with a linguistically homogeneous group. This is not surprising; there is no reason why the physical and cultural criteria of Bushmen should yield the same division into groups as linguistic criteria do. Whatever value the words "Bushman" and "Hottentot" may have, for the student of language they are linguistically useless. This is inconvenient, but it is a fact.

The source of the conflict between the traditional view and the recent proposal lies in the linguistic technique used to establish how closely languages are related. Two languages are said to be related, according to the latter system, as long as a set of rules can be formulated which could systematically convert a significant number of words in one language to comparable words in the other. The traditional view has never provided rules to show how the Northern, Central and Southern languages are related. It has relied rather on an appeal to the obvious resemblances: the use of clicks, grammatical similarities and a supposedly large number of cognate words. As a counter to this approach we could give linguistic examples which may appear to be related, but from which no set of rules could be obtained to justify claiming that the languages are related. Consider Table 7.

	Language			
	1	2	3	4
eye	/ga	!nun	ts ʔaxam	⊙oa
child	da ʔama	⊙wa ʔa	/u βa	ǂaams
ashes	to̩	ǂgoa	!kx ʔũi	ǂgue
sun	/am	//ʔan	//ʔui	tšhʔa

Table 7 The examples illustrate the problem of constructing rules of sound shift which would relate different languages.

If we compare the words for "eye", "child" and "ashes" in four different languages, we see that there are no regular sound changes, so that we could not use these words to show that languages 1-4 were related. The words for "sun" in languages 1, 2 and 3 look more promising, however. It might seem that rules like

(i) /→//ʔ (replace / with //ʔ)
(ii) m→n (replace m with n)

would show how languages 1 and 2 are related. Similarly, rules like

(iii) /→//ʔ
(iv) a→ui
(v) m→nothing (that is, delete the m)

might seem to relate languages 1 and 3. The trouble with these rules is that while they show the relationship between the various words for "sun", these rules cannot be applied to other groups of words. For example, if we attempt to use rule (iv) "in reverse", to relate the word for "ashes" in languages 1 and 3, we should predict incorrectly that the word should be something like *tã* in language 1. Or we might expect that the word for "eye" in language 1 ought to be *gam* because it is *!nun* in language 2, and rule (ii) says m→n. The unavoidable conclusion is that these rules have no generality whatsoever and that we have failed to show by this method that the four languages are related. Naturally, hundreds of examples like these would be necessary in order to sustain the conclusion that the four languages are unrelated. On such reasoning rests the claim that there are four completely unrelated languages in the traditional Khoisan group.

Which view is right? Let us try to decide by examining a bigger set of examples drawn from a number of "Bushman" languages. The question is: "How many language families do we have to recognise?"

One doesn't have to be an expert to read the message in Table 8. It is clear that languages A, B, C, D and K must be grouped together, and so must E, F and G. It is clear also that there is a small amount of overlap between these two groups in the words for "ashes" and "laugh". Language H appears to be unique except for one

	A	B	C	D	E	F	G	H	I	J	K
ashes	doa	≠gua	≠goa	se:sa	≠goa	≠goa	≠goa	≠nue	tǫ	!ui	≠numša
child	/oa	/ũa	/õa	/oa	⊙ǫa	⊙a̰	⊙a	ɟams	da ʔama	⊙wa	/goa
dog	ʔaba	ʔaba	ʔaba	a̰ruku	≠hei	≠hi	≠hi	tshu	g≠hwîya	!ogi	aba
ear	≠e	≠e	≠e	≠e	≠nohah	≠nuisi	≠nohoh	/õe	!wa≠eya	//no-iŋtu	≠e
eye	!xai	≠xai	!xai	≠xai	!ũɪ	!õe	!ʔũɪ	⊙oa	kxʔwa	tsaxau	tšai
fire	/ʔe	/e	/ẽ	/ʔe	/ʔã	/ʔã	/ʔã	⊙goa	//weya	/e	/e
head	mʔa	ma	ma	ʔama	/nan	/nɜn	/nɜn	ʔ⊙nũ	≠ʔalo	/na	hma
laugh	kxʔqae	kxʔãe	kxʔẽɪ	kʔqãe	kxʔai	kxʔai	kxʔqai	/gɣae	tshi	kurrikən	!a
sun	/am	/am	/am	/am	//ʔan	//an	//ʔan	tshʔa	/am	//õɪn	/am
water	tsha	tsha	tsha	tsha	!ha	!ha	!ha	džo	!kxʔa	!hwa	tsa

Table 8 Data from various "Bushman dialects". The problem is to determine how many distinct languages these data represent. For the distribution of these dialects see Ill. 10.7.

feature: it resembles E, F, G and J, but none of the others, in having the click written ⊙, the bilabial or "kiss" click.

On the traditional view, we should end up with the following classification: A, B, C and D are dialects of /gwi, K is Nharo; these five are Central (that is, Hottentot) languages. E, F and G are !xõ dialects, H is ≠hõa (Botswana) and J is /xam (Cape, now extinct); these five are Southern languages. I is !xũ, a Northern language. The whole lot are linguistic relatives of one another.

On the other view languages A–K would be classified as follows: A, B, C and D are dialects of /gwi, they are related to K (Nharo) and belong to the Tshukhoe branch of the "Hottentot" languages (Group A on page 143). Languages E, F and G are dialects of !xõ and belong to Group C. I is !xũ, of Group B. J is /xam, of Group D. H is indeterminate, because it was only recently discovered. But it doesn't seem to fit in anywhere, so we may have to create a new group. That would make five unrelated groups.

We are now in a better position to appreciate the problems. There are a significant number of overlaps between the language groups, but again it is not possible to provide general conversion rules. Even worse – and this point is crucial – it is not possible to provide general conversion rules for *obviously related* dialects (A–D and E–G). Yet no-one would wish to claim therefore that these are all separate languages; they are overwhelmingly and obviously similar. So it looks as if the mere lack of conversion rules is not an adequate reason for rejecting a relationship. But the cost of doing without these rules is high, because one is no longer constrained to show how languages and words are related; one merely asserts that they *are* related! The effect is chaotic, since it now becomes possible to relate !xõ to /gwi and as easily, if not as plausibly, to Polish, Greek, Latin and German. This has actually been attempted, so the danger is far from being imaginary.

What of the substantial overlap found in the words for "water", "fire" and "laugh" that cut across the various languages? For the traditionalists this would be strong support for establishing a single family containing A–K. Their opponents, on the other hand, cannot provide rules to support this, so they are forced to regard these similarities either as fortuitous or, more likely, as arising from linguistic borrowings. At this point the debate threatens to become sterile: on the one hand we have no sound shift rules and on the other hand significant overlaps are not acceptable as evidence that languages are related. No rules are forthcoming, nor is any explanation of the borrowings, so a stalemate is reached.

It is interesting to note that the most recent advances in our understanding of this problem are coming as the by-products of studies whose prime concern has been the description of particular languages, as opposed to the comparison of languages for the purposes of genetic classification. These descriptive studies have

10.6 Another "language" of the desert – the message of the *spoor* or tracks left by small and large animals. Here two !Kung hunters are reading the information encoded in the *spoor*: it is a form of reading vital to success in the hunt and to the survival of the Bushmen.

amassed vast amounts of new data on a number of languages and these have made more extensive comparison possible. The latest results suggest very strongly that past scholars have been looking in the wrong place for their evidence! Instead of comparing words like "sun", "moon", "fire", "kill" (so-called core vocabulary, and the stock-in-trade of the comparative linguist), they ought to have been comparing words like "butterfly", "tickle", "gravy", "slander", "inflorescence", "*Acacia giraffiae*" and other botanical names, and words corresponding to phrases in English like "point between the shoulder blades", "put on a distrustful look", "tighten a bowstring", "woman's rear apron", etc.

In the course of translating a dictionary of Kxoe (traditional Central) into !xũ (traditional Northern) recently, a research worker discovered 150 cognate forms, most of which were "esoteric" vocabulary. A comparison of these forms with !xõ (traditional Southern) yields 19 per cent cognates. Recall that, from one point of view discussed above, no two of these three are related! Of course, a demonstration like this is not sufficient in itself to settle the debate, because the possibility still remains that these forms could have been borrowed from a fourth language spoken by a culturally dominant people (Nama, for example). Nor does the discovery of some cognate words reduce the over-all diversity of the languages of the Khoisan area. It does, however, hold the promise of exciting new directions for an issue that has remained unsolved for the past century.

How could this diversity have arisen?

Rather than move away from the problem at so inconclusive a point, let us briefly explore a possible explanation for this state of affairs. It has been noted frequently by many investigators that a "Bushman" language can show a certain amount of fluidity in the pronunciation of certain words. Some examples of this sort of variation are given in Table 9.

146

Language	English word	Variant pronunciations
Khakhea Bushmen (Botswana)	African	≠kaba, //gabe, /kabe
/xam (Cape)	name of the tribe	/xam, !kham
	see	/na, /ne, /ni
/auni (Cape)	ostrich egg	≠nore, !ui, ≠ui
	water	//ka:a, kha, khaia
	men	≠ ʔe, ≠ui, ≠i

Table 9 Various pronunciations for a single word

Evidently, all these variant pronunciations are equally acceptable and would be found in the speech of a single individual. If this sort of "instability" of pronunciation was widespread in these languages, it would have tended to create great linguistic diversity amongst them. If we imagine this developing over thousands of years in the many small and isolated Bushman bands, it would hardly be surprising to find the situation described above.

One final point on inter-relatedness among these languages: speakers of !xũ (Northern), /gwi (Central), !xõ (Southern), /nuʰki (Southern) and //xegwi (Southern) are totally unable to understand one another. The linguistic distance between these languages is vast, and neighbouring groups of Bushmen, leading identical sorts of lives and sounding to the uneducated ear for all the world as if they speak the same language, would have to be bilingual to understand one another! The distribution of some of these languages is shown in Ill. 10.7.

Conclusion

The need for the continued study of these languages is an urgent one. While many of the linguistic communities are thriving, some consist of fewer than a dozen speakers. Where Nama boasts a Bible and a newspaper and !xũ a gospel and a few school readers, the remaining languages live only on the lips of their speakers. We know that in the last fifty years at least two whole linguistic communities of Southern Bushmen have disappeared; //xegwi, Korana and Griqua will be the next casualties, and the prognosis for //nuʰki cannot be good. This is a depressing state of affairs for a linguistic corner of the globe that is unique, and so important for our understanding of the varieties of human language.

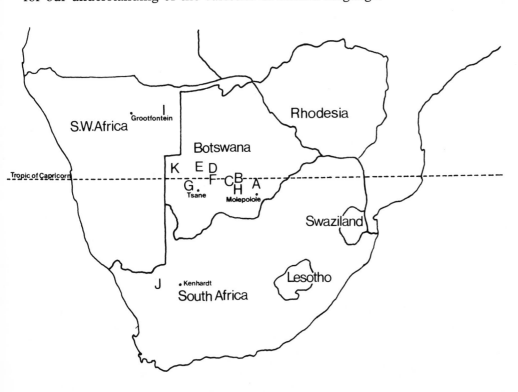

10.7 The distribution of some "Bushman" languages and their dialects. The so-called Central languages are linguistically Hottentot. All the languages are mutually unintelligible.

II
The Bushmen's Store of Scientific Knowledge

Hans J. Heinz

"The Bushman is the original scientist." This is a statement I have made on various occasions, and invariably it has been met by disbelieving, puzzled or sceptical expressions on the faces of my listeners. So now I happily grasp the opportunity of proving my point. All my observations and recording of the Bushmen's scientific knowledge were carried out on the !ko Bushmen living in the triangular area between the Takatshwane valley, 145 km (90 miles) south of Ghanzi in western Botswana, Massering Pan and the borehole 24 km (15 miles) south of Lone Tree Pan. However, experience has taught me that any Bushmen surviving in the Kalahari "desert" must have a comparable amount of "scientific" knowledge at their command.

The area of my research is mainly very sandy and varies from flat to slightly undulating, the monotony of the landscape being barely broken by the very shallow valleys and isolated pans. The annual rainfall of 305 to 380 mm (12 to 15 inches) or less falls during the extremely hot summer months. Winter days are usually mild to fairly warm, the nights being cold, with temperatures sometimes dropping below freezing point.

The whole of this arid or semi-arid area is waterless but for temporary small supplies of free water available in occasional pans. However, boreholes many kilometres apart are now interspersed along the 650 km (400 mile) long trek route for cattle that links Ghanzi with Lobatse.

The valleys may support a grassland in some parts, but more often only a sparse grass cover, accompanied by a variety of variously zoned low shrubs. The extensive areas lying between the valleys and pans are occupied mainly by thorny to non-thorny woodlands.

Such then is the adverse environment in which people live who either have fled to it as a last refuge in the face of ever-encroaching hostile strangers, or may well be the last remnants of a people once widely dispersed throughout southern Africa, but exterminated in all but the most inaccessible parts of the Kalahari. There are substantial arguments for either view. Of pertinence to the former is the valid observation of G. B. Silberbauer that survival in the Kalahari requires such specific and intimate knowledge of the plant and animal world that a stranger would not be able to learn a fraction of it, let alone the considerable knowledge required to satisfy his material needs. This can have been acquired only through many generations. Indeed, Bushmen taken into areas only 50 to 65 km (30 to 40 miles) from their own familiar environment are faced with many new plants that they can neither identify nor evaluate nutritionally. Yet, studies on the parasites Bushmen harbour suggest that they brought some of these long ago from humid areas much more favourable to their survival. I therefore freely own that the question of when and how the Bushmen came to the Kalahari has not yet been satisfactorily resolved in my mind.

To evaluate the Bushman's response to this taxing environmental challenge, it should be appreciated that this environment continuously impresses upon him his own impotence and the power of Him who rules over his destiny. This imposes on him what I interpret as a deep sense of religious humility. I shall return to this subject after I have discussed the main aspects of the Bushman's scientific repertoire.

Plants of the Bushman's world

As hunters and gatherers, the Bushmen are equally at home in their animal and plant worlds. We shall look first at their botanical knowledge, since plants supply a major part of their dietary. Thus there are ⊙ah ⊙ani ("wild plants") as opposed to ⊙aje ⊙ani ("wild animals").

The wild plants are broadly differentiated, according to their growth habits, as trees, shrubs, erect herbs or climbers. Even plant parasites are identified as such.

Our studies were carried out during a time when the plants were severely affected by drought. Hence our informant was frequently faced with the problem of having to identify material that would be regarded as quite inadequate for identification by a university-trained botanist. Except for a number of insignificant herbaceous members of the calcrete pan flora, our informant's knowledge of plants included virtually all species represented in the comparatively rich and diversified local flora. The relative ignorance of pan vegetation was explained by the fact that the !ko were not pan-dwellers. If one includes common plants not in evidence during the drought, it would seem that recognition and intimate knowledge of at least three hundred plants form part of the repertoire of an average Bushman woman. The command of such information, not to mention that of a more general nature, is not the discipline of a specialised Bushman botanist, but a knowledge shared by all adult and near-adult members of the band. The knowledge of the men is in no way inferior to that of the women, who perform the customary duties of food-gathering, and men may become acquainted with plants unknown in the home area.

The Bushman broadly recognises that plants, like animals, have basic growth requirements such as water and air, that the roots not only absorb moisture but grow towards a source of water, and that this water rises up the stem of a plant. However, beyond realising that the plant "breathes" and that it must also eat in order to live, he is unaware of how these processes are accomplished. Although some plant names have a very definite sexual connotation, the reason for the naming is obscure, since the !ko Bushman is ignorant of the sexual nature of reproduction in plants.

11.1 This young Bushman girl with her digging stick has just dug up a long white bush potato (*Vignia dinteri*). Plant foods supply a major part of the dietary of the Bushmen.

149

11.2 Bushmen are highly skilled practical ecologists. The very uniform and monotonous landscape seems to be visualised as a complex of smaller and larger plant communities. The position, shape, size and special composition of each such community is recognised and this contributes greatly to the success of the Bushmen in their uncompromising environment.

With the exception of the grasses, the !ko Bushman has no formalised system of taxonomy in which plants are divided into groups or categories reflecting their natural or genetic relationship to one another. None the less he is deeply concerned with the classification of those plant forms which we should define as "species".

A long heritage of intimate experience, coupled with remarkably keen powers of observation and appreciation of fine detail, has enabled the !ko to evolve a highly efficient working taxonomy which in several respects functions more satisfactorily than our own. Virtually all plant "species" are designated by a single short name, the system of naming being characterised by brevity and by the absence of a multitude of confusing synonyms. These names are highly specific: they refer to vegetation units quite as refined as species, or in some cases even more closely categorised than the units defined as species. The perplexing problem of differentiating between closely related and virtually identical plant forms is overcome by the use of criteria of generally accepted and proven reliability. These include reference to the habitat preferences of the plants concerned, and to their chemistry in the case of edible and medicinal plants.

11.3 Not only does the Bushman depend on plants for most of his food and, not infrequently, for much of his water too; but he relies on plants to provide the materials with which he makes almost all of his artefacts and articles of everyday use. Here women in the Dobe area fell saplings with which to start making huts.

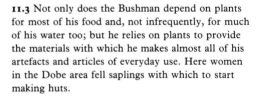

150

The Bushman's ability as a practical ecologist is likewise highly developed. His very uniform and monotonous landscape is seemingly envisaged as a complex of smaller and larger plant communities, the position, shape, size and peculiar constitution of each being recognised by him. This knowledge is essential to successful hunting and food-gathering and is vital to his own safety when moving about his seemingly uniform and usually waterless environment. Thus his surprising ability to orientate himself geographically, not only in his home area but even in surroundings previously unknown to him, stems from his capacity to imprint in his mind the types of plant communities, or even plant associations, which he sees between any given position and the place where he, say, cached a certain object. Obviously the sequence of these is of crucial importance in his orientation.

The peculiarly well-developed taxonomic and ecological aptitudes of the Bushman can be the outcome only of constant, deliberate and meticulous observation of all the perceptible natural phenomena in his uncompromising environment. The purpose of these observations is essentially utilitarian, since the greater his success at exploiting every potentially useful aspect of his environment, the more assured is his continued survival within it.

Not only is the Bushman dependent on plants for making almost all of his artefacts and substances of everyday use, but he relies on them for most of his food and, not infrequently, for much of his water too. Despite frequent periods of drought, these plant foods are usually more regularly available than meat.

Animals of the Bushman's world

Let us now turn to the fauna which populates a Bushman's environment. Here, as in plant taxonomy, the Bushman is far more concerned with "species" than category, but he does divide all animals (⊙aje ⊙ani) into two major groups: the si'isate, which are those that bite (or sting or do harm in some manner), and the non-biting animals, which also are called ⊙aje ⊙ani. The si'isate are broken down into the small ⊙xate ⊙ani and the larger thani ⊙ani. The ⊙aje ⊙ani are similarly divided into the ⊙aje ⊙ani proper, which include all antelopes, or meat-bearing animals (⊙aje means "meat" for human consumption), and the /uate, which embrace all birds, but omit tortoises as well as rodents (which the Bushman acknowledges belong to groups of their own). It is obvious that lions and leopards belong to the si'isate, while scorpions and snakes are also a part of it. Indeed snakes, which constitute such an ever-present hazard, are collectively called si'isa and are only secondarily referred to by their specific name, even though a Bushman is capable of differentiating between a poisonous and a non-poisonous snake. Though birds constitute a natural group, there are no terms which would refer to insects, probably because many of them belong to the ⊙xate ⊙ani. However, for reasons completely obscure, there is a harmless lizard of whose supposed, poisonous bite the !ko are convinced, and it therefore logically falls into the group of si'isate.

Of the entire fauna, the insects or arthropods play the least significant role in the life of a Bushman. For this reason, and because the life cycles of many arthropods are extremely difficult to elucidate, one would here expect to find – and indeed does find – the greatest lacunae in knowledge. What information does become available in many cases must command respect.

It is well known that the larva of the beetle *Diamphidia simplex* provides some Bushmen with an extremely effective arrow poison. It is not surprising, therefore, that he should know most aspects of its life cycle. Here are some items of entomological information recorded in my journals. The informants gave me the names of some 65 different insects, of which only certain species were grouped together. Thus all butterflies and moths are *thebi*, all mosquitoes are *me me*, all flies are ⊙*ate*, all lice are ⊙*ahnte* (qualified by the host on which they are found) and all dragon-flies are *n/ah/i*. But the !ko failed to combine many insects which obviously had common morphological features. Thus most ants have a specific name, and this applies to termites and harvester ants as well. On the other hand strange examples of synonymy were encountered. Why do the water beetle and the water bug have a common name, *!ebili*, but not the back swimmer, if a common habitat was responsible for this grouping? What is the grouping together of the bumble-bee and the leaf-cutter bee based on, or that of the zebra beetle and the green-protea beetle? Nevertheless, from a systematic point of view it is remarkable that so many insects have been given specific names and that these names feature in the vocabulary of a broad spectrum of the !ko population.

My informants appreciated the significance of the wedding flight of swarming females in the termite cycle, and knew that somewhere within the nest there is a "boss or captain", and that there are other types, some of which are there to fight. The cicadas sing to each other with an organ that lies under the wings. Little of the life cycle of the butterfly retains any mystery for them, and even the curled-up tongue with which the insect drinks the sap of flowers has been studied. The entire hatching or emerging process of the common fly has been observed in the greatest detail. Thus: "When the wings dry the fly opens them with its hind legs and is ready to fly away." Mud wasps make their nests from pan mud mixed with their own saliva(!). Sand is unsuitable because it will not stick.

The account given of the honey bee is perhaps one of the most interesting, because it is such a remarkable mixture of truth and fiction. "The honey bee comes from the north. In some years there are none at all. When they swarm, they hang in a tree, while some bees go off in search of a new nesting place. They look into every tree or ground hole, even into holes of termites, until they find a suitable large place. They then return to inform the others and all bees fly to the potential nesting site. A few bees precede the rest to see if the nesting place is safe. The leader is their captain. He is so harmless that he can be placed in one's mouth. The bees now begin to build their hives. There are three types of bees: long ones, which lay eggs that produce stinging bees, the captain, which lays eggs that produce only captains, and the males, which sting. The combs are made from a mixture of powder and sap. Some of the flower holes of the combs are filled with flower sap, while others which receive the eggs are filled with the powder the bees collect on their legs. The captain never leaves the nest, and has 'her' own comb which she makes for herself. Both males and females collect honey.

"In times of hunger the bees drink the honey which comes from the sap and they may even open closed honeycombs. When the nest hole is too small, the captain swarms with some of the bees. Swarming bees can separate several times. Those that stay behind remain until the combs are too old, then they also leave. There is a green bee (bee killer) which enters a nest and kills honey bees."

When I tried to correct some of the more obviously incorrect aspects of this account, especially about the egg-laying ability of the worker and drone bee, my explanation was rejected: "Perhaps your bees are like that, but ours are different." At other times, however, the Bushmen showed a keen interest and exhibited intelligent curiosity when I discussed some of their mistakes.

The Bushmen have given more attention to the life cycles of parasitic arthropods than to that of any other group. They are quick to point out that ecto-parasites are common on animals which are out of condition. In this low rainfall area mosquito plagues follow heavy rains, and the Bushmen understand that these bring a disease which kills people (malaria).

Finally, population explosions or fluctuations are generally explained on a meteorological basis, with regard not only to the actual amount of rain, but also to the time of year when rains are concentrated.

The ornithological knowledge of the Bushmen generally rests on a firmer basis. Indeed, it seems that some of the finer points are not necessarily a part of the repertoire of all Bushmen, and that there may well be some who are more interested in bird life than others. Men apparently have a greater degree of this knowledge than women, for often when asking the latter for the name of a bird, I was told only: "It's a bird, I don't know its name." Nevertheless we were able to obtain some 65 different names for the total number of 77 birds seen during the course of these investigations. Certain birds form very obvious groups, which are not broken down to the species unit. Thus: all vultures have the same name, likewise all ducks and geese, and most doves. But the Namaqualand dove alone has a distinct species name. All storks have a common designation, which in each case is qualified by a suffix indicating a specific attribute, thus: "stork, the grey one" or "stork, the white one". Other very obvious groups, such as the owls or francolins, were represented only by specific names for each different type within that group.

Thus a common name for owls, or for francolins, is missing. But if we were to mistake these shortcomings in nomenclature for ignorance, the Bushmen would be quick to correct us. Their ability to reproduce the song of each bird is astonishing. Not infrequently informants pointed out fine differences in song that established the separate identity of a bird which in appearance closely resembled another. The Bushman's knowledge of the biology of birds is equally extensive. He knows where he may expect to find the nest of any species of bird, and also when the young are to be found in the nest. A knowledge of nesting behaviour is necessary, if young birds constitute a part of a people's dietary. But understanding the food requirements of a specific bird would appear to be less utilitarian. Some girls taught me what the food of an ostrich chick was, and went with me to collect it. After a few weeks some of the plants were replaced by other species, with the remark: "They are now older and no longer eat these." Yet there were a few very puzzling lacunae in this repertoire of knowledge. The !ko had an intimate biological understanding of the violet-eared waxbill, and were even able to say when we should expect the birds to come to the drinking trough for water, yet they had no name for it. Similarly, the common buffalo weaver remained unnamed, as did the cattle egret and the swallow-tailed bee-eater, though it was nesting not 50 metres from our camp.

What I have discussed so far could, I believe, constitute knowledge acquired by any people who keep their eyes open and their ears close to the ground. However, at the level of the higher animals, such as smaller and larger mammals, we were increasingly astonished at the wealth of information proffered by the Bushmen. Here we can give only a cursory account of the data collected. In many cases I have been unable to determine whether field zoologists would agree with some of the opinions offered. Though I am still consulting specialists, I have found those that reply: "It may be so, we don't know, we have not had an opportunity to make such fine observations."

From all that has been said above, we should expect to have a detailed nomen-

11.4 Southern Bushwomen with a rich haul of tsamma melons.

153

clature of those mammals which live in the Kalahari. In fact, with the exception of some of the gerbils and some species of mice that have a common name, most mammals have very specific names. But it is in the realm of animal behaviour that we can learn so much from the Bushmen. Here are two pieces of factual information which I was at first not prepared to accept, so startling did they seem to me.

The !ko said that they had watched hyenas sleeping in their lairs and seen them wake up, rise and observe the flight direction of vultures in the sky before trotting off in a similar direction. Several years later Jane Goodall wrote: "Indeed, it is by closely watching the movement of vultures in the sky that many earth-bound predators are directed to new sources of food."

The spotted hyena, the !ko say, is rare in their area, and they claim that their knowledge of it is small. They do state that it is an animal which kills for its food, since it does not eat decayed meat. While hunting it attacks buck by the tail first, eating this before biting pieces out of the hind leg. The spotted hyena can run as fast as many buck, they say, and easily outpaces a horse.

In 1968 Kruuk surprised nature lovers, who were all convinced that the spotted hyena is a carrion eater, with his startling pictures of it pulling down a zebra. Jane Goodall, too, has demonstrated the hunting ability of this animal.

Much of the information given to me by Bushmen in the Kalahari about the behaviour of the Cape hunting dog could have been extracted from Jane Goodall's detailed account of this canine. The leopard, they say, has a mortal fear of the wild dogs. Two Bushmen, Dausa and Gocholu, quite independently of each other, gave evidence for this. Gocholu reported that a leopard, while killing a duiker, was surprised by a pack of dogs and quickly climbed a tree with its kill. The dog pack swarmed around the tree, so much so that the ground was swept clean by their feet. He saw that a dog had jumped up and been caught on a sharp branch, which pierced the dog's throat and emerged at the nose. The leopard, confronted with the pierced body, was so frightened that it did not eat for over twenty-four hours, though he had food. Only on Gocholu's approach did the leopard dare to flee. Dausa's leopard fared more badly, for it starved to death, transfixed by the stare of a dead dog caught in a similar manner.

The Bushman's stories of the black-backed jackal, "this clever old man", have a certain similarity to those told in Europe of Reynard the fox. Though highly anthropomorphic, they are all full of significant behavioural observations. The biology of all other jackals, too, is known in great detail.

We must bear in mind that the Bushman has a great advantage over the research worker trained as an observer of animal behaviour, and that is his ability to read and give the age of tracks. It is therefore easy for him to render a chronological account of what happened during the night, or before his arrival. A trained zoologist can at best evaluate the "finished product", the observed behaviour, with but the barest idea of the preceding sequence of events.

The curiosity of lions has often been documented, and especially friendly lions have made history. But few people other than Bushmen would report that a certain "very friendly male lion would approach humans with his ears flapping like a dog's. He never killed or harmed·anyone, though women would encounter him while they were collecting veldkos."

Many mammals of the Kalahari are nocturnal, so that much of their behaviour would escape us, particularly their mating ceremonies. Yet, of the caracal the !ko say that their courtship lasts over a period of four days, and that after mating the male leaves the female and does not return until the cubs are born. All this was written in the sand!

The black and white genet is separated from the rusty-spotted type by its sleeping preferences, the former preferring trees or mongoose holes, while the latter prefers to go under a fallen tree overgrown with grass. Of the scaly ant-bear, the Bushmen say that neither copulation activities nor the mating places have ever been seen, and that they suspect these animals mate underground. The porcupine, another nocturnal animal, "lives in lairs which it takes away from ant-bears by contaminating the hole with its own urine. Before copulating, porcupines play extensively at different places. After mating a union lasts for life."

The honey badgers, the !ko say, have a wide range of food which includes snakes, scorpions and even small antelopes. They may kill a python, fighting as a pair and intoxicating it with their scent. They have a few enemies. Only leopards and domestic dogs kill them, but the Bushmen stated that, because of its smell, no honey badger had ever been attacked by wild dogs.

These are only a small fraction of the detailed biologies described to me. Similar facts are available for most of the very small mammals as well, such as gerbils, shrews, mice, bats, mongooses and ground squirrels, only a very limited number of which are eaten or have any other utilitarian significance for Bushmen. However, information given about antelopes was most extensive and gave much food for thought. The !ko had something to say about heat, gestation period, the number of young, the age of the mother when she has her firstborn and, for each species, where the young is dropped. The Bushmen knew how the female hides her young and could imitate her calling the foal. In the realms of the social behaviour of antelopes, especially, they demonstrated their keen powers of observation.

For each species they knew whether it was solitary or social, whether there was a strict or a loose matriarchal system. They differentiated between those where bulls run together according to age groups and those where this behaviour is missing, or where there is only a father-son relationship, as in the kudu. On attitudes towards offspring, the informants said among other things that both male and female steenbok have been seen to run up to a Bushman crying and bleating for the release of a calf.

A "solitary bull", the Bushmen said, need not be an old bull. Whatever his age, he is morose. He eats, sleeps and walks without interest in others of his species, even in the period of rut. Though he sees them, he stays alone. He is usually fat. He may notice something suspicious, but he immediately forgets what drew his attention and continues to graze. Conversely a bull in the herd never fails to react to what he has seen.

The solitary bull acts as if he were abnormal. He is easy to shoot. Once a male is out of a herd, he can never join another herd, because each animal has its own herd smell. Not all solitary animals are abnormal. Among wildebeest, eland and hartebeest wounded animals which were unable to continue with their herd and have subsequently recovered are also forced to wander on their own. If two such animals meet, they stay and graze together, but passing herds will not let them in. Such males are not allowed to take females from passing herds. This type of behaviour does not apply to springbok, gemsbok and kudu.

The Bushmen's faunal information includes such aspects as behaviour towards the sick and the wounded, reaction towards the dead or towards other species, which includes symbiotic associations, such as with birds that warn. Regarding aspects of sexual behaviour, they report that all buck masturbate. They usually rub their horns against a soft bush or, if wildebeest, in a hole. Ejaculation is rapid. Duikers scratch holes into which they ejaculate and defaecate before leaving. Duikers or steenbok, which are very aggressive during rut, especially when they have lost their mate, may mount or "rape" a ewe of another species if she happens to be in their territory. Various informants were very emphatic that this occurs.

The Bushmen have detailed information also on fighting techniques of the bulls of various species, and also of species in which the cows fight. Interesting is the following statement about the gemsbok: "The lead cow is boss and is followed by a calf who will one day take her place. This position is therefore hereditary. If this calf is a male, he will hand over leadership to one of his sisters."

At a time when economic game husbandry is being increasingly recommended, knowledge on the times of activity of antelopes is not just of academic importance. At a recent congress it was reported that the oryx, or gemsbok, which can go for long periods without drinking, obtains its water requirements from hygroscopic plants by feeding at night, when these contain the highest degree of moisture. These studies, however, were not carried out on the Kalahari gemsbok. All my informants were adamant that the gemsbok does not feed at night and that, with the exception of moonlit nights, it rests much of the night, though it may also sleep during the heat of the day. Here again, I cannot give a personal opinion whether this is so.

Regarding sleep, my informants said that sleep and slumber are different.

During sleep flies cover the head of the animal and the ears hang down. In slumber the ears move back and forth slowly. When the animal is awake, the ears are erect and turn in all directions, listening. Except for lions, animals do not sleep in the middle of the day. They slumber and listen. Lions, however, are dead to the world when they sleep.

In closing this aspect of a Bushman's repertoire of biological knowledge, I recall one particularly significant item on animal senses and response to stimuli. Here, more than anywhere else, does the Bushman show not only his keen powers of observation, but his ability to make correct deductions from his observations.

All antelopes have good powers of smell but some, such as the wildebeest, depend on it more than certain others, such as the hartebeest. In winter the antelope's sense of smell is keener than it is in summer. It is also better in the morning and evening than at midday. When the ground is wet, game animals have a better sense of smell than when the ground is dry. However, rain can obliterate the smell of a person; besides, wet ground has a smell of its own. After rain of 2 to 3 days, game can smell very well, because the sun "pulls up" the "wet" and the smell "goes between the wet". Now the wind carries this. On such days even a man can smell game if the wind is right. But the wind is not essential to take human smell to an animal. A fly may sit on the hunter and then go to the buck, taking the man's smell along. This can happen on hot days, when he is sweating, and the antelope will be seen to dart off suddenly.

Anyone who has any idea of the molecular nature of smell and its distribution would not be astonished by this valid and correct deduction, for we know that a fly can indeed transport "smell" molecules on its feet and transmit these to the nose of an antelope!

Anatomy and physiology

Just as the Bushman has given virtually every creature its own specific name, so also has he named the bones, muscles and organs of the body. Indeed, we should feel disappointed at this stage were it not so. However, what is surprising is his ability to recognise the *homology* of muscles, bones or organs between different species. Thus, a particular muscle does not change its name, from one animal species to another, just because the muscle has a completely different appearance and shape.

The Bushman would describe the physiological function of the living body somewhat as follows:

"The air we breathe is the same as that which causes the wind and it has the same name. God *(Gu/e)* made it, and it is as necessary to animals and plants as to man. We do not know what happens to it in our bodies. If we do not get air we shall die. We do not understand the difference between inhaled and exhaled air; perhaps the air we exhale has changed. When we sleep under a skin or blanket we become frightened unless we let in fresh air. When we run we need more air, that is why we pant.

"A person who has stopped breathing cannot be made to start breathing again, neither can a baby be made to begin breathing if it fails to do so at birth. We do not know how air gets into our lungs, except that we cause it to enter by breathing, neither do we know what the air does in the lungs.

"When we run we become short of breath and perspire because the body is hot. The perspiration makes the body cold. The water comes from the muscles. The more we drink, the more we perspire. We also perspire in sickness because the pain that causes the sickness makes us hot. The perspiration of a sick person is not harmful. The smell of perspiration of a healthy person is powerful: when it is rubbed on the head of a sick person, it helps him. The perspiration is salty because it is dirty.

"We do not know the nature of spit, but we know that we need it to talk. When we are thirsty and hot after chasing an animal, the tongue sticks to the inside of the mouth. The spit comes from little holes under the tongue. There is only one kind of spit from under the tongue, but the spit which is hard comes from the chest. When we are sick with a cold, two different kinds of water come from the nose: that which is soft like spit, and that which is hard, but this is the same as the spit which comes from the chest. The hard spit is harmful to us because it brings the sickness from the chest. We do not know how our bodies make the hard spit.

"When we eat we swallow the food, and the tongue helps to move the food from the front to the back of the mouth. The food does not often go into the lungs, because there is something which closes the breathing tube. We cough when we have white matter in the lungs and we vomit when the stomach does not like the food we eat.

"In the stomach the food becomes more broken up and watery and there is water in the stomach called *ka'au*, which is different from spit because it is sour when we vomit. It is not harmful. Sometimes when we feel sick we bring up green vomit. This is called *na'an/e!ka* (the gall-bladder's water). From the stomach the food goes to the intestines. It moves through these because they 'contract' and squirt the food forwards. The food becomes bad in the intestines because of the heat. There are little muscles in the intestines which squeeze out the food needed by the body. This happens in all parts of the intestine.

"The faeces are dry because the water is needed by the body and returns to it. The faeces smell because they are rotten, but they are not harmful to man. The faeces are expelled from the body by muscles which contract during excretion.

"There is no gizzard in man or in animals except birds. In the gizzard the food goes rotten before it passes into the stomach. Some animals, such as the spring-hare, have a long tube (appendix), but we do not know whether man has one. The hyena has a small one.

"We do not know the purpose of the liver. The gall-bladder, which we remove before we eat, is found on the liver's under side. Neither do we know what the pancreas does.

"The heart moves the blood through the blood vessels, but we do not know why the heart has so many rooms. The heart of a bird is like that of other animals. There are different kinds of blood vessels. The thick-walled ones lie on the inside of the legs and arms, and they beat like the heart; the thin-walled ones lie on the outside of the limbs, but they do not beat. (One Bushman confused the different types of vessels, but was corrected by the others!) There is a large blood vessel (aorta) which goes directly from the heart to the body. The blood takes food from the stomach and intestines and turns it into fat. The colour of the blood varies. That which comes from the heart is light in colour.

"When we cut ourselves, the blood stops flowing because it dries and closes up the wound. There is something in it which makes it like a jelly. This we can see in the belly of a freshly killed animal.

"A white water sometimes comes out of a wound; it is like the water which makes us sweat.

"Human blood does not hurt us, unless it is a woman's blood of menstruation. This blood makes a man thin. A man does not have this blood. This woman's blood is also harmful to weapons because it takes the strength, not only from the arrow poison, but also from a bullet: an animal will run from such a bullet even though it has been badly wounded. The blood of a woman during childbirth is the same as that during menstruation and just as harmful. Only this type of woman's blood is harmful: her other blood does not harm us. A man's blood is not harmful to a woman. Sometimes we suck the blood from a cut with an animal's horn. This takes the sickness out of the body.

"The kidney returns some of the water we drink back to the body, and some to the bladder. The water passes to the bladder through a little tube. We do not know why the bladder does not drip all the time, but when it is full it makes us want to urinate.

"The testicles make the man's *!ghwa* (spermatic fluid). (Only one of the three informants was conversant with this fact.) The man's !ghwa passes into the penis through a little tube. We do not know what causes the penis to squirt. We also do not know what causes a man's penis to become stiff, but a baby's penis becomes stiff when it wants to urinate. Small children cannot copulate because they do not have the white !ghwa.

"The woman has a little head (ovary) at the top of the house (uterus) where the baby starts to grow before it goes to the uterus. In the beginning the baby is a little spot of blood in the ovary and the man's !ghwa comes there and this makes the

157

11.5 The Bushmen possess a wealth of information about the higher animals, such as the larger and smaller mammals. Many of the beliefs they have long held about the behaviour of hyenas and Cape hunting dogs have only recently been "discovered" by scientifically trained students of animal behaviour! A keen observer of animal life is !Xroma, shown here. He is a "headman" in the Dobe area of the north-western part of Botswana.

baby. The baby then passes to the uterus. The man's !ghwa and the woman's blood form a baby: this stops the monthly bleeding. It is the same with animals. The baby drinks the water in the uterus, but the mother also gives the baby food and blood through the cord. Inside the mother, the baby eats and drinks every day before it is born. The baby remains inside the mother for 4 to 7 months. (There was considerable variation in estimates of the duration of human pregnancy.)

"In the head we have the brain, which runs down into the spine. The function of it is to give us a headache. God made our eyes to see. We smell with the nose and not with the lungs. Animals can smell better than we do because they have better, not bigger noses. We taste with the tongue* and hear with the little holes of the ear. The earshell is there to stop the sound. Animals can hear better than we do because they have big ears and can move them. Men cannot do this. We think with our heart, for when we know we are doing wrong we say, '*n/n chue* (in the inside of my heart) I know that this is wrong.'

"When we have children we look at them to see whether they are ours. We look at their hair to see if it is lighter or darker, hard or soft. We look at the form of the ear and the colour of the eyes. Some of our people have black eyes, others brown. We also compare the lines of their hands with our own, and we sometimes observe that the teeth are spaced like those of the mother or father. Our children show a likeness both to the mother and to the father, because the man's !ghwa gives his features to the child. Some illnesses such as syphilis, the sickness that eats away your nose, or tuberculosis, the sickness that makes you cough blood, we also pass

---

*The author repeatedly saw children suck the end of the feather with which he cleaned his pipe. It is not easy to assess whether Bushmen have a predilection for bitter flavours. They state that they do not mind bitter things: one of the mainstays of their diet, the n//am *(Cucumis kalahariensis)*, is certainly bitter, and this applies also to some of their other vegetable foods.

on to the child. This applies to being born with six toes or fingers as well. Soon after the child is born we can see whether we are the parents, because the child will look like us or his grandparents."

The learning process

Impressed by such a wealth of factual knowledge, one wonders how, in the absence of a written language, all aspects of the Bushman's knowledge of plant and animal lore is transmitted. The Bushmen have no organised schooling, so that information can pass only by word of mouth. Generally the mothers teach their daughters when these accompany them on their *veldkos*-gathering trips, while the fathers teach their sons or answer their questions while hunting with them. But this is not the only way. Much information is transmitted within the children's societies, directly from the older to the younger, and only occasionally do they appeal to higher authority by running to their elders. Of importance also is the evening fire. Here the children sit with and between the elders, intently listening to, but never participating in, the conversation. The day's hunt or the trip to the melon patches gives rise to many subjects of conversation which register themselves in the impressionable mind of the young. The child is almost constantly exposed to processes of learning and teaching, although these are completely informal.

Knowledge and philosophy

At the beginning I said that the Bushman's inquiring mind regarding his environment deeply affects his "Weltanschauung" and his religious beliefs. It has become abundantly clear that the !ko Bushman is very much a realist, pragmatist and proto-scientist, in that he is capable of minute observations and correct deductions from his observations. He shows extensive curiosity, because his acquired biological knowledge often goes far beyond the utilitarian. It would therefore seem logical that this realism manifests itself in all aspects of Bushman "Weltanschauung". He lives in a world that he has studied intimately. In many

11.6 ". . . The woman has a little head (ovary) at the top of the house (uterus) where the baby starts to grow before it goes to the uterus. In the beginning the baby is a little spot of blood in the ovary and the man's !ghwa comes there and this makes the baby. The baby then passes to the uterus. The man's !ghwa and the woman's blood form a baby: this stops the monthly bleeding. The baby drinks the water in the uterus, but the mother also gives the baby food and blood through the cord. Inside the mother, the baby eats and drinks every day before it is born . . ."

11.7 ". . . When we have children we look at them to see whether they are ours. We look at their hair to see if it is lighter or darker, hard or soft. We look at the form of the ear and the colour of the eyes. Some of our people have black eyes, others brown. We also compare the lines of their hands with our own . . . Our children show a likeness both to the mother and to the father, because the man's !ghwa gives his features to the child . . . Soon after the child is born we can see whether we are the parents, because the child will look like us or his grandparents . . ."

cases his minute observations have made it possible for him to link cause with effect. Indeed, some of his observations on environmental phenomena are so accurate that he is able to make certain predictions about future developments that will affect his own life for better or worse. To mention but one example: impending droughts or wet periods are predicted as a result of his observing the behaviour of certain insects or the growth patterns of particular plants. However, having empirically obtained pertinent data, he attributes developing catastrophes to nothing less than the will of his God, Gu/e or /oa, and he knows there is little he can do to alter the course of events.

Many religions of other pre-literate people, even though pragmatic, realistic or even rational, seem to me to be characterised by fear, intimidation or haunting. This does not apply to the !ko religion, nor to any other Bushman religion. There is ample evidence from 14 years of observation that when a Bushman fears something, that fear is well founded. He fears things he knows to be dangerous and with which he is well acquainted, such as snakes, certain lizards (which he believes, for reasons unknown, are poisonous), leopards, lions and large animals such as elephants which impress him by their sheer size. He fears to walk from his village at night (and prevents me from doing so), not because there are spirits or demons about, but because this is the hunting time of snakes. He does not reject a camp site because it may be haunted, but because he sees a hole occupied by a mamba, or because he observes some bones lying about indicating that some animal died of a sickness which may still linger in the ground. (We should call it bacterial contamination.)

I have never observed the !ko Bushman to be genuinely intimidated by any person of his own kind (despite the existence of curses), by any natural phenomenon of his environment, nor by any unusual manifestation such as strange noises of an animal. On the contrary, he listens for these – even waking at night – and quickly draws correct conclusions as to their meaning. In an assessment of this kind it is necessary to differentiate between what the Bushman says and does. It is the foreign, the strange, that makes him uneasy. His fear of the Kau Kau Bushmen (the !kung) is rooted in respect for the strange and unknown. He has been told, or perhaps has even observed, that when Kau Kau Bushmen participate in his dances, the trance condition of a Kau Kau man differs from his. The Kau Kau, he believes, during this period of trance really has powers which go far beyond his own. He therefore attributes thoroughly unwarranted supernatural powers to a Kau Kau Bushman.

The !ko Bushman is not superficial in his religious beliefs because of his empirical and realistic approach. He is fully conscious of the shortcomings of his knowledge and his inability to understand and explain many of the observations and happenings about him. His original source of knowledge stems from "the old people". He feels and says that he cannot be held responsible for what "they" did not tell him. To this fund of learning we must add that which he has observed or experienced himself. But in studying his ethno-botany and especially his ethno-zoology, we are often tempted to ask the *why* and the *wherefore*. The moment this question goes beyond the observable, he does not conjecture, but parries with the reply "because Gu/e made it that way".

All the phenomena of life and death which he cannot *readily* understand are the work of a single power, Gu/e – God. But beyond this, all natural behaviour, even his own, comes about because God, Gu/e, made plants and animals to act as they do. Only Gu/e knows why this or that takes place. Gocholu told us that Gu/e terminates the human life cycle by sending a lion who steps over a score of sleeping people before picking his victim.

What he cannot understand by employing his powers of observation and deduction, the !ko Bushman readily attributes to the will of Gu/e. Indeed, even understandable behaviour comes about because "Gu/e made the creature to act that way". No mortal can, on his own, affect the life of a person, unless sent by Gu/e to do so. No "medicine" can imbue a doctor with the ability to go into a trance, unless such medicine be instilled by Gu/e's power; indeed, no therapeutic plant medicine is effective without Gu/e's backing. Animals do not harm man, not even a lion or leopard, unless willed to do so. None the less, one does not provoke Gu/e or /oa by acting recklessly in the presence of these beasts. A man does not step on a puff-adder through carelessness, for has he not trained eyes to see it? Gu/e hid the serpent to strike and kill him. Similarly, Gu/e keeps the steenbok from his arrow, for does his neighbour come home laden with meat? Such are the categorical statements given during many discussions.

The !ko, as we have said, unashamedly lay bare their own limitations and ignorance of things of this world. Thereby they exhibit their humility, that quality venerated by thinkers and philosophers of many cultures and societies.

12
Religion and Folklore
Megan Biesele

There is great variation among the cultural traditions of the various Bushman groups. Across South West Africa, Botswana and Angola today is spread a complex, interpenetrating patchwork of systems of belief and religious practice. Not long ago this patchwork was even vaster, extending across South Africa as well. Thus it is almost impossible to discuss Bushman religion and folklore without referring to specific groups, to specific places and historical times.

There is diversity of belief between groups and also within single groups. Explanations for this diversity include some of the forces that also account for the wide variations among Bushman languages. The picture is further complicated by outside influences. Another reason for the diversity is the great influence that outstanding individuals may exert, in Bushman culture, in the shaping of local tradition and practice. This process has been observed among modern-day *Zhũ/twãsi* (!Kung) and it may reasonably explain some of the complexity observable among other Bushman groups as well.

For instance, local conceptions of God's appearance are greatly influenced by accounts of local curers who have "visited the sky" while in a trance. Another instance of the effect of a single individual concerns the giraffe medicine dance, which is widely spread across South West Africa and western Botswana. Old Be (N!oshe), who "received the first giraffe song from God" when she was a woman in middle life, is still alive today in Tchum!khwe. According to Botswana !Kung, Be was alone in the bush one day. She saw a herd of giraffes running before an approaching thunderstorm. The rolling beat of their hooves grew louder and mingled in her head with the sound of sudden rain. Suddenly a song she had never heard before came to her entire, and she began to sing. God told her it was a medicine song.

Be went home and taught it to her husband. They sang and danced it together. He then taught it to others. There are old *Ĵũ/wã* men who can trace the people through whom the song spread into Botswana. This giraffe medicine tradition, stemming from a single inspired individual, has virtually replaced the earlier gemsbok dance over vast areas of the Kalahari. The change has occurred within living memory.

The beliefs of the Bushmen
Given this fluidity, this complexity, it is doubly difficult to answer the question of whether Bushmen believe in a single god or in many gods. Most Bushman groups believe in a greater and a lesser god. There are also some other supernatural beings, as well as the spirits of the dead. But to say that Bushmen are therefore *polytheistic* would be to set an extremely high valuation on the roles of the lesser supernatural beings.

In general the Great God is regarded among Bushman groups as a supreme good being. The !Kung say he created himself, declaring: "I am *chi dole*. I am unknown, a stranger. No one can command me." He then created bush-food *(veldkos)* and water, the earth and the air. He taught people the skills they would need to live their lives, and he gave them medicine dancing so they could cure themselves. He dwells in the eastern sky surrounded by his servants, the spirits of the dead.

The Great God sends good and bad fortune to men through these servants and through the Lesser God, who lives in the western sky. This Lesser God is treacherous and vengeful. But neither of the gods has much to do with the moral life of present-day Bushmen. Generally social wrongs are dealt with inside the

12.1 Folklore is passed on by word of mouth. //oka n!a is an old woman storyteller in the Dobe area of Ngamiland.

12.2 At Kauri in Ngamiland, /uka n!a has donned his dance finery, including a rare and fine aardwolf headpiece.

group. One important exception among the !Kung is that God may be angered if a person is neglected or ill-treated by his kin. To punish the group God may take the person away – that is, kill him. But usually the concept of sin as an offence against God is absent. However, the Great God may be displeased by other, non-social types of human activity, and may mete out punishment for these.

Though God is in the sky, he is not remote from men. He can be approached not only by the shamans, but by ordinary individuals, through informal prayer. Among the now extinct Cape Bushmen, prayers were most often addressed to the New Moon. These prayers were usually requests for rain and for food. The Moon was the creation of the mantis hero, /Kaggen, who threw his own shoe into the sky to give himself light. Travelling northward from the Cape today, we encounter traces of the belief that the Moon has command over the life-giving rain among other Bushman groups, notably the Nharo. However, from groups that are now extinct we have very little information about further religious observances regarding the moon and other heavenly bodies. It is questionable whether we are really justified in assuming that the few prayers that have been preserved add up to moon "worship".

It is certain that among the Botswana and South West Africa !Kung no active divinity is attributed to the heavenly bodies. There, prayers are addressed to a great anthropomorphic creator, who is called variously Hishe, Huwe, Kxo, !Gara, Erob, Thora, ≠Gao n!a, and other names. Some !Kung groups have as many as eight different names for the single Great God. The name Hishe or Heishe may be a corruption of Heitsi Eibib, a mythical Hottentot hero. That Huwe, too, refers to an anthropomorphic being we know from shamans' accounts of him and from

163

many folk tales. It is interesting, though, that the !o !Kung of Angola offer prayers to the Moon. In some cases, they even substitute the creator name Huwe for the name of the New Moon, //nui -se.

It is possible to see connections also between Hishe-Huwe and the Mantis of the Southern Bushmen. In the Cape, the Mantis is the central figure in the main cycle of stories. He is never worshipped, but he is believed to have created not only the Moon but also the various buck, and to be the protector of the buck. In Lesotho the Mantis was even more definitely the creator, causing life and death, controlling the abundance of gathered food and hunted game. He was connected also with the curing dance.

The Lesser God, called by various Bushman groups //gaũwa, //gawama, //ganga, //gauab, /gamab, /nawa, Gaua, Gauna, Khauna or Xamaba, is generally thought of as the destroyer. Among the Nama Hottentots, too, //gaunab was the black chief opposed to the creator and rain-giver, Tsui-//Goab. In all Bushman and Hottentot groups the Lesser God does both good and evil deeds, but the emphasis is definitely upon evil. The !Kung believe that this god walks in the treacherous whirlwind.

The Lesser God //gaũwa is subservient to the Great God, working evil on the world through harmful medicine he brings to man. Medicine men confront him at a trance-dance and scream: "Idiot! You have brought a bad medicine! It is going to kill someone. Take it back."

There is some resemblance between //gaũwa and !Khwa, the personification of the rain in the old Cape Bushman mythology. Rain appeared in these myths as a supernatural personage who himself "thundered" and "lightened". When Rain was angry, people might be carried off in a whirlwind. Certain observances thus had to be kept, in order not to provoke !Khwa's anger.

12.3 Men in a trance dance in the central Kalahari.

164

!Khwa often appeared in animal guise. In the form of a bull it carried off a young girl. Sometimes it was an eland. Generally it was an animal living in a waterhole. Rain-magicians had only to lead it forth over the countryside to ensure that life-giving rains would fall. These rain-animals, which figure so beautifully in many southern African rock paintings and in ethnographic fragments concerning rain magic recorded during the last century, have not been found in the present-day mythologies of the more northern Bushmen.

But the Zhũ/twãsi tell tales in which Rain, !Ga, is personified. They also make a sharp distinction between *!ga di*, or Female Rain, which is gentle and feared by none, and the violent Male Rain, *!ga !go*. They say that !ga !go should be referred to by means of a respect word, n/oi, so he will not be angered. Windy, frightening rain is often met with shouts of abuse similar to those used to upbraid the malevolent //gaũwa. The !o !Kung of Angola say in a rain storm that "//gaua thunders".

Dance and trance

The curing dance, which facilitates contact between the human world and the divine, is substantially the same among different Bushman groups today. The central focus of religious life for all groups that still live in anything like the ancient way is the dance with its attendant trance medicine. Apparently the dance was important in the past as well: there are striking rock paintings, from Rhodesia to the Cape Province, which bear testimony to its flourishing existence in prehistoric times.

There are a number of medicine songs, though some, like the giraffe songs, sometimes enjoy much greater popularity than others. The songs are named after "strong" things – honey, the elephant, the mamba – and are considered to possess

12.4 A dance may begin quite spontaneously and "for fun" . . .

12.5 Almost everyone in the encampment – and often from far around – is caught up in the dance. Old /uka n!a joins in.

medicine. This medicine is not a physical substance. It is instead a kind of latent power which may be activated by singing and dancing. Its presence is visible in its effects on the medicine-owners, who are people who have achieved the trance state and can use it to cure others.

Usually the women sit on the ground beside a fire and clap and sing while the men dance. There are, however, groups in which female curers are as numerous as male, and in some places special women's dances have developed. But mainly the music of the dance comes from the part-singing and complex clapping of women.

The structure of this music is most intricate. It is endlessly varied by disciplined

improvisation, within the bounds of repeated musical phrases. When the awesome sound of the men's rattles – long strings of dried cocoons wound around the legs – is added to the singing and sharply clapped cadences, a music of truly unearthly beauty is produced. This music is one of the basic vehicles of transcendence, enabling curers to achieve the altered state of consciousness called trance.

A dance does not begin on a high level of religious seriousness, however. It begins instead in play, in dancing for the delight of it. Children and adolescents often begin a dance and are joined later by the older people. As the night wears on, children drop out and go to sleep, often on their mothers' laps, while the adults dance on.

Thus the dance is an activity which can include people of all ages, at the level on which they are ready to participate in it. It is a social form potentially including everyone, but no-one who does not want to is coerced to join in. Some nights even the best of dancers may prefer simply to watch. Though there are high standards for excellent dancing, no mediocre dancer ever feels unwelcome. In this freedom lies a goodly part of the power of Bushman dancing.

12.7 At a very young age, a child will attempt to join in the dance.

12.8 Dancing and singing and clapping may continue throughout the night.

166

Dances are never scheduled, but are spontaneously initiated. They may take place as often as several times a week, but the average is once in ten days. Though they sometimes begin in response to a specific, pressing illness or shared anxiety, they most often start in fun. Then they may proceed to become serious, as various people go into trance and begin to cure. Or they may remain on a level of fun for many, many hours, and no-one may go into trance at all.

Dances usually last most or all of a night. During this time there may be numerous fluctuations of mood. The dancing may be lack-lustre or ardent, and there may be several periods of intense curing interspersed with periods during which no-one is in trance. Just at dawn there is invariably a great surge of energy, and the curing medicine is believed then to be very strong.

About half the adult men achieve trance at some time during their lifetimes. Some practise it for years and become accomplished curers. It is believed that when in trance these curers possess the power to draw out illness from the bodies of sick people. The illness is then cast away so that it may no longer harm anyone.

12.10 Sweating male dancers are near trance.

Sickness is believed among the !Kung and others to be caused by tiny, invisible arrows brought from God by the spirits of the dead. When a curer is in trance he goes to the sick person and lays fluttering hands on him to draw out these arrows into his own body. The curer works himself to an apex of excitement, at which point his entire body gives a violent shrug directed toward expelling the arrows through his upper back. At the same moment he utters a characteristic curing shriek.

In deep trance (semiconsciousness or unconsciousness), the spirit of the curer is believed to leave his body to do battle with the spirits of the dead and with the Lesser God in the dark beyond the ring of firelight. The dead are reviled for bringing all sorts of misfortune, not just sickness. The spirits of some great curers may also travel to the village of God, to plead there for the return of the spirits of the ill and dying.

In none of this is it believed that supernatural beings enter or speak through the bodies of the curers. The shamans themselves are active, it is believed, moving about earth and sky to benefit the group. But the curers, important as they are, readily acknowledge their absolute dependence upon the singers. The women sing

12.12 Central Kalahari dancers fall into a trance.

168

and clap to provide not only the impetus for trance, but also musical protection for the curers as their spirits travel outside their bodies. The trance dance is thus not only an art form in which all can participate, but a concerted effort of the entire community to banish misfortune. The fact that all members of a group participate personally in this effort accounts for much of its psychic and emotional efficacy. The dance is perhaps the central unifying force in Bushman life, binding people together in very deep ways which we do not fully understand.

Bushman folklore

For most people the reading of African folk tales has usually meant reading the folk tales of Bantu-speaking Negroes. But that Bushman folklore belongs to a completely different tradition from that of the Bantu-speakers is readily apparent. It imparts the flavour of a truly separate world. Borrowed stories, even when told in Bushman languages, are immediately detectable, though there have naturally been some true incorporations of Bantu-speakers' ideas. In general, Bushman stories show much more affinity with Hottentot stories than with those of the Bantu-speaking Negroes.

Within this separate world, the folklore of the different groups is perhaps even more varied than are the religious ideas. The stories collected a hundred years ago in the Cape revolve primarily about the Mantis, /Kaggen, and his family. In these stories the Mantis is a kind of trickster, shown sometimes as a bumbling fool, yet possessed of supernatural powers. His wife is the Dassie *(Hyrax capensis)*. They have three children: a daughter, Ywe-/naṅ-//kaintu; a son, !gaunu-ts'axau (!gaunu is the name of a certain star, and ts'axau means "eye"), who is killed by baboons and restored to life by his father; and another son, /kaggen-⊙pwa, the young Mantis. The Porcupine, !xo, is an adopted daughter of the Mantis. !xo is afraid to live with her own father, who is //khwai-hemm, the All-Devourer. She is married to /kwammanga, a being not identified with any animal, but seen in the rainbow. !xo and /kwammanga have two children, /kwammanga-⊙pwa, who is quiet like his father, and /ni, the talkative Ichneumon, who chides and advises his grandfather, /Kaggen. The Mantis also has two sisters. One is the Blue Crane and the other is the mother of his pet Springbok. These characters were all men and women once, believed to belong to a race on earth before the Bushmen. Now they have been changed into animals.

The Bushmen of Lesotho and the Orange Free State had a similar mantis hero for their tales. His name has been spelled by researchers there as Ohang, 'Kaang or Cagn. His wife is Ko or Coti. They have two sons, Cogaz and Gcwi. Cogaz is killed by baboons and restored to life by Cagn, just as is !gaunu-ts'axau in the Cape

12.14 Periods of intense curing may occur during the trance dances. At Dobe-Mahopa, in Ngamiland, /"ase !xumsi n!a is curing in a trance.

stories. Occasionally he fulfils the same function as does the Cape Ichneumon, /ni, in helping the Mantis out of some of his many scrapes.

Further north there are few remnants of the powerful Mantis figure. The !xõ Bushmen around Takatshwane, Botswana, have a few stories featuring a mantis. Zhũ/twãsi call the mantis "God's servant" and believe that it is bad to kill or injure one. But in general the present-day groups in the north have story traditions distinct from the old ones of the Southern Bushmen.

The /gwi trickster, for instance, is called Pisiboro or G//awama. He is anthropomorphic, but of super-normal dimensions. Pisiboro's leg was bitten by a python in South West Africa, around Gobabis. It became inflamed, and as the fever took hold on him, he developed a raging thirst. In his death throes, as he dragged his leg from South West Africa to Botswana looking for water, he scraped out the tortuous course of the Okwa *omuramba*. His body putrified and became the water of rivers, and his hair flew up in the sky and stayed there as black clouds of rain. This hero appears to be identified by the /Gwi with the Lesser God.

The !Kung story tradition is like the tale traditions of the more southerly Bushmen again, in that the protagonist in the old tales is connected to some extent with the Greater God. There are, however, some important differences between this protagonist figure and current conceptions of God. He is referred to in the tales as Huwe or Heishe, or as ≠Gao n!a or Gaoxa, which last is a term of respect rather than a name. Gaoxa's family includes his wives, on whom he plays a hilarious succession of dirty tricks. They play others back on him. He has two sons, Kã//ka and !xoma, who have various adventures. In one story they are killed by lions and buried in the stomach contents of an eland. But they are restored to life by their father, as was !gaunu-ts axau. Again like !gaunu-ts axau, they are identified with stars. Gaoxa also has a strange brother-in-law called !õ!õtsi/dasi, whose eyes are located on the insides of his ankles. Running through these stories is a great concern with proper family relationships, with delicate social arrangements involving the sharing, cooking and eating of food, and with the division of labour between the sexes.

The most enigmatic figure in !Kung tradition is Gaoxa's lovely daughter-in-law. Usually she is referred to as !xô//əmdima, a very obscure name which probably means "beautiful ant-bear maiden". But sometimes she is called !kxodi, or "elephant girl". At times she is married to an elephant and at times to the older brother of Kã//ka and !xoma. In some versions she is called !eu!eua or !eu!euadi, references to her little barking laugh. Around this daughter-in-law revolves a fascinating cycle of stories dealing with themes of marriage and marriage-service, murder and blood-vengeance, birth and the origin of meat, and the balance of power between men and women.

Besides the hero cycles there exists in Bushman folklore a great abundance of other tales, usually involving animals and containing explanations of how the world has come to be as it is. There is also a rich store of legends dealing with historical figures and actual events. Remote connections among the various tale traditions present a fascinating challenge to those interested in Bushman folklore. But all Bushman story traditions are homogeneous in this important respect: all the animals in the stories were originally people and only later became animals. At first glance this characteristic of Bushman folklore appears to be out of the ordinary: in most other traditions it is said that people were at first animals, rather than the other way around. It is interesting to speculate whether this peculiarity represents a genuine and important difference from other cultures.

There is one story which is easily recognisable in collections from all Bushman groups. This is the well-known story of the origin of death. There are as many versions of this story as there are storytellers, but basically death comes to the world because the Hare denies the Moon's assertion that men shall die but be forever reborn, just as the Moon itself is:

Once long ago the Moon and the Hare were arguing together. "When a person dies he will do as I do and come back from the dead," said the Moon. "He will die and return, die and return as I do," said the Moon.

But the Hare scorned him, saying: "Uh-uh! What makes you think a person who dies will not rot and smell foul? A dead person will not return."

12.15 Facial scarifications imitating the stripes of the beautiful zebra.

170

12.16 Musical interest starts early – with the first dance the children see. These Bushman children at Dobe are playing tunes on grass-stems.

The Moon thus spoke well and the Hare spoke badly. They argued and they fought. And as they were fighting the Hare scratched the Moon's face with his fingernails. To this day the Moon's face bears these black scratch marks. And the Moon in retaliation took a shoe and split the Hare's lip. And to this day the Hare's lip is split in two. These were the signs of their quarrel. Since then men have died and have not returned.

Ngamiland, 1971

This tale is found among Bushmen throughout southern Africa. Only in the Cape Province, however, has a definite prayer to this same Moon been recorded:

!Kábbĭ-ă yonder! Take my face yonder! Thou shalt give me thy face yonder! Thou shalt take my face yonder! That which does not feel pleasant. Thou shalt give me thy face . . . (with) which thou, when thou hast died, thou dost again, living return; when we did not perceive thee, thou dost again lying down come, that I may also resemble thee. For, the joy yonder, thou dost always possess it yonder, that is, that thou art wont again to return alive, when we did not perceive thee; while the Hare told thee about it, that thou shouldst do thus. Thou didst formerly say, that we should again return alive, when we died.

Katkop, 1875

So short a chapter cannot with any justice claim to be a proper introduction to the rich world of Bushman folklore and religion. Those who want to go through the folk tales for themselves, to know about the tiny medicine bows of gemsbok horn, about imitative games and dances, about the month-long winter ordeal of young men's initiation and the Eland dancing of girls' puberty; those who want to

171

12.17 Bushwoman (Ngamiland) with thumb piano.

read texts of prayers and of mood-songs to the thumb piano, verbatim descriptions of shamans' travels to the village of the dead, and accounts of how Bushmen believe the world and the heavens to be shaped, should look to some of the specialised studies in the Select Bibliography.

Interesting and important as these things are, greater interest lies in the fact that there exist today a few Bushmen who are still very much involved with them. We have access to first-hand information about how these beliefs and traditions fit in with ecological and social conditions prevailing in present-day environments. Thus we can ask Bushmen themselves to clarify their traditions for us, and hope to gain a more comprehensive view of the thinking behind the picturesque details we have glimpsed. Any such research would be a step toward the mutual understanding that is ever more necessary as the world – and with it southern Africa – grow smaller.

172

13
The Bushmen in a Changing World

Hans J. Heinz

From what has already been written here it becomes clear that the 20th century is advancing relentlessly into every niche into which the "wild" hunter-gatherer has withdrawn. There are romantics who are horrified at the thought of a planned programme for the future development of the Bushmen. "Why don't you let these people live their own happy life without interfering?" they ask. Yet they give little thought to the fact that they, and this very 20th century which they represent, are constantly altering the life-base of the Bushmen. It is precisely this process with which we must come to terms.

A further most significant point is often overlooked: the need for the Bushmen's social status to rise in the eyes of people with whom they come into contact (see Chapter 14). Unless and until this is achieved, the Bushmen will remain prisoners within a vicious circle that ensures their poverty, ignorance and lowly status. What is required basically, therefore, is the *means* by which the Bushmen can meet successfully the challenge of this century and by which they can rise in the social esteem of others.

Today the government of Botswana finds itself in a quandary. It is exposed to the most diverse outside pressures to do something for this minority group, the Bushmen. As a recipient of extensive international development aid, it realises the need to meet this challenge squarely. Yet Bushman rehabilitation programmes are costly. How can such monies be allocated or spent without some promise of success? The authorities consider themselves "let down" by the numerous students of Bushman cultures, who have come from some of the most distinguished institutions of the world, and to whom they have freely extended scientific – and social – hospitality. The scientists have come and gone. Hardly one has applied himself to the pressing social problems that face the government in dealing with the Bushman minority. For this reason, the authorities appear to be hesitant in dealing firmly with uninformed do-gooders and romantics who wish to "save" the Bushmen, for such actions might have serious repercussions in the world press. The authorities just do not seem yet to know what is the right thing to do. What is lacking is experience gained on the spot, in well-controlled, small-scale programmes, so that what has been learnt may be applied in a much larger project.

In the days of Tshekedi Khama, there were tribal schools to which capable Bushman boys on the cattle posts of the Bamangwato tribe had access, with financial support of the royal house. There are Bushmen who are today senior officers in the Botswana police force and who received their education in such schools. Today these school have been taken over by the State.

The present projects in Botswana are very limited. Basically they may be divided into mission projects and those of non-mission origin.

Mission projects for the Bushmen

The first that should be mentioned is the mission farm of D'Kar near Ghanzi. It is run by the Reformed Church of Aranos, South West Africa, and was started in 1968 on a donated farm. The missionaries, Mr Rampa and Mr Jerling, not only began ecclesiastical work, but also started a tannery, a farm and the first Bushman school. While the latter caters for children, some of whom are housed in a hostel, the tannery is there to train adults in the working of skins and the manufacture of simple articles such as saddles, bridles, shoes and *riems,* or thongs. The skins all come from the farm, where the Bushmen are exposed also to agricultural training. The school, which has a fluctuating attendance of about 90, presently admits non-Bushman children as well. There are two State-paid Tswana teachers. The child-

ren of D'Kar, as do all other children in Botswana, enjoy the benefits of a State-provided school-feeding scheme. The hostel, however, is run completely by the mission, which provides food and clothing for the children and pays the salary of the matron. The entire project, which was originally most promising with regard to vocational training, at present appears to be in a state of flux. The school, which adheres to the curriculum of the Botswana Department of Education, may therefore come under State management.

At Xanegas, near the border of South West Africa, there is a similar but larger project run by the Dutch Reformed Church under Miss V. Venter. The school was begun by the Coloured community for their children some twelve years ago. For the past four years, however, Bushman children have been admitted. They number about 40 today. A ratio of one-third Bushmen is maintained. These are mostly Nharo and come from the Coloured-owned farms of the surrounding area. The emphasis here is almost exclusively on primary education and no Bushman child has so far gone beyond Standard 4. The school runs two hostels, one of which is exclusively for Bushmen. One of the problems arising from a school system where children live in hostels is that they tend to become isolated or estranged from their home communities. Xanegas tries to avoid this by sending the children home periodically. As Xanegas is a thoroughly multiracial school, much is being done to avoid social stratification among the children. The school adheres closely to the syllabus of the Botswana Department of Education. It receives considerable fiscal aid both from central and local government. Thus the six teachers, the hostels and some of the classrooms are all supported or paid for from government sources, local or central.

Literacy classes have now been started for adult Bushmen. However, little development is apparent in the field of vocational training, either for children or adults. The area is highly overgrazed and it appears therefore to be undesirable that the Bushmen in this area become pastoralists, as are their employers. It is hoped that home industries and highly controlled farming may be encouraged among the Bushmen in this intensively farmed area.

Other mission work has been restricted to medical care. Thus the Seventh Day Adventist Mission of Kanye has been conducting a flying doctor service for several years. Much of this medical care reaches Bushmen who come to clinics in the Kalahari. In the case of Bere (see below), regular visits to the Bushman settlement have been conducted on a monthly basis. Soon, however, Danish medical students are expected to take over this service. The German Lutheran Mission wishes to become active in the southern or eastern Kalahari, which will bring medical aid to certain Bushman communities as well. At Sehitwa this mission plans to conduct courses on a "nurse aid" level for girls stationed in remote areas. A capable girl of the Bere Bushmen has been admitted to the first of these.

Non-mission projects for Bushmen

Some of the non-mission projects are still very much in their infancy. At Lone Tree, along the Ghanzi-Lobatse road, Mr A. Traill, a contributor to this volume, has begun an agricultural scheme among about 100 people. It owes its origin, I believe, in part to the effect radiating from the settlement at Bere, in part as well to the energy of Mr Traill. The Lone Tree scheme is concerned essentially with the transition of adults to an agricultural economic system. Promising young men from Lone Tree have been sent to the agricultural brigades so popular in other parts of Botswana. The scheme has received the moral and financial support of the State. Sooner or later funds will become available for sinking its own borehole as a source of water. However, one danger lies in the pressure exerted by Tswana tribesmen on "uninhabited grazing areas". As has been shown, land occupied by Bushmen is considered by these people to be "uninhabited".

Not more than 19 km (12 miles) away lies the Bushman Settlement Scheme of Bere, which was started at Takatshwane by relatively "wild" Bushmen, of their own volition. This was some seven or eight years ago, and the scheme has since been piloted by the writer. The impetus for the development was given when some of these people, accompanying the writer on eight of his expeditions to the north, saw the material advances of other Bushmen. The question posed at that time was: "Why can't we have goats, etc., etc., as they have?" (It is probable that this question posed by Lone Tree people returning from visits to Bere was also at the root of Mr Traill's scheme.) Money was raised for a borehole and the Takatshwane people, who amalgamated with a band from the Okwa valley, moved to a pan called Bere.

13.2 A group of Nharo Bushmen outside a hut in the area between Olifantskloof and Ghanzi. Among the world's last surviving hunters and gatherers, the San face an uncertain future.

13.3 That the hunting and gathering way of life will have disappeared off the face of the earth by the 21st century is virtually certain. The dilemma facing governments of all territories where Bushmen and other hunter-gatherers survive is how to buffer them against the developing cultures that surround them, without loss of their self-esteem, and at the same time to smooth their transition into the developing world into which they are inevitably moving, without sacrificing all of their own cultural heritage.

13.4 Schools and self-help schemes are a part of the needs of the moment; so are medical services and supplies.

13.5 One of the important aspects of the entire problem is the Bushman's identification with the land. We have seen how important it was in the historical past – in the 200 Years' War – and it is no less crucial today. Much of the Bushman's social system has been destroyed because he has ceased to feel an identification with the land where the opportunity to do so has been denied to him.

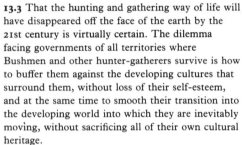

Today Bere boasts a school run by a young New Zealand lady, a small, licensed general dealer's shop run by a San girl, a permanent house for each of the two, an ablution block, a workshop, a tannery, a two-roomed dispensary, two guest houses and the first two permanent Bushman houses. Bere has its own air strip, built by the Bushmen on their own initiative, and a 16 km (10 miles) access road, also cleared by them before subsequent grading. The livestock consists of about 104 high-grade cattle, the same number of goats, 4 horses and numerous donkeys.

Financial support has come from various sources. While initially the writer drew support from private sources, State aid was received after the infrastructure had been completed. Such aid largely serves to insure the smooth running of the school. Recently, the United States Self-help Aid programme has brought money into the Scheme, as have also the Max Planck Gesellschaft and the firm Hoechst of Germany.

The achievements at Bere are mentioned to show that the emphasis is on *total* development. Paternalism is meticulously avoided. Experts in various vocational fields are encouraged to visit Bere as teachers for those Bushmen showing interest in certain trades. Thus there have come a thatcher, a master mason, a carpenter, an expert in animal husbandry and an expert in the tanning of skins. The people are encouraged to employ their traditional skills in the manufacture of curios of high standard, so that appropriate and fair remuneration may be obtained. (Only in this way was it possible to obtain the means to buy quality livestock.) Those few who are more talented are encouraged to refine their skills.

The school at Bere does not fall under the Botswana Department of Education and is therefore free to work out its own syllabus. The step from a hunter-gatherer culture to that of a present-day settled society is so great that it is better for children of the first generation to learn only the three R's. Provision is made, however, to send especially gifted youngsters to a secondary school. Unfortunately experience has shown that children who have been away at boarding school return as misfits in their home society. The emphasis in the school is on breaking down band differences and on moulding the people of Bere into one; on establishing pride in achievement and a sense of responsibility; on creating an awareness in these people that they are all citizens of Botswana, with rights, duties and obligations equal to those of all other Botswana citizens.

Bere has achieved much, but it has serious problems in spite of the lessons which have been learned. Perhaps the greatest one concerns discipline and the subjugation to authority. The concept of headmanship in a Bushman society has been a volitional one. Yet at Bere 95 people are obliged to live together permanently because they have their immovable property and their water there. Living together in peace is a lesson which the Bere Bushmen are still learning (as, indeed, is the rest of the world). It is a particularly difficult lesson, because for the first time there is a forceful headman, in the person of the writer. However, he has no other disciplinary authority than force of personality. As a pilot scheme, therefore, Bere serves a very important purpose. It is a testing ground for policies which are to be of significance in the implementing of the Okwa River Project (see below).

Further development schemes

Dr Silberbauer in his chapter points out the grave social problems posed by the unemployed Bushmen of the farming community of Ghanzi. The Bushmen who squat on Ghanzi farms constitute a sizeable unemployment and under-employment problem and a drain on the resources of the farming community. They live largely on hand-outs given to them by people sympathetic to their plight. The slaughter and theft of cattle by these unemployed Bushmen have become endemic. It is estimated that R70 000 per year is spent in maintaining and controlling the squatters, a great proportion of which represents the value of cattle stolen and food given out for subsistence.

In order to make the Bushmen self-sufficient again and to relieve the pressure on the farming community at Ghanzi, three interrelated schemes have been proposed which, it is hoped, would help Bushmen adapt to the fast-evolving economy of Botswana. The proposed schemes would consist in:

a. Expanding the existing facilities for educating and training the Bushmen. This is already reflected in State support given to Xanegas, D'Kar, Bere and Lone Tree.
b. Establishing a settlement scheme for Bushmen in the Okwa valley (or perhaps even several similar schemes).
c. Investigating the possibilities of a wildlife culling scheme.

Regarding the Okwa valley project, it is proposed to establish a settlement for Bushmen over a period of five years in the Okwa valley, 80 km (50 miles) south of Ghanzi and slightly east of the Tschwane borehole. An area 19 by 19 km (12 by 12 miles) would be set aside, fenced and divided into four paddocks. Prospective squatters would be selected from the "squatter community" on the basis of recommendations made by an anthropologist conducting research among the Bushmen. The settlement would be supervised by a settlement officer with some training in animal husbandry and agriculture. The settlement officer would be assisted during the initial period by a sociologist who would work hand in hand with an ecologist.

The settlers would be taught the fundamentals of animal husbandry, stock management and the principles of stock ownership. The leadership of the settlement community would be the responsibility of a headman chosen by the community from its members. The ecologist, with the assistance of the game department, would ensure sound conservation practices, so that the veld should not suffer from overstocking.

The manufacture of curios would be encouraged and marketing would be done through a handicraft marketing organisation. Thus it is considered that this scheme would assist in the essential process of integrating the Bushmen into the economy of the country.

This brings us to the final programme, the wildlife cropping scheme, which was long ago suggested by the writer and recently by Dr Silberbauer. At this stage it is still on the drawing board. However, it essentially affects Bushmen of the Central Kalahari Reserve, whose future position is not at all clear. One group in the southern part of the Reserve has a borehole where livestock such as goats and horses drink. These Bushmen are anxious to develop along the lines of Bere and have said so on various occasions. This, incidentally, demonstrates the effect radiating from Bere, which is more than 160 km (100 miles) away. Basically the Government has no opposition to this desire, as long as Tswana pastoralists are not encouraged to enter the area with their cattle. The northern half of the Reserve would be proclaimed a national park. No village would be allowed to develop there and livestock would not be permitted to enter. It is not clear yet which of the areas in central Botswana would be earmarked for game culling, but it is reasonable to assume that the thoroughly "wild" Bushmen living in the Central Kalahari Reserve would be given ample opportunity to seek employment in such ventures.

One of the most important aspects of the entire Bushman problem is that of the Bushman's identification with the land. Much of the Bushman's social system has been destroyed because he ceased to feel an identification with his land or because this was denied him. It is becoming increasingly clear in Gaborone that it is most essential to give back to the Bushmen areas which they have called or can call their own, whether this be a farm around Bere or land in the Okwa valley.

Positive development work has been started in Botswana, but much more can be done if dedicated workers come forward to help and to put their experience at the disposal of the authorities. It would be well if some of those scholars who have been in Botswana or who periodically visit it were to turn their attention to the socio-economic problems associated with the survival of a people who have a unique contribution to make – not only to Botswana, but to all of mankind.

14
The Future of the Bushmen

George B. Silberbauer

The question of the future of the Bushmen is complicated by several factors. First, there are the contrasting ideological orientations of the governments of the countries in which they live. Secondly, Bushmen have been subjected to differing cultural influences in their varying localities, and these influences have, to varying extents, effected changes in their cultures. Thirdly, there is much diversity among the Bushman cultures themselves. In some parts of Botswana and Angola the Bushmen have a long history of close contact with Tswana and other Bantu-speaking Negro peoples, and have become so closely integrated with them and so extensively acculturated that little remains of the original Bushman culture. Others have had shorter, more peripheral contact, but have adjusted their lifestyle to one of partial dependence on Negro and White cattlemen; it is only with great difficulty that these could return to their traditional hunter-gatherer way of life. The great majority of Bushmen fall into these two categories, and it is only the remaining 15 per cent, living in the remoter parts of the central and northern Kalahari, who still live as hunters and gatherers.

14.1 Bushmen have been subjected to differing cultural influences in their varying localities for centuries. These influences have in different degrees effected changes in their cultures. Even before their exposure to this diversity of outside impacts, there is little doubt, the Bushmen varied enormously from group to group and from area to area. Here we show Bushman ladies and adolescents singing and clapping to make the age-old musical accompaniment to the dancing of their menfolk.

South West Africa/Namibia

The early settlement of the Gobabis district of South West Africa by Whites dispossessed the local Bushmen of their land. This resulted in their gradual displacement eastwards into Botswana to join their fellow Nharo, or northwards and eastwards to their fellow !Kung and ≠ao//ei. The few who have remained in the Gobabis district are farm labourers, with no effective security regarding tenure of jobs or residence. The commitment of the South West African government to the ideology of separate development has hitherto precluded permanent rights of residence in this area for these Bushmen, so that their future probably lies with their fellow tribesmen across the border, or in the !Kung country north of the Gobabis district.

In the 1950s the South West African administration initiated a programme of training and permanent settlement of Bushmen in the !Kung country. The aim was to stabilise the locally migrant hunter-gatherers in permanent settlements and to convert them from food-gathering to food-growing. This northern region enjoys a higher rainfall and has better-quality soils than do other parts of the Kalahari, and the type of small-scale farming to which the Bushmen were introduced is feasible. The scheme has the merits of safeguarding the Bushmen's occupation of their land and allowing them a measure of freedom in determining the conduct of their own affairs. The lack of integrative developments has, however, left unaltered the unfavourable image of Bushmen in the rest of the country. Other peoples in South West Africa (as in southern Africa generally) tend to regard the Bushmen as an inferior minority, pampered by being allowed to waste potentially productive land. As long as this image persists, there is a latent threat to the Bushman's identity and to his right to occupy his own land.

14.2 Planning the future of the Bushmen in South West Africa/Namibia: Mr Geelbooi Zowa/'Waaj is the leader of the San or Bushman delegation at the Turnhalle Conference in Windhoek on the future of South West Africa/Namibia. *(Photo by courtesy of The Star, Johannesburg)*

Botswana

Serfs

The majority of Bushmen in Botswana have largely abandoned their locally migrant hunting and gathering life and have attached themselves, permanently or seasonally, to the villages and cattle-posts of Bantu-speaking Negro pastoralists. They perform variable amounts of unskilled labour and render certain specialist services for the Negro cattlemen. In many cases, stable and permanent master-serf relationships have developed. In the last decade or so, the arrangement has come to be regarded as something of a liability, in that the serfs' consumption of food and other resources outweighs the productivity of their labour. Because of the low regard in which they are held, the Bushmen are not exposed to effective acculturation and socialisation and so have never really learnt the principles underlying the economic, social and political systems in which they participate. Their lack of comprehension perpetuates their low standing. It also inhibits motivation towards advancement, and denies them opportunity for improving their usefulness and productivity as workers. Not only are they wasted manpower in sparsely inhabited areas where human resources are scarcest, but they are virtually low-intensity parasites on the marginally successful agriculture and cattle-raising of the villagers and cattle-post owners.

Impelled by their desire for improved living standards and assisted by technological innovations, the peasant pastoralists will inevitably increase the efficiency of their enterprises. Unless the vicious circle locking the serfs in the culture of poverty is broken, the Bushmen on the cattle-posts will suffer the same fate as have those on the farms (see below). Education, specific training and more rational use of the special skills of the Bushman (for example, in the field of handicrafts) are the most promising means of redirecting the trend. It would then be possible for the Bushmen to make more useful and rewarding contributions and, eventually, to capitalise and undertake stock-raising on their own account.

Farm Bushmen

The most urgent problems are those of Bushmen whose territory was allocated to White farmers who settled in the Ghanzi district of Botswana at the end of the 19th century. The farms were only roughly surveyed and freehold title was not granted to the settlers. Partly for these reasons, but also because of their remoteness in those days, development of the farms proceeded slowly. Although the settlers built houses and sank wells, they did not fence their properties. The local Bushmen remained in occupation of the area, gathering plant foods and hunting the game which roamed across the farms until the late 1950s. The traditional foods were supplemented by rations given in return for work, as more and more Bushmen drifted into employment as cattle-herds and labourers. They adopted a more sedentary pattern of residence and families settled more or less permanently on particular farms to become, in effect, serfs of the farmers.

This phase represented a satisfactory mutual adaptation for the 50 or 60 years of its duration; co-operation was rewarding to both parties, and did not entail irksome restrictions on the activities of either. However, the initiation of a new and enlarged settlement scheme during the last 15 years brought an influx of new cattlemen with capital and more modern techniques of husbandry. Properties were resurveyed and freehold title was granted; farms were fenced and cattle-herds dispensed with; improved and more valuable breeds of cattle were imported and stocking densities rose. The days of casual, intermittent, unskilled labour interspersed with periods of hunting and gathering were gone. Cash wages were instituted and rates of pay rose rapidly. Unemployment, an almost meaningless concept when the rotating labour market and natural food resources combined to care for all, became a serious problem. By 1964 only 10 per cent of the 4 000 Bushmen on the Ghanzi farms held jobs, and the remaining 3 600 had either to parasitise the workers or to resort to stock-theft to avoid starvation, in an area suddenly without game or plant foods.

There was a head-on clash of interests. The farmers had invested money, materials, work and stock in enterprises which, if they were to succeed, could not bear the burden of a steady drain of valuable stock being stolen. Nor could they

14.3 ≠oma, a Bushman youth in the Dobe district, wears an imported shirt – just one sign of the cultural changes which are entering with increasing rapidity into San society.

181

14.4 A mere 25 years ago, traditional clothing was almost universal among the Bushmen; imported items of clothing were at that time scarcely ever encountered. Today they stand as merely one visible symbol of the far-reaching and less superficial changes that are sweeping over Bushman life everywhere.

afford to feed the large numbers of hangers-on made unemployable by the new techniques of farming. The Bushmen, quite simply, had been dispossessed of their land and livelihood, despite the undertaking by the government of the then Bechuanaland Protectorate, at the time of settlement, that the Bushmen's rights to land would not be disturbed. Both farmers and Bushmen were forced into competing for the land and its resources and made to bear the brunt of a situation which was not of their making. The farmers have shown commendable restraint and compassion, and the Bushmen have exhibited remarkable patience and fortitude under these very trying conditions.

Economic deprivation among the Bushmen has been accompanied by serious social disruption. The solidarity and the system of mutual dependence of the old communities have largely disappeared and the groups of labourers on the farms

182

are now little more than loose and temporary aggregations, lacking a shared identity and common purpose. Social control has been undermined. With little to promote harmony within the group, the social fabric is torn by dissent and friction, as those who once depended on and supported one another are forced to compete ruthlessly for jobs and scarce means of survival. The economic role of women, once the main providers of food, was negated by the disappearance of food plants from the heavily grazed farms, leaving the women totally dependent on the men as wage-earners or stock-thieves. Promiscuity and prostitution have taken the place of the fidelity of the old community life, and deserted wives and unmarried mothers are now numerous.

Degraded, disintegrated and demoralised as they are, the farm Bushmen have no means of extricating themselves from a position which, already intolerable, will continue to deteriorate unless determined, skilled help is given, and unless that help is sensitive to the needs of the Bushmen, including that of expressing their own ethos and identity.

The first aim of the rescue operation is necessarily to realign the vectors of interest from their present diametric opposition to a convergence on common aims; competition must be restructured to achieve co-operation. To relieve the pressures of competition between Bushmen and farmers for land and livelihood, the Bushmen should be allocated their own areas of land and supplied with the means of living on it. In the selection of land, consideration must be given to such obvious factors as the availability of groundwater, vegetation and soil, and accessibility to labour and produce markets. Consideration must be given also to the ethnic diversity which exists among farm Bushmen and their traditional division of the country into tribal territories. It is not practicable to provide only one area; it is necessary to give each group its own land within its own traditional territory.

In itself, relocation will not solve problems. The process must necessarily be voluntary, which entails the effective communication of the purpose of relocation, and of the idea that worthwhile aims can be achieved through moving. These aims, and the means of achieving them, can be decided in any detail only after the possibilities have been investigated and the results explained to the Bushmen, so that they may determine for themselves their choices among the available alternatives. The aridity and low fertility of the area severely restrict the range of economic alternatives. It is highly unlikely that these Bushmen will choose to return to hunting and gathering for the main part of their subsistence. The social organisational context of the hunter-gatherer lifestyle has been attenuated to the point of ineffectuality, and most of the Bushmen have lost the knowledge and skills needed for this kind of life. A population of 4 000 hunter-gatherers would require between 42 000 and 62 000 km² (roughly 16 000 and 24 000 square miles) and there is not that amount of unoccupied land. A combination of stock-raising and partial dependence on game and food-plant resources seems to be the most promising initial means of subsistence.

Whatever range of feasible choice is offered them, the farm Bushmen must be given the opportunity also to acquire skills and knowledge applicable outside the field of mere subsistence. The farms provide a small but growing market for employment. Apart from the regular labour requirements, there is a developing need for contractors and other specialists. There is also a potential for the development of trades based on the by-products of stock-raising, in which many of the traditional Bushman skills in handicrafts would be relevant. For example, tanning, leatherwork, spinning and weaving have provided useful incomes for Blacks in southern Africa, and for aborigines in Australia. If properly taught and organised, they could be considered as possible supplements to the other activities of rehabilitated farm Bushmen.

It is certain that local resources would be inadequate for a programme on even the minimum scale at which assistance would be effective. It can be argued that, as the instigator of farm settlement, as guarantor of Bushman land rights, and as recipient of the proceeds of the sale of the land, the old Bechuanaland Protectorate government incurred responsibility for the dispossessed Bushmen. The present government of the Republic of Botswana inherited its predecessor's responsibilities but, bearing the heavy burden of national development, it is probably unable to field the necessary manpower and funds needed to discharge this obligation in time to avert a disastrous crisis. Rehabilitation of farm Bushmen will almost certainly require international aid.

The desert dwellers

The farm Bushmen are in a desperate situation which calls for the immediate application of remedies, but in a sense they are already committed to a particular line of development, which narrows down the field of possible policies. The question of the future of those Bushmen who are still hunters and gatherers involves a longer perspective and poses more searching and profound problems of policy.

Hunters and gatherers exploit the unimproved resources of their habitat and therefore depend on these remaining in a state of undisturbed equilibrium. Under these conditions man is an integral but largely neutral element in the ecosystem; the pressures which he exerts in exploiting resources are of magnitudes small enough for the plant and animal communities to tolerate. Except for localised and temporary effects, the processes of self-regulation correct man-made disturbances; resources are neither depleted nor increased by human activity. The human population density is low (between 10 and 15 km², or about 4 to 6 square miles, per person in the central Kalahari) and the over-all rate of exploitation is therefore also low. As the hunters and gatherers feed off a wide spectrum of food-plants and animals, the human load is spread over many species, and as man's ecological niche overlaps those of several herbivores and carnivores, the pressures which he imposes within the ecosystem are low.

Where man utilises a more developed and complex technology, even the relatively primitive technology of the peasant pastoralist, his role changes from that of a neutral, integrated participant in the ecosystem to that of manipulator and manager of ecological factors. He becomes a capitalist, wresting an annual dividend of harvest and progeny from his investment of crops and stock. To achieve this he must alter the ecosystem, giving his crops and stock pre-eminence in their niches, reducing competition by excluding other species. Furthermore, he must suppress the normal processes of ecological succession to avoid development towards climax communities, and he must hold the ecosystem at an early *sere,* or stage of succession, where gross productivity is maximal. The ecological manipulation and competition for space that characterise more advanced food-production techniques constitute a danger to the hunter-gatherer's subsistence base and, hence, to his whole way of life.

That the remaining hunting-gathering Bushmen have not had to face that competition, but have been allowed to continue in their traditional way of life, is due only to the fact that they live in areas which nobody else wants. They have remained relatively isolated and undisturbed because it has not been worth the while of more than a handful of people to overcome the difficulties of reaching them.

As pressures on other, better-favoured land mount and as technology overcomes the environmental barriers which until now have prevented exploitation of the resources of the remote parts of the Kalahari, the threat of competition grows. That ethic which Max Weber called Protestant, but which equally possesses Roman Catholic, Jew, Moslem or devotee of the Lord Buddha, will assert itself and demand that resources be exploited. He who utilises the greatest amount at the greatest rate earns thereby the right to oust all others who, by narrow economic criteria, are unworthy of the privilege of occupying land – land which has been theirs in the whole course of the memory of man. This, at least, has been the pattern of all the history of contact between Bushman and non-Bushman, between hunter-gatherer and pastoralist, farmer, industrialist and miner. The desire for economic gain has occasionally been reinforced (and sometimes camouflaged) by such idealistic motives as the provision of medical services or the propagation of the gospel. To resist these imperatives requires considerable political courage, and the choice of policy is made more difficult by the fact that, in many significant respects, the "wild" Bushmen are no longer isolated.

Settlement and hunting on its borders have already reduced the numbers of game animals which migrate into and across the Central Kalahari Reserve. Depletion is not yet critical, but the processes which could bring eventual crisis have been at work for many years. The present isolation of the Bushmen in the Reserve is no longer sufficiently complete to avoid the spread of infectious diseases, for which contact provides a vector, and these Bushmen have not yet developed physiological or cultural means of resisting these diseases. Furthermore, the slight, intermittent contact which has existed has sufficed to introduce such cultural changes as a reliance on iron for arrowheads and spearheads, knives and other artefacts. Those whose territories are within convenient reach of the farms have developed the habit of migrating to them in times of drought in search of food and water.

For these reasons a simple policy of isolation and non-intervention is inappropriate and inadequate. The situation requires management of the points of articulation between the Bushmen and the outside world, and of the inputs and other traffic across these contacts, so as to allow the hunter-gatherers to retain their identity and meaningful ways of expressing it. This does not imply that processes of change must be halted and all developments stultified. Rather, it means that the desert dwellers need protection from influences which, in their forcefulness and unfamiliarity, would be beyond the capacity of the Bushmen to meet, absorb and usefully employ. The culture of these Bushmen is not fossilized and static; they themselves recognise its dynamism and propensity for change in response to the variations in their environment. Both psychologically and socially they are well prepared for adaptive change in certain directions. Provided development is consistent with this directional predisposition, and articulates with their existing knowledge, values and practices so as to retain cultural coherence, it is possible to enhance the Bushmen's capacity to deal with outside influences and to assist them to reach a stage where they can be integrated with the other inhabitants of Botswana, yet retain their distinctive way of life and govern their affairs according to their own values, without threat of subjection to an alien ethos.

It is not only on ethical grounds that the culture of hunting-gathering Bushmen should be defended, although moral considerations are sufficient reason for this. Plant geneticists and animal breeders have stated the need for preserving wild flora and fauna in order to retain the genetic diversity needed for the development of future specialised strains. If the predictions of such environmentalists as Commoner, Dubois and Ehrlich on the future needs of man are at all accurate, there is much in the expert knowledge, cognition and outlook of the "wild" Bushmen which is of value to the rest of the world in confronting the environmental crisis. The intellectual and spiritual resources contained in the cultures should not be extinguished.

As I have indicated, the practical political problem in a conservation scheme is that the "Protestant Ethic" demands demonstration of the pay-off from that which is to be conserved. The need of conservation of the Bushmen's cultures could be met by a scheme in which the desert dwellers cropped the larger species of Kalahari antelope, as a commercial undertaking yielding an economically useful return.

Antelope are better adapted to Kalahari conditions than are cattle. Cattle-raising is the principal industry in the Kalahari and Botswana generally, but it is a costly and marginally successful undertaking in all but the most favourable parts of the Kalahari. Antelope have the advantage over cattle in that:

(i)   they do not require daily access to water in order to thrive;
(ii) they feed off a wider portion of the total vegetation spectrum than do cattle, obtaining more food per unit area;
(iii) they convert food into body material with greater efficiency;
(iv) for the preceding two reasons, low-quality pasture and browsing support a higher biomass when turned over to antelope than when grazed by cattle;
(v)   under natural conditions, antelope are less susceptible to a wide range of diseases than are cattle;
(vi) antelope do not require the high capital and maintenance costs that are necessary to successful cattle-raising.

From the point of view of the Bushmen, game cropping is advantageous in that:

(i)   it does not require relocation of the Bushmen;

(ii) it is an activity which makes use of their existing knowledge and skills and does not require extensive new training;

(iii) it does not require drastic changes in the existing social and economic organisation of the Bushmen;

(iv) a yield valued by the outside world is economic justification for leaving intact the ecosystem on which the Bushmen depend for their livelihood and way of life.

There are several aspects which must be investigated before a scheme of this nature can be initiated. The main problem areas are:

(i) the means of preparing and marketing the product, namely game meat;

(ii) the optimum rate of cropping of each species in each locality under varying conditions of rainfall, season, etc.

As an adjunct to game-cropping, a handicraft industry could be developed comparable with that suggested for farm Bushmen. This would be based on the processing of game by-products and could make use also of other traditional skills of these Bushmen, such as beadwork.

A scheme of this nature is certainly not a final solution; it deals principally with the problem of protecting the Bushmen and their habitat from intrusion and disruption by others. Other problems remain and will continue to arise. These will have to be dealt with in continuing consultation with the Bushmen. This is no more than a foundation for a future which leaves open to the Bushmen the widest range of options in deciding the direction and nature of later development.

This is only a brief sketch of the main features of the most pressing problems threatening the future of the Bushmen. There are many others which are capable of solution, such as medical problems. However, to attack them in a piecemeal fashion will be of little avail, unless the social, economic and political status of the Bushmen is improved to a stage where they are no longer a despised minority, but are accepted as equal but distinctive members of their various nations, with rights and opportunities to lead their lives and express their identity in ways consistent with their own values. The measures which are suggested here are intended as first steps in the building of foundations upon which stable and happy Bushman communities can develop.

The ethnic identity and cultural heritage of the 50 000-odd survivors of this people who once occupied the whole of the southern third of Africa are precious elements. The tragedy of cultural extinction has occurred too often in the past. The lifestyles of the Bushmen should be conserved, not in order to perpetuate living museum exhibits or fairground side-shows, but because they are viable and valid socio-cultural systems of human beings. The world has the wisdom to value cultural diversity and the means of conserving the elements which make up that diversity. It also has the compassion to stay its hand from destroying the means and values by which a people lives. What is needed is to extend to the Bushmen help in defending themselves against the forces which, quite unnecessarily and avoidably, threaten their way of life. Without such help the Bushmen will be lost.

Glossary

Phillip V. Tobias

alleles
various versions of the same gene capable of occupying the same locus or site along the members of a pair of corresponding chromosomes.

blood groups
a system of inherited chemical substances located on the surface of the red blood cells. Each blood group is produced by two or more genes that may be alleles (q.v.) or they may be different genes situated closely together along the length of the same chromosome.

blue wildebeest, blouwildebees
the brindled gnu, African antelope of the species *Connochaetes taurinus*.

bolas
two or three balls, generally of stone, connected by a strong cord: when whirled through the air and thrown, the bolas could bring down man's prey by entangling its limbs.

BP, B.P.
"Before Present" – a conventional way of expressing prehistoric dates determined by radio-isotope techniques, such as the radiocarbon method and the potassium-argon method.

buchu
"Hottentot tea"; the dried leaves of several species of the plant genus *Agathosma,* a shrub belonging to the family *Rutaceae*. Khoisan people mixed the powdered leaves with animal fat and rubbed it into their bodies. Its medicinal properties include carminative and diuretic effects.

bywoner
a farm tenant; a person who lives on a farm and in return for his services enjoys certain privileges, such as free housing, pasturage and a share of the produce.

dassie
the "rock-rabbit" or "rock-badger" or "hyrax": generally applied in southern Africa to the hyracoid species *Procavia capensis* (= *Hyrax capensis*). Two other genera of this mammalian order are found in Africa, *Dendrohyrax* (the tree hyrax) and *Heterohyrax* (the rock hyrax or yellow-spotted dassie).

ectomorphic body build
a variety of human physique dominated by linear build, with little participation of the fatty component and with a relatively lightly constructed skeleton and musculature.

epicanthic fold
a fold of skin that passes from the upper eyelid downwards adjacent to the side of the root of the nose.

gemsbok
the oryx, a large straight-horned African antelope of the genus *Oryx*.

haemoglobin, hemoglobin
the red pigment that transports oxygen from the lungs to the tissues of the body: this red protein is to be found in the erythrocytes or red blood-cells.

haptoglobin
a protein in blood serum that has the capacity to combine with haemoglobin. There are different types of haptoglobin and the varieties are produced by different genes.

infibulation
to fasten with a clasp (or "fibula"): the term is applied especially to the practice of placing a clasp or stitches across the vulva of the female or the foreskin of the penis to prevent sexual intercourse.

karos(s)
a cloak or mantle of animal skins, with the hair on and worn by the San and other African peoples.

knobkerrie, knopkierie
a short stick or wooden club with a knobbed head.

landdros(t)
a magistrate.

longinymph
see *tablier*.

lumbar lordosis
hollow-back or saddle-back: an accentuated curvature of the lumbar part of the spinal column with its convexity towards the front and its concavity towards the back.

macronympha
see *tablier*.

molapo
a basin between two sand dunes.

mongongo
Tswana word for the nuts, fruit and trees also known as mangetti (*Ricinodendron rautanenii* Schinz). The nuts are tasty and nutritious, being rich in protein and oils. They form one of the most highly sought of the plant foods of the Bushmen.

Monomotapa
a reputed 15th century African kingdom situated more or less in the area between the Limpopo and Zambesi rivers. The fact that gold was to be found there gave rise to legends of the fabulous riches of Monomotapa. Maps of the 16th century show it with a great southerly extension.

neoteny or paedomorphism
the tendency to retain into adulthood features which in other populations or species are regarded as those of immature stages of development.

omuramba
a shallow, dry, ancient water-course, hollowed somewhat below the general surface of the land (plural *omirimbi*).

paedomorphism
see *neoteny*.

palaeolithic
term applied to the Old Stone Age, the time during which men cultivated no plants and domesticated no animals, and made stone tools by chipping or flaking rather than by grinding. Roughly the first 99 per cent of human prehistory.

pap
soft, semi-liquid food; in southern Africa, applied to porridge made of maize meal ("mielie meal").

penis rectus
term applied to the male genital organ or penis when, in the relaxed state, it is nearly horizontal in position rather than pendulous.

Pleistocene
the geological epoch that began about 2 million years ago and during which extensive continental glaciation ("Ice Ages") occurred, especially in the northern hemisphere. The Pleistocene is classified as the sixth epoch of the Cenozoic Era (that began about 70 million years ago); it also marks the first epoch of the Quaternary Period.

polymorphism
the occurrence within one and the same population of several distinctive and discontinuous features (or of the differing forms of a gene governing such a set of features), even the rarest of which variants is more frequent than we could account for by recurring mutations of the gene or genes concerned.

riem
a leather thong.

secular trend
a long-term trend of change in a population, manifest over a generation or more; applied more commonly to the tendency of human populations in developed, industrialized countries to mature more rapidly and to attain a greater adult average height than their predecessors. Of pre-industrial, developing communities, the San, like aboriginal Australians, show such a trend. Most other developing communities, however, show no secular trend or a negative secular trend, i.e. a trend to attain shorter adult average stature than their immediate forebears.

sickle-cell trait
a hereditary defect caused by a recessive mutant form of the gene that controls the structure of haemoglobin; when this form of the gene is present in double dose, it causes a serious illness, sickle-cell anaemia; when it is present in single dose (that is, when this form of the gene has been inherited from only one of the two parents), it produces resistance against malaria.

skerm

a shelter or wind-break made by the Bushmen.

steatomeria

isolated deposits of fat over the thighs, in persons who are not otherwise obese.

steatopygia

isolated deposits of fat over the buttocks, in persons who are not otherwise obese.

steroid hormones

hormones belonging to a large family of chemical substances, all of which are variations on the theme of a common organic chemical formula. Cortisone, oestrone (estrone), progesterone and testosterone all belong to the family of steroid hormones.

Strandloper

a beach-comber, seashore hunter in rock pools, tidal pools, sea-fish traps, etc.

tablier

macronympha, longinymph, "Hottentot apron" – enlargement of the labia minora (part of the external genitalia of the female).

tsamma, tsama

a succulent melon, related to the watermelons, though not as sweet. It belongs to the species *Citrullus vulgaris*. Mrs Lorna Marshall describes how she observed /Gwi Bushmen living for a month without any water but with tsama melons. These melons grow in great communities in the Central Kalahari.

veldkos

wild foods: term applied especially to vegetable foods gathered by hunters, such as fruits, nuts, berries, bulbs, corms and tubers.

voorloper (or touleier)

the person who leads a team or span of oxen.

wildebeest, black wildebeest, swartwildebees

the gnu, African antelope of the genus *Connochaetes*; the white-tailed or black wildebeest belongs to the species *Connochaetes gnu*.

Classified Bibliography on the San or Bushmen

Phillip V. Tobias

This Bibliography is not only a reading list for those who wish to dip into one or other aspect of the Bushmen or San. It is a source list for students and research workers who wish to follow up some phase of the numerous writings on the Bushmen and to probe the depths of it.

To make it easier to find one's way about the 290 titles in this list, they have been classified under a number of headings.

The first section deals with historical writings, most of which were published before 1910. These give a record of the early contacts with the Bushmen and of the gradual awakening of interest in them.

Section 2 lists a number of general works as well as popular works. Each publication in this section covers more than one, sometimes many, aspects of the San or Bushmen.

The remaining six sections deal with specific facets; many of the items listed here are not books but articles that have been published in scientific and other periodicals or journals. The aspects covered are:

    Section 3 Archaeology and Rock Art
    Section 4 Ecology and Survival, Demography, Social Organisation
    Section 5 Biological Anthropology, including Medical Aspects
    Section 6 Psychology and Ethology
    Section 7 Linguistics
    Section 8 Beliefs, Ritual, Myths, Folklore

In compiling this Bibliography, the Editor has been able to avail himself of short lists of references furnished by many of the writers of chapters. Valuable help was rendered by Elizabeth Dey, the Librarian (Reference and Research) of the University of the Witwatersrand, Johannesburg.

Historical Writings

Alexander, Sir James Edward (1838): *An Expedition of Discovery into the Interior of Africa, through the hitherto undescribed Countries of the Great Namaquas, Boschmans, and Hill Damaras.* London: Henry Colburn (2 Volumes). 1-302; 1-306.

Anderson, Andrew A. (1887): *Twenty-five Years in a Waggon in the Gold Regions of Africa.* London: Chapman & Hall (2 Volumes). 1-307; 1-253.

Andersson, Karl Johan (1856): *Lake Ngami; or, Explorations and Discoveries, during Four Years' Wanderings in the Wilds of South Western Africa.* London: Hurst & Blackett (2nd Ed.). 1-546.

Andersson, Karl Johan (1861): *The Okavango River: a Narrative of Travel, Exploration, and Adventure.* London: Hurst & Blackett. 1-364.

Andersson, Karl Johan (1875): *Notes of Travel in South Africa.* London: Hurst & Blackett. 1-338.

Arbousset, T., and Daumas, F. (1846): *Narrative of an Exploratory Tour to the North-East of the Colony of the Cape of Good Hope.* Cape Town: A. S. Robertson. 1-330.

Baines, Thomas (1864): *Explorations in South West Africa.* London: Longman, Green, Longman, Roberts & Green. 1-535.

Barrow, John (1801): *An Account of Travels into the Interior of Southern Africa, in the years 1797 and 1798.* London: T. Cadell & W. Davies. Volume I, 1-419. (1804) Volume II, 1-452.

Bartel, K. (1893): *Völkerbewegungen auf der Südhälfte des afrikanischen Kontinents.* Leipzig: Mitteilungen des Vereins für Erdkunde. 1-90.

Bertin, G. (1886): "The Bushmen and their native language". *Journal of the Royal Asiatic Society* (London), Volume 18, Part 1.

Bleek, W. H. I. (1875): *A Brief Account of Bushman Folk-Lore and other Texts.* Second Report concerning Bushman Researches, presented to both Houses of Parliament of the Cape of Good Hope, by command of His Excellency the Governor. London: Trübner; Cape Town: Juta. 1-21.

Burchell, William J. (1824): *Travels in the Interior of Southern Africa.* London: Longman, Hurst, Rees, Orme, Brown & Green (2 Volumes).

Campbell, John (1815): *Travels in South Africa undertaken at the request of the Missionary Society.* London: Black & Parry. 1-582.

Chapman, James (1868): *Travels in the Interior of South Africa.* London: Bell & Daldy (2 Volumes). 1-454; 1-480.

Dornan, S. S. (1907): "Notes on the Bushmen of Basutoland". *Transactions of the South African Philosophical Society,* Volume 18, 437-450.

Dowd, Jerome (1907): *The Negro Races: A Sociological Study.* New York: The Macmillan Co. 1-493.

Elffers, Hubertus (1902): *Through the Thirst Land. A Story of the Kalahari.* Cape Town: Juta. 1-38.

Farini, G. A. (1886): *Through the Kalahari Desert : a Journey to Lake N'Gami and Back*. London: Sampson Low, Marston, Searle & Rivington. 1-475.

Fritsch, Gustav (1868): *Drei Jahre in Süd-Afrika*. Breslau: Ferdinand Hirt. 1-416.

Fritsch, Gustav (1872): *Die Eingeborenen Süd-Afrikas ethnographisch und anatomisch : beschrieben, mit Atlas*. Breslau: Ferdinand Hirt. 1-528.

Galton, Francis (1853): *Narrative of an Explorer in Tropical South Africa*. London: John Murray, 1-314.

Hahn, Theophilus (1870): "Die Buschmänner: Ein Beitrag zur südafrikanischen Völkerkunde". *Globus,* Volume 18, 65-68, 81-85, 102-105, 140-143, 153-155.

Harris, William Cornwallis (1838): *Narrative of an Expedition into South Africa, 1836-37*. Bombay: printed at the American Mission Press. 1-406.

Holub, Emil (1881): *Seven Years in South Africa*. London: Sampson Low, Marston, Searle & Rivington (2 Volumes). 1-479; 1-426.

Kolben, Peter (1731): *The Present State of the Cape of Good Hope : or, a Particular Account of the several Nations of the Hottentots*. Translated from High German by Mr Medley. London: W. Innys (2 Volumes). 1-365; 1-363.

Leyland, J. (1866): *Adventures in the Far Interior of South Africa including a Journey to Lake Ngami*. London: George Routledge. 1-282.

Lichtenstein, Hinrich (1811-1812): *Reisen im südlichen Afrika in den Jahren 1803, 1804, 1805 und 1806*. Berlin: C. Salfeld (2 Volumes). 1-685; 1-661.

Livingstone, David (1857): *Missionary Travels and Researches in South Africa*. London: John Murray. 1-711.

Moodie, Donald (1841): *The Evidence of the Motives and Objects of the Bushman Wars, 1769-77*. Cape Town: A. S. Robertson; London: J. M. Richardson. 1-64.

Passarge, Siegfried (1907): *Die Buschmänner der Kalahari*. Berlin: Dietrich Reimer. 1-144.

Paterson, William (1789): *A Narrative of Four Journeys into the Country of the Hottentots and Kaffraria*. London: J. Johnson. 1-171.

Philip, John (1828): *Researches in South Africa*. London: James Duncan (2 Volumes). 1-403; 1-450.

Pöch, Rudolf (1910): "Reisen im Innern Südafrikas zum Studium der Buschmänner in den Jahren 1907-1909". *Zeitschrift für Ethnologie,* Volume 42, 357-361.

Pöch, Rudolf (1911): "Die Stellung der Buschmannrasse unter den übrigen Menschenrassen". *Korrespondenzblatt der deutschen Gesellschaft für Anthropologie, Ethnologie und Urgeschichte*. Volume 42, Part 8/12, 75-80.

Schinz, Hans (1891): *Deutsch-Südwest-Afrika. Forschungsreisen durch deutschen Schutzgebiete Gross-Nama und Herero-land, nach dem Kunene, dem Ngami-See und der Kalahari 1884-1887*. Oldenburg and Leipzig: Schulzesche Hof-Buchhandlung. 1-586.

Smith, Andrew (1829): "Observations relative to the Origin and History of the Bushmen". Read at the South African Institution on 31st August, 1829. 171-180.

Sparrman, Anders (1785): *A Voyage to the Cape of Good Hope, towards the Antarctic Polar Circle, and round the World, but chiefly into the Country of the Hottentots and Caffres, from the Year 1772, to 1776*. Dublin: White, Cash & Byrne (2 Volumes).

Stow, George W. (1905): *The Native Races of South Africa : a History of the Intrusion of the Hottentots and Basutu into the Hunting Grounds of the Bushmen, the Aborigines of the Country, with numerous illustrations* (G. M. Theal, Ed.). London: George Allen & Unwin. 1-618.

Sutherland, J. (1845): *Memoir respecting the Kaffers, Hottentots, and Bosjemans, of South Africa*. Cape Town: Pike & Philip (2 Volumes). 1-432; 1-720.

Sutherland, J. (1847): *Original Matter contained in Lieut.-Colonel Sutherland's Memoir on the Kaffers, Hottentots, and Bosjemans, of South Africa*. Cape Town: Pike & Philip. 1-580.

Theal, George McCall (1897-1910): *History of Africa South of the Zambesi* (to 1795). Volumes I to IV. London: George Allen & Unwin.

Theal, George McCall (1907-1910): *History and Ethnography of Africa South of the Zambesi, from the settlement of the Portuguese at Sofala in September 1505, to the Conquest of the Cape Colony by the British in September 1795*. London: George Allen & Unwin (3 Volumes). Volume I (1907) 1-501; Volume II (1909) 1-523; Volume III (1910) 1-499.

Theal, George McCall (1910): *The Yellow and Dark-skinned People of Africa, South of the Zambesi*. London: Swan Sonnenschein. 1-397.

Transvaal Native Affairs Department (1905): *Short History of the Native Tribes of the Transvaal*. Pretoria; reprinted by State Library, 1968. 1-67.

Vaillant, François le (1790): *Voyage dans l'interieur de l'Afrique*. Paris: Leroy (2 Volumes).

Vaillant, François le (1790): *Travels into the Interior Parts of Africa by the Way of the Cape of Good Hope in the Years 1780, 81, 82, 83, 84 and 85*. London: G. G. J. & J. Robinson (2 Volumes). 1-395; 1-403.

Vaillant, François le (1790): *Travels from the Cape of Good-Hope into the Interior Parts of Africa, including many interesting Anecdotes*. London: William Lane (2 Volumes). 1-442; 1-464.

Vaillant, François le (L'an 3 [1794-5]): *Second Voyage dans l'interieur de l'Afrique*. Paris: H. J. Jansen (3 Volumes).

Vedder, Heinrich (1912): "Die Buschmänner". *Allgemeine Missions Zeitschrift,* Volume 39, 403-416.

Werner, H. (1906): "Anthropologische, ethnologische und ethnographische Beobachtungen über die Heikum- und Kung-Buschleute". *Zeitschrift für Ethnologie*, Volume 38, 241-268.

General and/or Popular Works

Almeida, Antonio de (1954): "Dos Bosquimanos e Hotentotes na história e na ciência". *Boletim da Sociedade de Geografia de Lisboa*, Series 72a, April-June, Numbers 4-6, 191-217.
Almeida, Antonio de (1965): *Bushmen and other Non-Bantu Peoples of Angola. Three Lectures*. Johannesburg: The Institute for the Study of Man in Africa. 1-43. (With a Preface by P. V. Tobias, v-viii.)
Almeida, E. de C., de Castro, C., and Lampreia, J. D. (1964): *Bibliografia do Centro de Estudos de Etnologia do Ultramar. Ia Parte: Etnografia*. Lisbon: Centro de Estudos de Antropobiologia. 1-163.

Balsan, François (1952): *L'Expédition Panhard-Capricorne*. Paris: Amiot-Dumont. 1-260.
Bjerre, Jens (1960): *Kalahari*. London: Michael Joseph. 1-227.
Bleek, Dorothea F. (1928): *The Naron, a Bushman Tribe of the Central Kalahari*. Cambridge: University Press. 1-67.

Cowley, Clive (1968): *Fabled Tribe: a Voyage to discover the River Bushmen of the Okavango Swamps*. New York: Atheneum. 1-232.

Dornan, S. S. (1925): *Pygmies and Bushmen of the Kalahari*. London: Seeley, Service & Co. 1-318.
Duggan-Cronin, A. M., and Bleek, Dorothea F. (1942): *The Bushman Tribes of Southern Africa*. Kimberley: The Alexander McGregor Memorial Museum. 1-15 and 40 Plates.
Dunn, E. J. (1931): *The Bushman*. London: Charles Griffin. 1-130.
Du Plessis, J. (1911): *A History of Christian Missions in South Africa*. Reprinted by Struik, 1965. 1-494.

Ellenberger, Victor (1953): *La Fin Tragique des Bushmen*. Paris: Amiot-Dumont. 1-264.
Elliot Smith, G. (1930): *Human History*. London: Jonathan Cape. 1-509.

Fischer, Adolf (1936): *Menschen und Tiere in Südwestafrika*. Berlin: Safari Verlag. 1-301.
Fourie, L. (1928): "The Bushmen of South West Africa". In: *The Native Tribes of South West Africa*. Cape Town: Cape Times. 81-103.

Gusinde, Martin (1954): "Bei den Buschmännern in Südafrika". *Umschau*, Volume 54, 463-496.
Gusinde, Martin (1966): *Von Gelben und Schwarzen Buschmännern: Eine untergehende Altkultur im Süden Afrikas*. Graz: Akademische Druck- und Verlagsanstalt. 1-225.

Hastings, Macdonald (1956): *The Search for the Little Yellow Men*. London: Hulton Press. 1-176.
Hirschberg, Walter (1934): "The problem of relationship between Pygmies and Bushmen". *Africa*, Volume 7, Number 4, 444-451.
How, M. W. (1962): *The Mountain Bushmen of Basutoland*. Pretoria: J. L. van Schaik. 1-63.

Jackson, Agnes (1956): *The Bushmen of South Africa*. London: Oxford University Press. 1-32.

Maingard, L. F. (1935): "The first contacts of the Dutch with the Bushmen until the time of Simon van der Stel (1686)". *South African Journal of Science*, Volume 32, 479-487.
Marshall, Lorna (1965): "The !Kung Bushmen of the Kalahari Desert". In: *Peoples of Africa* (J. L. Gibbs, Ed.). New York: Holt, Rinehart & Winston. 241-278.
Marshall, Lorna (1976): *The !Kung of Nyae Nyae*. Cambridge, Massachusetts: Harvard University Press. 1-433.
Moodie, D. (1838-1841): *The Record, or a Series of official Papers Relating to the Condition and Treatment of the Native Tribes of South Africa*. Reprinted by Balkema, 1960. Various paging.

Quinton, J. C., and Lewin Robinson, A. M. (Gen. Eds.) (1973): *François le Vaillant – Traveller in South Africa, and his Collection of 165 Water-Colour Paintings*. Cape Town: Library of Parliament (2 Volumes). An English, an Afrikaans and a French edition.

Rheinallt Jones, J. D., and Doke, C. M. (Eds.) (1937): *Bushmen of the Southern Kalahari*. Johannesburg: Witwatersrand University Press. 1-283.

Sahlins, M. D. (1960): "The Origin of Society". *Scientific American*, Volume 204, 76-87.
Schapera, I. (1926): "A preliminary consideration of the relationship between the Hottentots and Bushmen". *South African Journal of Science*, Volume 23, 833-866.
Schapera, I. (1930): *The Khoisan Peoples of South Africa*. London: Routledge & Kegan Paul. 1-450.
Schapera, I. (1939): "A survey of the Bushman question". *Race Relations*, Volume 6, Number 2, 68-82.
Schoeman, P. J. (1957): *Hunters of the Desert Land*. Cape Town: Howard Timmins. 1-161.
Schwarz, E. H. L. (1928): *The Kalahari and its Native Races*. London: H. F. & G. Witherby. 1-244.
Seligman. C. G. (1957): *The Races of Africa*. London: Oxford University Press (3rd Ed.). 1-236.
Sollas, W. J. (1924): *Ancient Hunters and their Modern Representatives*. London: Macmillan (3rd Ed.). 1-689.
Spilhaus, M. W. (1966): *South Africa in the Making*. Cape Town: Juta. 1-422.

Theal, G. M. (1910): *Ethnography and Condition of South Africa before A.D. 1505*. London: George Allen and Unwin. 1-466.
Thomas, E. M. (1959): *The Harmless People*. London: Secker & Warburg. 1-266.

Tobias, P. V. (1959): "The Nuffield-Witwatersrand University Expeditions to Kalahari Bushmen, 1958-59". *Nature:* Volume 183, 1011-1013.

Tobias, P. V. (1970): "Bushmen". *Standard Encyclopaedia of Southern Africa,* Volume 2, 617-624.

Tobias, P. V. (1975): "Fifteen years of study of the Kalahari Bushmen or San". *South African Journal of Science,* Volume 71, 74-78.

Van der Post, Laurens (1958): *The Lost World of the Kalahari.* London: Hogarth Press. 1-256.

Van der Post, Laurens (1961): *The Heart of the Hunter.* London: Hogarth Press. 1-256.

Vedder, H. (1966): *South West Africa in Early Times.* London: Frank Cass. 1-525.

Willet, Shelagh M. (1965): *The Bushman: A Select Bibliography 1652-1962.* Johannesburg: University of the Witwatersrand. 1-38.

Wilson, M., and Thompson, L. (Eds.) (1969): *The Oxford History of South Africa,* Volume I. Oxford: University Press. 1-502.

Wright, J. B. (1971): *Bushman Raiders of the Drakensberg 1840-1870.* Pietermaritzburg: University of Natal Press. 1-235.

Archaeology and Rock Art

Battiss, W. W., Franz, G. H., Grossert, J. W., and Junod, H. P. (1958): *The Art of Africa.* Pietermaritzburg: Shuter & Shooter. 1-140.

Breuil, H. (1948): "South African races in the rock paintings". In: *Robert Broom Commemorative Volume.* Cape Town: Royal Society of South Africa. 210-214.

Breuil, H. (1949): *Beyond the Bounds of History.* London: P. R. Gawthorn. 1-100.

Breuil, H. (1949): "The age and the authors of the painted rocks of Austral Africa". *South African Archaeological Bulletin,* Volume 3, Part 9, 2-11.

Burkitt, M. C. (1928): *South Africa's Past in Stone and Paint.* Cambridge: Cambridge University Press. 1-183.

Clark, J. D. (1959): *The Prehistory of Southern Africa.* Harmondsworth: Penguin Books Ltd. 1-341.

Cooke, C. K. (1965): "Evidence of human migrations from the rock art of Southern Rhodesia". *Africa,* Volume 35. 263-285.

Cooke, C. K. (1969): *Rock Art of Southern Africa.* Cape Town: Books of Africa. 1-166.

Goodall, E., Cooke, C. K., and Clark, J. D. (1959): *Prehistoric rock art of the Federation of Rhodesia and Nyasaland* (R. Summers, Ed.). Rhodesia and Nyasaland, National Publications Trust. 1-267.

Impey, S. P. (1926): *Origin of the Bushmen and the Rock Paintings of South Africa.* Cape Town and Johannesburg: Juta. 1-102.

Laidler, P. W. (1929): "Hottentot and Bushman pottery of South Africa". *South African Journal of Science,* Volume 26, 758-786.

Lebzelter, Viktor (1930): *Die Vorgeschichte von Süd- und Südwestafrika.* Leipzig: Karl W. Hiersemann. 1-220.

Lebzelter, Viktor (1934): *Eingeborenenkulturen in Südwest- und Südafrika.* Leipzig: Karl W. Hiersemann. 1-306.

Lee, D. N., and Woodhouse, H. C. (1970): *Art on the Rocks of Southern Africa.* Cape Town and Johannesburg, London: Purnell. 1-165.

Leith, Brünhilda (1958): *On the Spoor of the Bushman: a chapter written in stone. Compiled from Lectures of the late George Leith.* Privately published, Somerset West. 1-43.

Luschan, F. von (1908): "Über Buschmann-Malereien in den Drakensbergen". *Zeitschrift für Ethnologie,* Volume 40, 665-687.

Mason, Revil J. (1962): *Prehistory of the Transvaal.* Johannesburg: Witwatersrand University Press. 1-498.

Pager, Harald (1971): *Ndedema: A documentation of the rock paintings of the Ndedema Gorge.* Graz: Akademische Druck- und Verlagsanstalt. 1-375.

Rosenthal, E., and Goodwin, A. J. H. (1953): *Cave Artists of South Africa.* Cape Town: Balkema. 1-80.

Rudner, J. and I. (1970): *The Hunter and His Art – a survey of rock art in Southern Africa.* Cape Town: Struik. 1-278.

Schoonraad, Murray (Ed.) (1971): "Rock Paintings of Southern Africa". Special Publication Number 2, South African Association for the Advancement of Science. *Supplement to the South African Journal of Science,* Number 2, May 1971. Johannesburg. 1-104.

Stow, G. C., and Bleek, Dorothea F. (1930): *Rock Paintings in South Africa from parts of the Eastern Province and Orange Free State.* London: Methuen. 1-28 and 72 plates.

Thesen, Hjalmar (1963): *The Echoing Cliffs.* London: Hutchinson. 1-143.

Tongue, Helen (1909): *Bushman Paintings.* Oxford: University Press. 1-48 (text) and 54 coloured plates, etc.

Van Riet Lowe, C. (1941): *Prehistoric Art in South Africa.* Pretoria: Government Printer. 1-38 (English); 1-37 (Afrikaans).

Vedder, H. (1925-1926): "Ueber die Vorgeschichte der Völkerschaften von Südwestafrika. I. Die Buschmänner". *Journal of South West African Scientific Society,* Volume 1, 5-16.

Vinnicombe, Patricia (1967): "Rock-painting analysis." *South African Archaeological Bulletin*, Volume 22, 129-141.

Vinnicombe, Patricia (1976): *The People of the Eland*. Pietermaritzburg: University of Natal Press. 1-388.

Willcox, A. R. (1956): *Rock Paintings of the Drakensberg*. London: Max Parrish. 1-96.

Willcox, A. R. (1963): *The Rock Art of South Africa*. Johannesburg: Thomas Nelson. 1-96.

Willcox, A. R. (1975): "The Archaeology of the Drakensberg Region of Natal". *Natal Town and Regional Planning Reports*, Volume 30. Pietermaritzburg: Natal Town and Regional Planning Committee. 1-27.

Ecology and Survival, Demography, Social Organisation

Allchin, Bridget (1966): *The Stone-tipped Arrow: Late Stone-Age Hunters of the Tropical Old World*. London: Phoenix House. 1-224.

Bicchieri, M. G. (Ed.) (1972): *Hunters and Gatherers Today. A Socioeconomic Study of Eleven Such Cultures in the Twentieth Century*. New York: Holt, Rinehart & Winston. 1-494.

Bijlsma, U. G., and Waard, F. de (1957): "'n Pylvergif van die Boesmans in Suid-Afrika". *Suid-Afrikaanse Tydskrif vir Geneeskunde*, Volume 31, 115-120.

Dart, R. A. (1937): "Hut distribution, genealogy and homogeneity of the /?auni- ≠ khomani Bushmen". *Bantu Studies*, Volume ii, 159-174.

Draper, P. (1976): "!Kung women: contrasts in sexual egalitarianism in the foraging and sedentary contexts". In: *Toward an Anthropology of Women* (R. Reiter, Ed.).

Heinz, H. J. (1966): *The Social Organization of the !Ko Bushmen*. Thesis accepted for the degree of M.A., University of South Africa, Pretoria. 1-247.

Heinz, H. J. (1973): "Territoriality among the Bushmen in general and the !Ko in particular". *Anthropos*, Volume 67, 405-416.

Joyce, J. W. (1938): "Report on the Masarwa in the Bamangwato Reserve, Bechuanaland Protectorate". *League of Nations Publications, VI, Slavery, C112, M.98*, Volume 6, 57-76.

Lee, R. B. (1968): "What hunters do for a living: or, how to make out on scarce resources". In: *Man the Hunter* (R. B. Lee and I. DeVore, Eds.). Chicago: Aldine Press. 30-48.

Lee, R. B. (1969): "!Kung Bushman Subsistence: an input-output analysis". In: *Environment and Cultural Behaviour: Ecological Studies in Cultural Anthropology* (A. P. Vayda, Ed.). New York: The Natural History Press. 47-79.

Lee, R. B. (1972): "The intensification of social life among the !Kung Bushmen". In: *Population Growth: Anthropological Implications* (B. Spooner, Ed.). Cambridge: Massachusetts Institute of Technology. 343-350.

Lee, R. B., and DeVore, I. (Eds.) (1968): *Man the Hunter*. Chicago: Aldine Press. 1-415.

Lee, R. B., and DeVore, I. (Eds.) (1976): *Kalahari Hunter-Gatherers: Studies of the !Kung San and their Neighbors*. Cambridge, Massachusetts: Harvard University Press. 1-384.

Marshall, John (1956): Film: *The Hunters*. Cambridge, Massachusetts: Center for Documentary Anthropology.

Marshall, Laurence and Lorna (1956): "The !Kung Bushmen of South West Africa". *South West Africa Annual*, 11-27.

Marshall, Lorna (1957): "The kin terminology system of the !Kung Bushmen". *Africa*, Volume 27, Part 1, 1-27.

Marshall, Lorna (1959): "Marriage among !Kung Bushmen". *Africa*, Volume 29, Part 4, 335-365.

Marshall, Lorna (1960): "!Kung Bushman bands". *Africa*, Volume 30, Part 4, 325-355.

Marshall, Lorna (1962): "!Kung Bushman religious beliefs". *Africa*, Volume 32, 221-251.

Potgieter, E. F. (1955): *The Disappearing Bushmen of Lake Chrissie*. Pretoria: Van Schaik. 1-64.

Service, E. R. (1962): *Primitive Social Organization*. New York: Random House. 1-211.

Service, E. R. (1966): *The Hunters*. Englewood Cliffs, New Jersey: Prentice-Hall. 1-118.

Silberbauer, G. B. (1964): "A Stone Age Race in Modern Africa". *Optima*. Volume 14, Number 4, 207-215.

Silberbauer, G. B. (1965): *Report to the Government of Bechuanaland on the Bushman Survey*. Gaborone: Bechuanaland Government. 1-138.

Silberbauer, G. B., and Kuper, A. J. (1966): "Kgalagari masters and Bushman serfs". *African Studies*, Volume 25, 171-179.

Story, R. (1958): "Some plants used by the Bushmen in obtaining food and water". *Memoirs of the Botanical Survey of South Africa*, Number 30. 1-115.

Tanaka, J. (1969): "The ecology and social structure of Central Kalahari Bushmen". *Kyoto University African Studies*, Volume 3, 1-26.

Tobias, P. V. (1956): "On the survival of the Bushmen". *Africa*, Volume 26, 174-186.

Tobias, P. V. (1961): "The physique of a desert folk". *Natural History*, Volume 70, Number 2, 16-25.

Tobias, P. V. (1964): "Bushman Hunter-Gatherers: a study in human ecology". In: *Ecological Studies in Southern Africa* (D. H. S. Davis, Ed.). *Monographiae Biologicae* XIV, 67-86. The Hague: W. Junk.

Van der Merwe, S. (1960): "Die Boesmans van Suidwes-Afrika". *Staatsamptenaar*, Volume 40, Number 11, 32-35.

Biological Anthropology, including Medical Aspects

Barnicot, N. A., Garlick, J. P., Singer, R., and Weiner, J. S. (1959): "Haptoglobin and transferrin variants in Bushmen and some other South African peoples". *Nature,* Volume 184, 2042.

Beighton, P. (1972): "Pituitary dwarfism in a Kalahari Bushman". *South African Medical Journal,* Volume 46, 881-882.

Bronte-Stewart, B., Budtz-Olsen, O. E., Hickley, J. M., and Brock, J. F. (1960): "The health and nutritional status of the Kung Bushmen of South West Africa". *South African Journal of Laboratory and Clinical Medicine,* Volume 6, 187-216.

Broom, R. (1923): "Contribution to the craniology of the yellow-skinned races of South Africa". *Journal of the Royal Anthropological Institute,* Volume 53, 132-149.

Broom, R. (1941): "Bushmen, Koranas and Hottentots". *Annals of the Transvaal Museum,* Volume 20, 217-249.

Charlton, R. W., and Bothwell, T. H. (1961): 'Primaquine sensitive red cells in various races in Southern Africa". *British Medical Journal,* Volume i, 941-944.

Coon, C. S. (1955): *The History of Man from the First Human to Primitive Culture and Beyond.* London: Jonathan Cape. 1-437.

Cummins, H. (1955): "Dermatoglyphs of Bushmen (South Africa)". *American Journal of Physical Anthropology,* Volume 13, 699-709.

Dart, R. A. (1937): "Racial Origins". In: *The Bantu-speaking Tribes of Southern Africa* (I. Schapera, Ed.). London: Routledge & Kegan Paul. 1-31.

Dart, R. A. (1937): "The physical characters of the /?auni-≠khomani Bushmen". In: *Bushmen of the Southern Kalahari* (J. D. Rheinallt Jones and C. M. Doke, Eds.). Johannesburg: Witwatersrand University Press. 117-188 and 33 tables.

De Villiers, H. (1961): "The tablier and steatopygia in Kalahari Bushwomen". *South African Journal of Science,* Volume 57, 223-227.

Drennan, M. R. (1929): "The dentition of a Bushman tribe". *Annals of the South African Museum,* Volume 24, 61-87.

Drury, J., and Drennan, M. R. (1926): "The pudendal parts of the South African Bush race". *Medical Journal of South Africa,* Volume 22, 113-117.

Griffiths, S. B. (1953): "Absence of the sickle-cell trait in the Bushmen of South West Africa". *Nature,* Volume 171, 577.

Harpending, H. C., and Jenkins, T. (1974): "!Kung population structure". In: *Genetic Distance* (J. F. Crow and C. Denniston, Eds.). New York: Plenum Press.

Jeffreys, M. D. W. (1951): "Pygmies – human and otherwise". *South African Journal of Science,* Volume 47, 227-233.

Jenkins, T. (1965): "Ability to taste phenylthiocarbamide in Kalahari Bushmen and Southern Bantu". *Human Biology,* Volume 37, 371-374.

Jenkins, T. (1972): *Genetic Polymorphisms of Man in Southern Africa.* M.D. Thesis, University of London.

Jenkins, T., Blecher, S. R., Smith, A. N., and Anderson, C. G. (1968): "Some hereditary red-cell traits in Kalahari Bushmen and Bantu". *American Journal of Human Genetics,* Volume 20, 299-309.

Jenkins, T., and Cleaton-Jones, P. (1966): "The ABH secretor status of Kalahari Bushmen". *South African Journal of Medical Sciences,* Volume 31, 42-44.

Jenkins, T., Harpending, H. C., Gordon, H., Keraan, M. M., and Johnston, S. (1971): "Red cell enzyme polymorphisms in the Khoisan peoples of southern Africa". *American Journal of Human Genetics,* Volume 23, 513-532.

Jenkins, T., Lane, A. B., Nurse, G. T., and Tanaka, J. (1975): "Sero-genetic studies on the G/wi and G//ana of Botswana". *Human Heredity,* Volume 25, 318-328.

Jenkins, T., Lehmann, H., and Nurse, G. T. (1974): "Public health and genetic constitution of the San ('Bushmen')". *British Medical Journal,* Volume ii, 23-26.

Jenkins, T., and Steinberg, A. G. (1966): "Some serum protein polymorphisms in Kalahari Bushmen and Bantu". *American Journal of Human Genetics,* Volume 18, 399-407.

Kaminer, B., and Lutz, W. P. W. (1960): "Blood pressure in Bushmen of the Kalahari Desert". *Circulation,* Volume 22, 289-295.

Keith, A. (1948): *A New Theory of Human Evolution.* London: Watts. 1-451.

Kennelly, B. M., Truswell, A. S., and Schrire, V. (1972): "A clinical and electrocardiographic study of !Kung Bushmen". *South African Medical Journal,* Volume 46, 1093-1097.

Krut, L. H., and Singer, R. (1963): "Steatopygia". *American Journal of Physical Anthropology,* Volume 21, 181-187.

Metz, J., Hart, D., and Harpending, H. C. (1971): "Iron, folate and vitamin B_{12} nutrition in a hunter-gatherer people. A study of the !Kung Bushmen". *American Journal of Clinical Nutrition,* Volume 24, 229-242.

Miller, K., Rubenstein, A., and Åstrand, P. O. (1968): "Lipid values in Kalahari Bushmen". *Archives of Internal Medicine,* Volume 121, 414-417.

Nurse, G. T., and Jenkins, T. (1974): "Lactose intolerance in San populations". *British Medical Journal,* Volume iii, 809.

Nurse, G. T., and Jenkins, T. (1977): "Health and the Hunter-Gatherer. Biomedical studies on the hunting and gathering populations of southern Africa". *Monographs in Human Genetics,* Volume 8. Basel: S. Karger. 1-126.

Pacher, H.-M. (1961): "Anthropologische Untersuchungen an den Skeletten der Rudolf Pöch'schen Buschmannsammlung". *Österreichische Akademie der Wissenschaften, Rudolf Pöchs Nachlass*, Serie A: Physische Anthropologie. Volume XII, Vienna. 1-12.

Pijper, A. (1932): "Blood groups of the Bushmen". *South African Medical Journal*, Volume 6, 35-37.

Schultze Jena, Leonhard (1928): *Zur Kenntnis des Körpers der Hottentotten und Buschmänner*. Jena: Gustav Fischer. 147-227.

Seiner, Franz (1912): "Beobachtungen und Messungen an Buschleuten". *Zeitschrift für Ethnologie*, Volume 44, 275-288.

Seiner, Franz (1913): "Beobachtungen an den Bastard-Buschleuten der Nord-Kalahari". *Mitteilungen der Anthropologischen Gesellschaft in Wien*, Volume 43, 311-324.

Singer, R. (1960): "Some biological aspects of the Bushman". *Zeitschrift für Morphologie und Anthropologie*, Volume 51, 1-6.

Singer, R. (1970): "Investigations on the biology of Hottentot and Bushman populations in Southern Africa". *Materialy i Prace Antropologiczne, Wroclaw*, Number 78, 37-48. (IBP Biology of Man in Africa, Warsaw Meeting, 1968.)

Singer, R., and Weiner, J. S. (1963): "Biological aspects of some indigenous African populations". *Southwestern Journal of Anthropology*, Volume 19. 168-176.

Stern, J. T., and Singer, R. (1967): "Quantitative morphological distinctions between Bushman and Hottentot skulls: a preliminary report". *South African Archaeological Bulletin*, Volume 22, 103-111.

Tobias, P. V. (1955-56): "Les Bochimans Auen et Naron de Ghanzi: contribution à l'étude des 'anciens jaunes sud-africaines' ". *L'Anthropologie*, Volume 59, 235-252, 429-461; Volume 60, 22-52, 268-289.

Tobias, P. V. (1956): "The evolution of the Bushman". *American Journal of Physical Anthropology*, Volume 14, 384.

Tobias, P. V. (1957): "Bushmen of the Kalahari". *Man*, Volume 57, 33-40.

Tobias, P. V. (1961): "Fingerprints and palmar prints of Kalahari Bushmen". *South African Journal of Science*, Volume 57, 333-345.

Tobias, P. V. (1961): "New evidence and new views on the evolution of man in Africa". *South African Journal of Science*, Volume 57, 25-38.

Tobias, P. V. (1962): "On the increasing stature of the Bushmen". *Anthropos*, Volume 57, 801-810.

Tobias, P. V. (1966): "The peoples of Africa south of the Sahara". In: *The Biology of Human Adaptability* (P. T. Baker and J. S. Weiner, Eds.). Oxford: Clarendon Press. 111-200.

Tobias, P. V. (1972): "Recent human biological studies in southern Africa, with special reference to Negroes and Khoisans". *Transactions of the Royal Society of South Africa*, Volume 40, 109-133.

Tobias, P. V. (1975): "Stature and secular trend among Southern African Negroes and San (Bushmen)". *South African Journal of Medical Sciences*, Volume 40, part 4, 145-164.

Tobias, P. V. (1975): "Anthropometry among disadvantaged peoples: studies in Southern Africa". In: *Biosocial Interrelations in Population Adaptation* (E. S. Watts, F. E. Johnston and G. W. Lasker, Eds.). The Hague: Mouton. 287-305.

Toerien, M. J. (1958): "The physical characters of the Lake Chrissie Bushmen". *South African Journal of Medical Sciences*, Volume 23, 121-124.

Truswell, A. S., and Hansen, J. D. L. (1968): "Medical and nutritional studies of !Kung Bushmen in northwest Botswana: a preliminary report". *South African Medical Journal*, Volume 42, 1338-1339.

Van Reenen, J. F. (1966): "Dental features of a low-caries primitive population". *Journal of Dental Research*, Volume 45, 703-713.

Ward, J. S., Bredell, G. A. C., and Wenzel, H. G. (1960): "Responses of Bushmen and Europeans on exposure to winter night temperatures in the Kalahari". *Journal of Applied Physiology*, Volume 15, 667-670.

Wells, L. H. (1929): "Fossil Bushmen from the Zuurberg". *South African Journal of Science*, Volume 26, 806-834.

Wells, L. H. (1952): "Physical measurements of Northern Bushmen". *Man*, Volume 52, 53-56.

Wells, L. H. (1960): "Bushman and Hottentot statures: a review of the evidence". *South African Journal of Science*, Volume 56, 277-281.

Wyndham, C. H. (1965): "The adaptation of some of the different ethnic groups in South Africa to heat, cold and exercise". *South African Journal of Science*, Volume 61, 11-29.

Wyndham, C. H., and Morrison, J. F. (1956): "Heat regulation of Masarwa Bushmen". *Nature*, Volume 178, 869-870.

Wyndham, C. H., and Morrison, J. F. (1958): "Adjustment to cold of Bushmen in the Kalahari Desert". *Journal of Applied Physiology*, Volume 13, 219-225.

Wyndham, C. H., Strydom, N. B., Ward, J. S., Morrison, J. F., Williams, C. G., Bredell, G. A. G., Von Rahden, M. J. E., Holdsworth, L. D., Van Graan, C. H., Van Rensburg, A. J., and Munro, A. (1964): "Physiological reactions to heat of Bushmen and of unacclimatized and acclimatized Bantu". *Journal of Applied Physiology*, Volume 19, 885-888.

Zoutendyk, A., Kopec, A. C., and Mourant, A. E. (1953): "The blood groups of the Bushmen". *American Journal of Physical Anthropology*, Volume 11, 361-368.

Psychology and Ethology

Balfour, H. (1902): "The Goura, a stringed-wind musical instrument of the Bushmen and Hottentots". *Journal of the Anthropological Institute*, Volume 32, 156-175.

Draper, P. (1973): "Crowding among hunter-gatherers: the !Kung Bushmen". *Science,* Volume 182, 301-303.
Draper, P. (1976): "Social and economic constraints on !Kung childhood". In: *Kalahari Hunter-Gatherers* (R. B. Lee and I. DeVore, Eds.). Cambridge, Massachusetts: Harvard University Press.

Eibl-Eibesfeldt, I. (1971): "'!Ko Buschleute (Kalahari) : Aggressives Verhalten von Kindern im vorpubertären Alter". Parts I and II. *Homo,* Volume 22, 267-278.
Eibl-Eibesfeldt, I. (1972): "!Ko Buschleute (Kalahari): Mutter-Kind-Interaktionen. Frauen mit Säuglingen, Liebkosen und Spielen". Parts I and II. *Homo,* Volume 23, 285-291.
Eibl-Eibesfeldt, I. (1972): "Die !Ko-Buschmann-Gesellschaft". *Monographien zur Humanethologie,* I. Munich: Piper.
Eibl-Eibesfeldt, I. (1973): "The expressive behaviour of the deaf and blind-born". In: *Social Communication and Expressive Movement* (M. V. Cranach and I. Vine, Eds.). London: Academic Press.
Eibl-Eibesfeldt, I. (1974): "The myth of the aggression-free hunter and gatherer society". In: *Primate Aggression, Territoriality, and Xenophobia* (R. L. Holloway, Ed.). New York: Academic Press. 435-437.
England, N. M. (1968): *Music among the ʒũ/'wã-si of South West Africa and Botswana.* Ph.D. dissertation, Harvard University, Cambridge, Massachusetts.

Heinz, H. J. (1967): *Conflicts, Tensions and Release of Tension in a Bushman Society.* The Institute for the Study of Man in Africa, ISMA Papers Number 23, 1-22.
Helmut, H. (1967): "Zum Verhalten des Menschen: die Aggression". *Zeitschrift für Ethnologie,* Volume 92, 265-273.

Kirby, Percival R. (1936): "A study of Bushman music". *Bantu Studies,* Volume 10, 206-252.
Kirby, Percival R. (1937): "The musical practices of the /?auni and ≠khomani Bushmen". In: *Bushmen of the Southern Kalahari* (J. D. Rheinallt Jones and C. M. Doke, Eds.). Johannesburg: Witwatersrand University Press. 1-59.

Marshall, Lorna (1961): "Sharing, talking and giving: relief of social tensions among !Kung Bushmen". *Africa,* Volume 31, 231-249.

Reuning, Helmut (1959): "Psychologische Versuche mit Buschleuten der Kalahari". *Die Umschau in Wissenschaft und Technik,* Volume 17, 520-525.
Reuning, H., and Wortley, W. (1973): "Psychological studies of the Bushmen". *Psychologia Africana,* Monograph, Supplement 7, 1-113.

Sbrznesny, Heidi (1974): *Die Spiele der !Ko Buschleute unter besonderer Berücksichtigung ihrer sozialen Funktion.* Thesis accepted for degree of Ph.D., Munich University, Dept. of Zoology.
Schmidbauer, W. (1971a): "Methodenprobleme der Human-Ethologie". *Studium Generale,* Volume 24, 462-522.
Schmidbauer, W. (1971b): "Zur Anthropologie der Aggression". *Dynamische Psychiatrie,* Volume 4, 36-50.
Schmidbauer, W. (1972): *Die sogenannte Aggression.* Hamburg: Hoffmann & Campe.

Linguistics

Beach, D. M. (1938): *The Phonetics of the Hottentot Language.* Cambridge: Heffer. 1-329.
Bleek, Dorothea F. (1928): "Bushman grammar". *Zeitschrift für Eingeborenensprachen,* Volume 19/20, 81-98, 161-174.
Bleek, Dorothea F. (1929): *Comparative Vocabularies of Bushman Languages.* Cambridge: University Press. 1-94.
Bleek, Dorothea F. (1936): "Special speech of animals and moon used by the !Xam Bushmen; from material collected by Dr W. H. I. Bleek and Miss L. C. Lloyd between 1870 and 1880". *Bantu Studies,* Volume 10, 163-199.
Bleek, Dorothea F. (1939-1940): "A short survey of Bushman languages". *Zeitschrift für Eingeborenensprachen,* Volume 30, 53-72.
Bleek, Dorothea F. (1956): *A Bushman Dictionary.* New Haven: American Oriental Society. 1-773.
Bleek, W. H. I. (1862-1869): *A comparative Grammar of South African Languages.* London: Trübner (2 Volumes). 1-92, 93-322.
Bleek, W. H. I. (1869): "The Bushman language". In: *The Cape and its People and Other Essays* (R. Noble, Ed.). Cape Town: Juta. 269-284.
Bleek, W. H. I. (1873): "Scientific Reasons for the study of the Bushman language". *Cape Monthly Magazine,* New (Second) Series, Volume 7, 149-153.
Bleek, W. H. I. (1873): *Report of Dr Bleek concerning his Researches into the Bushman Language, presented to the Hon. the House of Assembly, by command of His Excellency the Governor.* Cape of Good Hope. (British Museum Library.)

Cole, D. T. (1963): "Bushman Languages". In: *Encyclopaedia Britannica,* 1963: 467-470.

Doke, C. M. (1936): "An outline of the phonetics of the language of the !xũ Bushmen of the North-west Kalahari". *Bantu Studies,* Volume 10, 434-460.
Doke, C. M. (1937): "An outline of ≠khomani Bushman phonetics". In: *Bushmen of the Southern Kalahari* (J. D. Rheinallt Jones and C. M. Doke, Eds.). Johannesburg: Witwatersrand University Press. 61-88.
Doke, C. M. (1942): "Native Languages of South Africa". *African Studies,* Volume 1, 135-141.
Dornan, S. S. (1917): "The Tati Bushmen (Masarwas) and their language". *Journal of the Royal Anthropological Institute,* Volume 47, 37-112.

Greenberg, J. H. (1955): *Studies in African Linguistic Classification*. New Haven: The Compass Publishing Company. 1-116.

Lanham, L. W., and Hallowes, D. P. (1956): "An outline of the structure of Eastern Bushman". *African Studies*, Volume 15, 98-118.
Levy, L. (1968): *A preliminary list of publications referring to the non-Bantu click languages*. Communication Number 33 of the School of African Studies, University of Cape Town. 1-21, 1-14 [2 parts in 1 volume].

Maingard, L. F. (1937): "The !khomani dialect, its morphology and other characteristics". In: *Bushmen of the Southern Kalahari* (J. D. Rheinallt Jones and C. M. Doke, Eds.). Johannesburg: Witwatersrand University Press. 237-275.
Maingard, L. F. (1957-1958): "Three Bushman Languages. The Third Bushman Language." *African Studies*, Volume 16, 37-71, and Volume 17, 100-115.

Stevens, C. M. (1877-1878): "Remarks on 'clicks' with an investigation of the etymon of some South-African Native geographical names". *The Transactions of the South African Philosophical Society*, Volume 1, Part 1, 51-60.
Snyman, J. W. (1970): *An Introduction to the !xu Language*. Cape Town: Balkema. 1-208.
Stopa, R. (1972): *Structure of Bushman and its Traces in Indo-European*. Warsaw: Polska Akademia Nauk. 1-218.

Traill, Anthony (1973a): *The Compleat Guide to the Koon*. Research report on linguistic fieldwork undertaken in Botswana and South West Africa, July 1972 and January 1973. 38 pages, photos and maps.
Traill, Anthony (1973b): " 'N4 or S7': another Bushman language". *African Studies*, Volume 32, Part 1, 25-32.
Traill, Anthony (1973c): "A preliminary sketch of !xo Bushman phonetics". *Work in Progress, Department of Linguistics, Edinburgh University*, Volume 6, 1-21.

Vedder, H. (1910-1911): "Grundriss einer Grammatik der Buschmannsprache vom Stamm der !kũ Buschmänner." *Zeitschrift für Kolonialsprachen*. Volume 1, 5-24, 106-117.

Westphal, E. O. J. (1962): "A re-classification of Southern African Non-Bantu Languages". *Journal of African Languages*, Volume 1, 1-8.
Westphal, E. O. J. (1963): "The linguistic prehistory of Southern Africa: Bush, Kwadi, Hottentot and Bantu linguistic relationships". *Africa*, Volume 39, Number 3, 237-265.
Westphal, E. O. J. (1971): "The click languages of Southern and Eastern Africa". In: *Current Trends in Linguistics*, Volume 7: *Linguistics in Sub-Saharan Africa* (T. A. Sebock, Ed.). The Hague: Mouton. 367-420.
Wilhelm, J. H. (1922): "Aus dem Wortschatz der !Kun- und der Hukwe-Buschmannsprachen". *Zeitschrift für Eingeborenensprachen*, Volume 12, 291-304.
Wuras, C. F. (1920): "An outline of the Bushman language". *Zeitschrift für Eingeborenensprachen*, Volume 10, 81-87.

Beliefs, Ritual, Myths, Folklore

Bleek, Dorothea F. (1934-1935): "!Kung mythology". *Zeitschrift für Eingeborenensprachen*, Volume 25, 261-283.
Bleek, W. H. I., and Lloyd, L. C. (1911): *Specimens of Bushman Folklore*. London: George Allen & Unwin. 1-468.
Bleek, W. H. I., and Lloyd, L. C. (1924): *The Mantis and his Friends: Bushman Folklore*. Cape Town: Maskew Miller. 1-68.

Fouché, Abraham (1967): *Weeskinders van die Hemelgod*. Cape Town: Human & Rousseau. 1-40.

Hahn, T. (1882): *Tsuni-Goam, the Superior Being of the Khoi-Khoi*. London: Trübner. 1-154.
Heinz, H. J. (1971): "The ethno-biology of the !ko Bushmen: the anatomical and physiological knowledge". *South African Journal of Science*, Volume 67, 43-50.

Lee, R. B. (1967): "Trance cure of the !Kung Bushmen". *Natural History*, November 1967, 30-37.

Marais, E. N. (1959): *Dwaalstories*. Cape Town: Human & Rousseau. 1-31.
Markowitz, Arthur (1956): *With Uplifted Tongue: Stories, Myths and Fables of the South African Bushmen told in their manner*. South Africa: Central News Agency. 1-77.
Markowitz, Arthur (1971): *The Rebirth of the Ostrich, and other Stories of the Kalahari Bushmen told in their manner*. Gaborone, Botswana: National Museum and Art Gallery. 1-76.
Marshall, Lorna (1962): "!Kung Bushman religious beliefs". *Africa*, Volume 32, 221-252.

Partridge, A. C. (Ed.) (1973): *Folklore of Southern Africa*. Cape Town and London: Purnell. 1-129.
Phillips, Mary (1961): *The Bushman Speaks*. Cape Town: Howard Timmins. 1-59.

Story, R. (1964): "Plant Lore of the Bushmen". In: *Ecological Studies in Southern Africa* (D. H. S. Davis, Ed.). The Hague: W. Junk. 87-99.

Thomas, E. W. (1950): *Bushman Stories*. London: Oxford University Press. 1-75.

Vedder, H. (1937): "Die Buschmänner Südwestafrikas und ihre Weltanschauung". *South West African Journal of Science*, Volume 34, 416-436.

About the Writers of this Book

Phillip Vallentine Tobias, M.B.B.Ch., Ph.D., D.Sc., F.R.A.I., F.R.S.S.Af., F.L.S., in 1959 succeeded R.A. Dart as Professor of Anatomy at the Medical School, University of the Witwatersrand, Johannesburg. From 1956 to 1973 he was Chairman of the Kalahari Research Committee, which mounted many expeditions to the San people. He led expeditions to study the San, Khoikhoin, !Kora, Griqua, Zambian Tonga, Kafue Twa and other African peoples. He was founder and first President of the Institute for the Study of Man in Africa. Human ancestry is one of his abiding interests and he has studied early fossil hominids of South, East and North Africa, Europe, Israel, Indonesia and Australia. He is the author of diverse books such as *Chromosomes, Sex-cells and Evolution* (1956), *Olduvai Gorge* (Volume II) (1967), *The Brain in Hominid Evolution* (1971), *Man's Anatomy* (1963-64, 1967, 1977), monographs such as *The African in the Universities* (1954), *The Meaning of Race* (1961, 1972), *Man's Past and Future* (1969, 1971), *IQ and the Nature-Nurture Controversy* (1974), *The Sixth Freedom* (1977); chapters in books and numerous articles. He has edited many volumes and scientific periodicals.

Megan Biesele, Ph.D., devoted her doctoral thesis, presented to the Harvard University Department of Anthropology, to the study of Bushman ritual and folklore in the Dobe area of Botswana. On this subject she has published a number of papers, while her dissertation is now to be published as a book by Harvard University Press. She has completed a year of development-oriented research and liaison work for the Botswana Government among the !Kung Bushmen of north-western Botswana. As one who takes a deep interest in all aspects of the lives of the Bushmen, she is a founder and treasurer of the Kalahari Peoples' Fund, of Cambridge, Massachusetts, an organisation concerned with the future of the Bushmen.

Irenäus Eibl-Eibesfeldt, Ph.D., was born in Vienna. He is Professor at the University of Munich and Head of the Research Unit for Human Ethology of the Max Planck Institute. He has led several expeditions and published numerous papers and books, including *Galapagos* (1960), *Land of a Thousand Atolls* (1964), *Ethology: the Biology of Behaviour* (1967), *Love and Hate* (1970), *Die !Ko-Buschmanngesellschaft* (1972), *Der vorprogrammierte Mensch, das Ererbte als bestimmender Faktor im menschlichen Verhalten* (1973), *Krieg und Frieden aus der Sicht der Verhaltensforschung* (1975).

Hans Joachim Heinz, Ph.D., has been a research fellow of the former University of Botswana, Lesotho and Swaziland, and is an Associate of the Research Unit for Human Ethology of the Max Planck Institute. Whilst a staff member of the University of the Witwatersrand, he participated in some of the expeditions of the Kalahari Research Committee – and as a result his career underwent a dramatic change from medical parasitology to ethnology. He has conducted many research expeditions to the !Xo San as well as to the "River Bushmen". He was responsible for a pioneering settlement scheme for the San at Bere in Botswana. His published work includes studies on ethnology, ethno-biology and medical aspects of the San, as well as problems associated with settlement schemes.

Ray R. Inskeep, M.A., F.S.A., is Assistant Curator at the Pitt Rivers Museum, Oxford University. Formerly he was Head of the Department of Archaeology at the University of Cape Town, where he trained a number of archaeologists working today in South Africa. He has conducted extensive archaeological fieldwork in East, Central and southern Africa. Apart from papers published in periodicals, he has contributed chapters to several books, including the *Oxford History of South Africa*. For many years he edited the *South African Archaeological Bulletin*.

Mervyn David Waldegrave Jeffreys (1890-1975), M.A. (Oxon.), Dip. Soc. Anthrop., Ph.D. (London), served for many years in the civil service of Nigeria, including a period on the Bench in 1936. For more than ten years he was a staff member of the Department of Social Anthropology at the University of the Witwatersrand in his native Johannesburg. He made a great number of contributions to scientific bodies and periodicals, based partly on his extensive field experience, especially in West Africa, and partly on his intimate acquaintance with an enormous body of literature on man in Africa and in other parts. His personal library ran to well over 20 000 books and other items: this superb collection was left by him to the Witwatersrand University when he died in March 1975, less than two months before his 85th birthday. He published over 350 articles, mostly in scientific journals.

Richard Borshay Lee, Ph.D., a Canadian, teaches anthropology at the University of Toronto. He has carried out extensive research on the !Kung Bushmen in the Dobe area of northwestern Botswana, his special fields of interest being ecology, social organisation and ritual. His doctoral dissertation at the University of California

(Berkeley) dealt with the subsistence ecology of the !Kung Bushmen. His published works include *The New Native Resistance* as well as numerous research chapters and papers. With I. DeVore he edited *Man the Hunter* (1968), a book that surveys intensively the once universal hunting stage of man's development. Together, also, they edited *Kalahari Hunter-Gatherers: Studies of the !Kung San and their Neighbors* (1976), recently published by Harvard University Press.

Jalmar Rudner (Town Planner to the Cape Town City Council) and his wife, **Ione** (of the South African Museum, Cape Town), have shared archaeology and ethnology as an all-consuming hobby for over twenty-five years. For many years he was Honorary Curator of Archaeology at the South African Museum, Cape Town, in whose Palaeontology Department his wife works. They have undertaken many expeditions to parts of South Africa, South West Africa, Rhodesia, Angola, Lesotho and Botswana. Their most important publications are a monograph, *Strandloper Pottery from South and South West Africa* (1968) and a book on rock art in southern Africa, *The Hunter and his Art* (1970). They have also produced several translations from the Swedish of accounts of early travels in southern Africa.

George B. Silberbauer, Ph.D., was born in Pretoria and educated at the universities of Stellenbosch, the Witwatersrand and London. He spent fifteen years in the British Colonial Service and, in the former Bechuanaland, was District Commissioner for Ngamiland and Ghanzi, as well as Bushman Survey Officer to the Administration of Botswana. He is Senior Lecturer in the Department of Anthropology and Sociology at Monash University, Melbourne, Australia. His researches include fieldwork among Bushmen in Botswana and among aboriginal Australians. Apart from anthropological articles, he is the author of the authoritative *Bushman Survey Report* (1965).

Ronald Singer, M.B. Ch.B., D.Sc., F.R.A.I., is the Robert R. Bensley Professor in Biology and Medical Sciences, Professor and Chairman of the Department of Anatomy, Professor of Anthropology, and a member of the committees on Evolutionary Biology, Genetics and African Affairs at the University of Chicago, U.S.A. While on the staff of the Anatomy Department of the University of Cape Town, he was Director of the Universities of Cape Town and Oxford Research Expedition to South West Africa, as well as further expeditions to study Khoikhoin, San, Rehobothers and other African populations. He has contributed to our knowledge of the human biology of the Khoisan and other sub-Saharan Africans as well as to palaeo-anthropology.

Anthony Traill, B.A. Hons., Dip. Appl. Ling., M. Litt., is Senior Research Fellow in the African Studies Institute, University of the Witwatersrand, Johannesburg, and has been Senior Lecturer in the Department of Phonetics and General Linguistics of the same university. For more than six years he has conducted linguistic fieldwork amongst the Bushmen, concentrating on the !xo bands of south-western Botswana and Aminuis, South West Africa. He first drew attention to the existence of the hitherto unrecognised Eastern hua language of the Salajwe area, Botswana. His research findings have been published in a number of papers and he is the author of *The Compleat Guide to the Koon* (1974) and editor of *Bushman and Hottentot Linguistic Studies* (1975).

Alex R. Willcox, F.R.S.S.Af., F.S.A., F.R.A.I., although a quantity surveyor by profession, has found himself drawn more and more to archaeology over the past thirty years. He has long been a leading authority on South African rock art and he perfected the technique of photographing rock paintings. In his first book he showed how greatly superior colour photography is to tracing for reproducing the tone features of the art. He is the author of *Rock Paintings of the Drakensberg* (1956), *The Rock Art of South Africa* (1963), *The Archaeology of the Drakensberg* (1975), *Southern Land* (1976) and more than a score of scientific papers and articles. He has built up a remarkable collection of colour transparencies of rock paintings.

Index